Genocide Perspectives VI

The Process and the Personal Cost of Genocide

Edited by
Nikki Marczak and Kirril Shields

Australian Institute for
Holocaust and Genocide Studies

Genocide Perspectives Series

UTS ePRESS
University of Technology Sydney
Broadway NSW 2007 AUSTRALIA
epress.lib.uts.edu.au

Copyright Information
This book is copyright. The work is licensed under a Creative Commons Attribution
Non Commercial-Non Derivatives License CC BY-NC-ND

http://creativecommons.org/licenses/by-nc-nd/4.0

First Published 2020
© 2020 in the text and images, the author/s of each article
© 2020 in the book design and layout, UTS ePRESS
© in the original cover artwork: © Vernon Ah Kee
Title of artwork: lynching 2012
Charcoal on canvas, 150 x 90 cm
Courtesy of the artist and Milani Gallery
Artist: Vernon Ah Kee, Photo: Carl Warner, Cover design: Megan Wong

Publication Details
DOI citation: https://doi.org/10.5130/aaf
ISBN (Paperback): 978-0-9775200-3-9
ISBN (PDF): 978-0-9775200-4-6
ISBN (EPUB): 978-0-9775200-5-3
ISBN (Mobi): 978-0-9775200-6-0

Peer Review
This work was peer reviewed by disciplinary experts.

Declaration of conflicting interest
The editors declare no potential conflicts of interest
with respect to the research, authorship, and/or publication of this book.

Funding: Australian Institute for Holocaust and Genocide Studies

UTS ePRESS
Manager: Scott Abbott
Books Editor: Matthew Noble
Enquiries: utsepress@uts.edu.au

For enquiries about third party copyright material reproduced in this work,
please contact UTS ePRESS.

OPEN ACCESS
UTS ePRESS publishes peer reviewed books, journals and conference proceedings
and is the leading publisher of peer reviewed open access journals in Australasia.
All UTS ePRESS online content is free to access and read.

Suggested citation
Marczak, N. and Shields, K. (eds) 2020. *Genocide Perspectives VI: The Process
and the Personal Cost of Genocide.* Sydney: UTS ePRESS. DOI: https://doi.org/10.5130/aaf.
License: CC BY-NC-ND.

To read the free, open access version of this book online,
visit https://doi.org/10.5130/aaf or scan this QR code with
your mobile device:

For Sandra and Pam, and for Karen, Simon and Paul

Contents

Acknowledgements — ix

The Process and the Personal Cost of Genocide — 1
Nikki Marczak and Kirril Shields

Chapter 1. Fateful Choices: Political Leadership and the Paths to and from Mass Atrocities — 7
Alex J. Bellamy and Stephen McLoughlin

   Leadership and mass atrocities — 10
   The role and impact of leaders — 15
      Risk makers and risk breakers — 15
      Drivers and inhibitors — 19
      Prolongers and terminators — 27
   Conclusion — 30

Chapter 2. Freedom of Religion in the Genocidal Process and Group Destruction in the Holocaust and Armenian and Cambodian Genocides — 33
Melanie O'Brien

   Right to freedom of religion — 35
   Violations during the Armenian Genocide — 37
   Violations during the Holocaust — 40
   Violations during the Cambodian Genocide — 43
   Freedom of religion and genocide: definition and prevention — 47

Chapter 3. Post-memory and Artefacts: The Gelber/Altschul Collection — 53
Katharine Gelber

   The obligation of second generation storytelling — 54
   My father and his parents — 56
   The Altschuls — 59
   The Gelbers — 62
   Reflections — 68

Chapter 4. 'If You're Different Are You the Same?': The Nazi Genocide of Disabled People and Les Murray's Fredy Neptune   69
Amanda Tink

   Impairment and disability   72
   Silence and silencing   73
   Dehumanising language   75
   Eugenic thinking and acting   79
   Irreducible impairment   82
   Futures of worth   83
   Consequential lines   83
   Conclusion   85

Chapter 5. Nursing in Nazi Germany and the 'Euthanasia' Programmes   87
Linda Shields and Susan Benedict

   A framework for killing   88
   Eugenics and 'euthanasia'   91
   The children's 'euthanasia' programme   92
   The adult 'euthanasia' programmes   95
   Nurses and adult 'euthanasia'   99
   'Euthanasia' as a template for the Final Solution   102
   Wild or decentralised 'euthanasia'   102
   What happened to the nurses after the war?   105
   Conclusion   106

Chapter 6. Genocide and Suicide   107
Colin Tatz

   Connections and disconnections   107
   Defining the factors   109
   For and *against* suicide   110
   Indigenous suicides   115
   Aboriginal Australia   116
   Native North America   122
   Lost connections   125

Chapter 7. Apprehending the Slow Violence of Nuclear Colonialism: Art and Maralinga — 129
Jacob G. Warren

- Slow violence, cold genocide and radioactive contamination — 133
- Nuclear colonialism and the wasteland desert — 136
- Against the mirage of the desert as wasteland — 140
- Maralinga nullius — 143
- From ground zero to downwind — 145
- The bush yam — 149
- 'The colonisation of the future' — 151
- Conclusion — 152

Chapter 8. The 2017 Myall Creek Massacre Commemoration Speech — 155
Mark Tedeschi AM QC

Chapter 9. Long Shadows—The Great War, Australia and the Middle East: From the Armenian to the Yazidi Genocide — 159
Caroline Schneider and Hans-Lukas Kieser

- I — 160
- II — 162
- III — 163
- IV — 167
- V — 171
- Conclusion — 173

Chapter 10. 'It's Happening Again': Genocide, Denial, Exile and Trauma — 177
Armen Gakavian

- Exile and trauma — 178
- Responses to the genocide and to Turkish denial — 180
- Repression, rationalisation, resignation and reconciliation (1918–1965) — 180
- Rage and revenge (1965–2001) — 182
- Engagement (2001–present) — 185

Unresolved trauma, re-traumatisation and 'history repeating'	187
Conclusion	191
Biographies	193
Index	197

Acknowledgements

To members of the Australian Institute for Holocaust and Genocide Studies, thank you for the opportunity to edit this collection of essays, the sixth in the *Genocide Perspectives* Series. We would like to thank UTS ePRESS for enabling academic works such as *Genocide Perspectives* to reach a wide audience, and particularly to Scott Abbott and Matthew Noble.

Finally, a very heartfelt thanks to Vernon Ah Kee for allowing his artwork to appear on the cover of *GPVI* (and to Jacob G. Warren for facilitating that opportunity). Ah Kee's art represents themes of genocide and atrocity, both of which are explored in the *Genocide Perspectives* Series, and we are honoured that such a high calibre and moving artwork accompanies this book.

The Process and the Personal Cost of Genocide

Nikki Marczak and Kirril Shields

It is with a mixture of sadness and appreciation that we include, in this edition of *Genocide Perspectives*, the final published text of Professor Colin Tatz. The father of Australian genocide studies, and Founding Director of the Australian Institute for Holocaust and Genocide Studies (AIHGS), Professor Tatz passed away on 19 November 2019. In the wake of his death he has been honoured by individuals he inspired, organisations he worked with, and communities whose experiences he shed light on and for whom he advocated tirelessly throughout his life. He has been hailed as a 'doyen of genocide studies academics',[1] celebrated on ABC and SBS radio, by Armenian and Jewish communal representatives, and the universities at which he taught.[2] His dedication to challenging racism has been at the forefront of tributes, and his courage and rebellious streak

---

[1] 'Colin Tatz Has Passed Away at 85', *J-Wire*, November 19, 2019, https://www.jwire.com.au/colin-tatz-has-passed-away-at-85/.

[2] Phillip Adams, 'Remembering Colin Tatz', *Late Night Live*, ABC Radio, November 20, 2019, https://www.abc.net.au/radionational/programs/latenightlive/remembering-professor-colin-tatz/11722570; 'Vale Emeritus Professor Colin Tatz', November 22, 2019, https://politicsir.cass.anu.edu.au/vale-emeritus-professor-colin-tatz.

How to cite this book chapter:
Marczak, N. and Shields, K. 2020. The Process and the Personal Cost of Genocide. In: Marczak, N. and Shields, K. (eds.) *Genocide Perspectives VI: The Process and the Personal Cost of Genocide*. Pp. 1–6. Sydney: UTS ePRESS. DOI: https://doi.org/10.5130/aaf.a. License: CC BY-NC-ND.

admired by all those who knew him.[3] To us and the other members of AIHGS, he was Colin—our mentor and friend, and we will always remember him.

Colin adapted some of his 2019 book, *The Sealed Box of Suicide: The Contexts of Self-Death*, for an essay in this collection, and it is perhaps fitting that his last topic of writing relates to existential questions around life and death, personal choices, and the legacy of trauma, grief, and mourning.

Professor Tatz was never one to shy away from unorthodox and original theses, but his views were always informed by decades of practical, collaborative work with Indigenous communities. In his paper 'Genocide and Suicide', Tatz draws connections between the two. Sometimes they are co-existent, as noted through the Holocaust and Armenian cases, but in the main he focuses on Aboriginal communities in Australia, arguing that the high rates of suicides are not the result of mental illness, nor a phenomenon that can be medicalised or treated within a 'mental health' framework. Rather, he positions suicide as arising from centuries of colonisation, theft of land, and destruction of identity, families ripped apart under government policy, institutional sexual abuse, the Western legacy of drug and alcohol abuse, and from a cycle of socio-economic disadvantage. It is the consequence of decades of trauma and exacerbated by a sequence of paternalistic government policy, Tatz argues, that denies Aboriginal and Torres Strait Islander peoples' self-determination. But Tatz goes further, asserting that in this context, suicide may be a rational choice, to escape one's existence in the absence of hope. Low life expectancy in Aboriginal communities means that funerals are constantly being held; children are exposed to death regularly and from an early age. Sadness and grief are not the same as mental illness, but they are so intrinsic to many Aboriginal lives that suicide must be *understood* as a response and a valid choice.

Tatz's contribution sets the tone of *Genocide Perspectives VI* as a volume that offers new insight into the past, reinvigorating debate and providing scholarly contemplation on the 'crime of crimes', genocide. In this edition, among other topics, contributors explore the causal factors in the emergence of genocide, and reveal the impact of the Holocaust on individuals and families. Aspects of Indigenous Australian experiences are discussed, so too the persecution of particular groups by the Nazis. The legacy of the Armenian Genocide is explored through the 'long shadows' of the Ottoman era that are currently influencing atrocities in the Middle East, while the role of global governments in halting or fuelling the process of genocide is a key focus.

Once again, in the spirit of AIHGS, we have chosen to emphasise Australian scholarship, providing a platform for both established scholars and emerging ones. Australian scholars are at the forefront of genocide studies and have their own historical perspective living in a post-colonial, post-genocidal nation.

---

[3] Nikki Marczak and Meher Grigorian, 'A Rebel with a Cause and a Teacher with Heart', *Plus61J*, November 25, 2019, https://plus61j.net.au/plus61j-voices/rebel-cause-teacher-heart/.

Authors represented here, we believe, portray the diverse areas of study and research undertaken in the country, and their contributions are valuable to the expanding literature on genocide.

Genocide Perspectives VI begins with a densely analytical, evidence-based thesis on how political leadership can either fuel the fires that lead to mass atrocity or, alternatively, divert a nation away from conflict and violence. Alex J Bellamy and Stephen McLoughlin are respected experts on the United Nations endorsed concept of the Responsibility to Protect, which holds that states have a responsibility to protect peoples within their borders from atrocity crimes, and that where a state manifestly fails to do so, the international community has a responsibility to intervene. In this essay, Bellamy and McLoughlin explore the role of political leaders in driving the course of a country either towards violence, or diffusing the conditions that could lead to it. Although much research has been undertaken on the influence of leaders such as Adolf Hitler and Josef Stalin in pushing countries, indeed continents towards genocide, little is understood about the strategies leaders can effectively use to pull back from the brink. Providing a plethora of examples, from Kenya to post-Apartheid South Africa, Tunisia to Macedonia, Bellamy and McLoughlin show how decision making by leaders, even in nations that have the preconditions for atrocity crimes, can prevent mass violence. The stark comparison with recent examples of protracted conflict marred by attacks against civilians, such as the case of Syria, is extremely impactful. Their argument that leadership plays an important role in atrocity prevention must prove to be a cornerstone of atrocity prevention scholarship.

Similarly, Melanie O'Brien looks at genocide as a process rather than a one-off event, showing how violation of the right to freedom of religion manifested in a range of case studies. O'Brien examines the tactic of genocidal regimes of breaching the human right of freedom of religion in order to destroy the victim group, through the lens of the Holocaust, the Cambodian Genocide and the Armenian Genocide. Even when the target group is not defined purely as a religious group, O'Brien argues, the violation of freedom of religion contributes to the genocide. With a strong foundation in human rights law, this essay shows the journey of a gradual violation of rights towards mass atrocity crimes.

In the third essay, Katharine Gelber gives us a highly personal view of the sorts of rights violations O'Brien describes. As a child of a Holocaust survivor who never spoke of his experiences, Gelber grew up with minimal insight into her father's past, and it was only after he died in 2017 that she 'discovered a trove of objects, artefacts of a life I knew almost nothing about but which he had had in his possession for decades'. Gelber spoke at The University of Queensland's *Yom HaShoah*, or Holocaust Memorial Day event in 2019, and presented her findings from a two year research journey that has culminated in her donating her father's belongings to the Sydney Jewish Museum as The Gelber/Altschul Collection. Just as important, her journey has shed light on aspects of her family history that have left both visible and hidden scars

—intergenerational effects that are common to many children of survivors, even (perhaps especially) when they were told nothing of their parents' trauma.

The impact of Nazi persecution is told from a very distinct but equally personal perspective by Amanda Tink, who frames her essay with the continual consciousness that as a person with a disability, she would have suffered a terrible fate had she been born in the Nazi era. Tink writes, 'As with all genocides, its roots are in our language, and language around disability remains resolutely dehumanising'. Tink explores the Nazi genocide of people with mental and physical disabilities through Australian author Les Murray's text, *Fredy Neptune*. Murray was mildly autistic and he draws on his own experiences as well as those of his autistic son to convey prejudice and violence against people with disabilities. These are told through the eyes of two characters—Fredy, also autistic, who develops a physical and emotional reaction (superhuman strength and loss of pain) after witnessing a brutal act of murder during the Armenian Genocide, and Hans, an intellectually impaired young man whom Fredy rescues from Germany in 1933. Once again, the nature of genocide as an evolving and escalating process of prejudice, discrimination, language, violation of rights, and finally violence, is emphasised in Tink's paper, first with the ideology of eugenics permeating language around those with disabilities, deeming them as inferior and unworthy of life, and then, with their rights gradually taken away over time, eventually even their right to life.

The role of perpetrators in the Nazi 'euthanasia' programme discussed in Tink's paper is explored in detail in Linda Shields and Susan Benedict's essay on the role of nurses in Nazi Germany. Despite being one of the 'caring professions', nurses participated, with varying degrees of willingness, in the murder of disabled people—a category that the Nazis did not hesitate to expand to take in more and more victims. Shields and Benedict provide background about the propaganda of eugenics that was designed to convince those working in the Nazi system that their actions were not only legally required but morally right, and outline the processes undertaken in hospitals to determine which individuals were no longer 'worthy of life'. The question of how medical professionals could starve children, force feed people lethal doses of drugs, or leave victims outside in the cold to die remains unanswered, but Shields and Benedict's essay provides insight into the often banal and sometimes ideologically driven motivations for perpetrators of genocide.

Complementing Tatz's piece by exploring the exploitation and trauma of Indigenous Australian communities from a different point of view, is Jacob G. Warren's essay on Maralinga and nuclear colonialism. Warren describes the pain and 'violent realities' of seeing Maralinga, this 'invisibly scarred and toxic region only two hours north of the much-used Eyre Highway'. Just as Tink analysed genocide through literature, so too does Warren examine Indigenous genocide (the destruction of the peoples, identity, and land) via visual art. Warren describes the sand-covered painting *Maralinga* by Jonathan Kumintjara Brown and the five-metre tall installation *Thunder Raining Poison* by Yhonnie

Scarce, drawing connections with the image of the desert as 'void', *terra nullius*, the notion that the land was uninhabited, and environmental injustice a form of slow violence. Like many of the other essays in this collection, Warren grapples with the understanding of genocide as a slow gradual process but still evident today in the artworks depicting the nuclear destruction of Maralinga.

Another site of historical violence against Indigenous Australians is Myall Creek, where a massacre took place in 1838 of 28 men, women and children of the Kamilaroi nation. Each year that event is commemorated, and it is well known because it was one of the only massacres of Aboriginal people that resulted in prosecution against the perpetrators. Mark Tedeschi QC, who wrote a book on the event titled *Murder at Myall Creek*, gave a speech at the 2017 commemoration that he has generously allowed us to publish here. Tedeschi contemplates the significance of the unique prosecution of convicts for the murder of Aboriginal people and highlights the role of those individuals who refused to remain silent in the face of this horrendous crime. He points out the similarities between the case and modern war crimes trials, although war crimes as a concept had not been invented. Indeed, Tedeschi asserts that the 'actions of the Myall Creek murderers were war crimes and part of a deliberate, state-sanctioned genocide of the Aboriginal people that today would be punishable by the rules of international criminal law'.

Australian history, and the legacy of genocide, are two topics explored by Caroline Schneider and Hans-Lukas Kieser in their essay based on the 2018 exhibition in Canberra, 'Long Shadows—The Great War, Australia and the Middle East'. The exhibition and the essay look at the connections between the ANZAC experience and the Armenian Genocide, drawing on experiences of Australian soldiers who witnessed genocidal crimes as well as humanitarian efforts by Australian organisations to assist Armenian victims, all the while asking why the Armenian Genocide does not have a more prominent place in Australian and ANZAC history. The authors draw yet another important connection, between the persecution of the Ottoman era against ethnic and religious minorities, and the echoes, or 'long shadows', in the Middle East today, most clearly seen in the 2014 genocide of the Yazidis in Northern Iraq. The parallels between the two cases must compel us to ask why we still have not learnt from history, taking us back to Bellamy and McLoughlin's analysis of leadership and atrocity prevention.

Schneider and Kieser mention the transgenerational impact of the Armenian Genocide on the Armenian community and this issue is analysed in depth in the final essay of the collection, '"It's Happening Again": Genocide, Denial, Exile and Trauma', by Armen Gakavian. First examining how survivors and their descendants have responded to the ongoing trauma of the genocide over the past three decades, Gakavian goes on to identify two newer responses. The first—engagement with Turkish government, civil society and individuals has an 'outward, positive focus' whereby diasporan Armenians are willing to engage with Turkish peers in the more neutral environments of North

America, Europe, and Australia. Likewise, there has been a shift among some segments of the Turkish community that have proven willing to honestly confront their nation's history. The second more recent response, Gakavian argues, is one of fear among Armenian communities that the genocide 'is happening again'. Gakavian looks at responses to the 1988 earthquake, the conflict in Nagorno-Karabakh, and the recent conflicts in the Middle East especially in Syria, analysing how Armenians view such events through the lens of their unresolved trauma and Turkish denial.

We are very privileged to have co-edited this timely and original contribution to the *Genocide Perspectives* Series and to genocide studies literature more broadly. We thank the AIHGS for the honour, and all the contributors for their hard work.

CHAPTER I

Fateful Choices

Political Leadership and the Paths to and from Mass Atrocities

Alex J. Bellamy and Stephen McLoughlin

Syria's President, Bashar al-Assad, had an important decision to make on 30 March 2011. His country had been engulfed by protests for the past two weeks, triggered by the security force's overreaction to anti-regime graffiti scrawled on a school wall by a group of teenagers and fuelled by the tumults of the 'Arab Spring'. Now, the President was to deliver his first televised address to the nation since the protests began. Assad had a real choice to make; his counsellors were divided. Indeed, there is some suggestion that there were even two—very different—draft speeches.[4] Some, like Manaf Tlass, a close confidant to Bashar and his father Hafez al-Assad before him, and Brigadier General in Syria's elite Republican Guard, advised restraint. The President should align himself with the protesters, sack corrupt officials and offer political and economic reform, Tlass argued. Above all, he should rein in the security forces, end the use of force against peaceful protesters and prosecute those responsible.

---

[4] David Lesch views the speech as a pivotal turning point and documents the background and debates in impressive detail. See David W Lesch, *Syria: The Fall of the House of Assad* (New Haven: Yale University Press, 2013), 75–82.

How to cite this book chapter:
Bellamy, A. J. and McLoughlin, S. 2020. Fateful Choices: Political Leadership and the Paths to and from Mass Atrocities. In: Marczak, N. and Shields, K. (eds.) *Genocide Perspectives VI: The Process and the Personal Cost of Genocide.* Pp. 7–31. Sydney: UTS ePRESS. DOI: https://doi.org/10.5130/aaf.b. License: CC BY-NC-ND.

The people still believed in him, Tlass told his President. Moderation and accommodation would dampen the protests and secure the regime—just as it had in neighbouring Jordan.[5] Others disagreed. Hesitation and restraint would be taken as signs of weakness, they argued, just as in Egypt, where the army's refusal to fire on protesters had sealed President Mubarak's fate six weeks earlier. Assad would have no such problem persuading the feared security services, the *Mukhabarat*, and elite military units loyal to the government to attack the protesters. The President should denounce the protesters and step up the crackdown, they argued.

It was a close-run thing. On the day itself, moderates inside Assad's inner circle believed the President would offer a hand of conciliation to the protesters. Millions of Syrians tuned in to watch, most hoping that their President would offer words to unite the country and stem the escalation of violence. They were to be bitterly disappointed. Assad chose instead to pour fuel on the fire; to send Syria on a path towards civil war, mass atrocities and utter destruction, all in order to protect his family's hold on power. The President denounced the protesters as part of a great foreign-backed conspiracy that was using sedition to weaken and destroy Syria itself. All part of a masterplan supposedly orchestrated by Israel. The government, he argued, must take a firm hand. The touchpaper was lit and many Syrians left bitterly disappointed. But beneath all that lay the hard realisation that the state was positioning itself against the people, that the government would not reform and that violence was inevitable.

It is true that genocides and other mass atrocities do not emerge out of nowhere, that they are processes often long in the making.[6] All too often, however, a focus on the structural causes and pathways of escalation that lead to mass violence obscures the role of human agency, the fact that along the way leaders make decisions that push their countries towards, or away from, mass violence. Syria's recent history might have been very different had Assad chosen a different path. Likewise, Slobodan Milošević might have led Serbia in a different direction, Salva Kiir and Riek Machar might have pursued a more peaceful way of resolving their differences in South Sudan and Aung San Suu Kyi's government of Myanmar might have dished out citizenship rights not atrocity crimes in Rakhine state. Decisions made by leaders line the path to mass atrocities, yet they can also forge a path away from mass atrocities.

There are uncomfortable truths here for those invested in atrocity prevention, too. In May 1998, UN Secretary-General Kofi Annan gave a speech in Kigali, Rwanda, in which he underscored an undeniable—if uncomfortable—

---

[5] Tlass later defected. For an account based on his testimony see Sam Dagher, *Assad or We Burn the Country: How One Family's Lust for Power Destroyed Syria* (New York: Little, Brown and Co., 2019).

[6] Except where specifically noted, we use the terms 'mass atrocities' and 'mass violence' as shorthands for the atrocity crimes of genocide, war crimes, ethnic cleansing and crimes against humanity.

truth about the genocide there four years earlier. For all that the international community could be condemned for failing to confront the mass slaughter, the genocide itself 'was a horror that came from within'.[7] Atrocity crimes do not emerge from nowhere but arise out of deep-seated fear and practices of discrimination, marginalisation and conflict. On most occasions both the forces that push societies towards the abyss, and those that inhabit such moves, are propelled not by international actors but by national governments, civil societies and private sectors animated by decidedly local concerns.[8] As Scott Straus recently argued, international actors can play a 'supporting role' but 'it is very difficult, if not impossible, for international actors to impose new political narratives or to impose peace on ruling elites who do not want to compromise'.[9] The hard truth is that more often than not, the actors primarily responsible for determining whether or not a country will experience the horror of atrocity crimes are those within the country itself.[10]

In this essay, we explore the role of national leaders in committing, stopping and preventing mass atrocities. We argue that leaders play crucial but poorly understood roles in determining whether or not mass atrocities occur, as well as the degree to which they do and how they are terminated. To begin to better understand the role of leadership in causing and preventing mass atrocities, this essay unfolds in two main parts. First, we build a case for the importance of understanding the influence that leaders have had. We do this by pointing out the tendency on the one hand to accept as a given that such leaders as Josef Stalin, Pol Pot and Adolf Hitler were central to perpetration of genocide and mass violence, yet on the other there is very little interest in investigating what leaders have done to navigate things in a different direction. We then draw on examples to explore the role and impact of leaders in three ways: in creating or inhibiting risk; in pulling societies back 'from the brink'—or pushing them over it—in times of crisis; and in halting—or prolonging—atrocities that have already started. In better understanding the decisions that leaders have

---

[7] Stanley Meisler, *Kofi Annan: A Man of Peace in a World of War* (New York: John Wiley & Sons, 1997), 172.

[8] The importance of the local in driving atrocities is emphasised by Scott Straus, *The Order of Genocide: Race, Power and War in Rwanda* (Ithaca: Cornell University Press 2008) and, more generally, Stathis N Kalyvas, *The Logic of Violence in Civil Wars* (Cambridge: Cambridge University Press, 2006).

[9] Scott Straus, *Making and Unmaking Nations: War, Leadership, and Genocide in Modern Africa* (Ithaca: Cornell University Press, 2015).

[10] For an account of the different types of roles played by individuals with respect to atrocity crimes, see Edward C Luck and Dana Zaret Luck, 'The Individual Responsibility to Protect', in *Reconstructing Atrocity Prevention*, eds. Sheri P Rosenberg, Tibi Galis, and Alex Zucker (Cambridge: Cambridge University Press, 2015), 214–32.

made historically, which have led to both the perpetration and avoidance of mass atrocities, and why they have made such decisions, what becomes clearer are the circumstances within which leaders make such decisions, the reasons behind their decisions and how preventive strategies can be better calibrated to deal with different types of leaders.

Leadership and mass atrocities

Historians have written dozens, if not hundreds, of volumes about the central role that leaders such as Hitler, Stalin and Pol Pot played in planning, authorising and orchestrating mass violence.[11] But we lack a broader understanding of the role of leadership, the choices that leaders make and the factors that influence those choices. In particular, because we tend to focus only on the most notorious of genocidal leaders, we tend not to see the other paths that were open to them and the impact other leaders have had on halting atrocities that have started. And almost completely ignored are those leaders who succeeded in steering countries away from violence entirely during times of upheaval and dangerous risk escalation.[12] We know much about Bashar al-Assad's fateful decision, much less about how Jordan's King Abdullah II or Tunisia's Ben Ali and then Hamadi Jebali navigated more peacefully the same winds that destroyed Syria (though not entirely peacefully in Ben Ali's case). When it comes to leadership and mass atrocities, the dogs that do not bark are never heard. As a result, we have only a partial understanding of the role that leaders play—one that provides relatively little advice for the prevention of mass atrocities.

There is broad consensus that mass atrocities are processes that are deliberately planned, rather than spontaneous outbursts of violence.[13] There is also good evidence that authoritarian political regimes are more prone to perpetrate such violence than others, and that those regimes that promoted exclusionary ideologies are especially prone.[14] But these contextual factors, and

---

[11] See, for example, Alan Bullock, *Hitler and Stalin: Parallel Lives* (New York: Knopf, 1992); Ben Kiernan, *The Pol Pot Regime: Race, Power, and Genocide in Cambodia under the Khmer Rouge 1975–1979* (New Haven, Connecticut: Yale University Press, 2008).

[12] See, for example, Helen Fein, *Accounting for Genocide: National Responses and Jewish Victimization during the Holocaust* (New York: Free Press, 1980); Leo Kuper, *Genocide: Its Political Use in the Twentieth Century* (New Haven: Yale University Press, 1983); Jacques Semelin, *Purify and Destroy: The Political Uses of Genocide and Massacre* (New York: Columbia University Press, 2007).

[13] For example, see Adama Dieng, 'Seeing Atrocity Crimes as Processes, Not Single Events', interview by YJIA, *Yale Journal of International Affairs* 9, iss. 1 (2014): 85–90.

[14] Straus, *Making and Unmaking*, 326.

the impact they have on the course of events, are mediated by human agency, meaning that similar sets of factors create different effects in different settings because the people who are taking decisions and acting upon them are different. As the historian Margaret Macmillan points out, no two settings are ever the same precisely because the people involved are different. These regimes are more often than not headed by a prominent, sometimes 'charismatic', leader. What matters—when we are looking for evidence of processes or risk factors—is the collective impact these have on the choices that leaders make across time and space. The way we understand mass atrocities and their prevention therefore needs to be 'saturated with agency' to a much greater extent than it is.[15]

On the one hand, structural or contextual factors associated with heightened risk of mass atrocities matter only inasmuch as they influence the decision making of individuals and groups, and little is more consequential than the decision making of political leaders. On the other, it is important to recognise that contextual factors are often themselves produced by the conscious decisions of national elites. Forms of government, patterns of discrimination, the quality of the rule of law, the character of national ideologies—all of these factors associated with heightened risk are human artifices usually constructed by national elites. In relation to each one, national leaders could have chosen to follow more propitious paths, as indeed they tended to do in those countries that successfully navigated their way through moments of potential crisis.[16]

For example, in explaining why Côte d'Ivoire 'retreated from the brink' in early 2011 while Rwanda spiralled into genocide 16 years earlier, Scott Straus points to the distinct approaches each country's inaugural post-colonial leader took. Rwanda's Grégoire Kayibanda repeatedly emphasised the threat that ethnic Tutsis represented, while Côte d'Ivoire's Houphoet Boughny 'preached the values of inter-ethnic cooperation, dialogue and tolerance'.[17] Another study investigated the domestic factors that were instrumental in three countries—Botswana, Zambia and Tanzania—navigating long-term risk associated with mass atrocities following independence in the 1960s. It found that effective long-term risk mitigation was in large part the product of the inclusiveness of vision, and corresponding inclusive policies implemented by these states' founding leaders: 'This in itself highlights the importance of individual agency in the long-term prevention of mass atrocities'.[18] Evidently, not only do leaders

---

[15] To borrow a phrase used by Christopher Clark, *The Sleepwalkers: How Europe Went to War in 1914* (London: Penguin, 2012), xxvii.

[16] This way of thinking about the relationship between human agency and social structures in the context of mass violence draws from Alex J Bellamy, *East Asia's Other Miracle: Explaining the Decline of Mass Atrocities* (Oxford: Oxford University Press, 2017), 11.

[17] Scott Straus, 'Retreating from the Brink: Theorizing Mass Violence and the Dynamics of Restraint', *Perspectives on Politics* 10, no. 2 (2012): 353–55.

[18] Stephen McLoughlin, *The Structural Prevention of Mass Atrocities* (London: Routledge, 2014), 159.

matter in the prevention of mass atrocities, but often their agency plays a central role in shaping and limiting scenarios of risk.

That mass atrocities tend to be deliberative and well planned is well established. This suggests the importance of leadership, and historical experience seems to bear this out. Scholars have long argued that leaders are of central importance in making purposeful decisions that lead to such violence. They argue that the leader is often the key agent responsible for instrumentalising pre-existing divisions and prejudices that escalates tensions and mobilises populations to either take part in violence, or turn a blind eye to the violence directed against collective groups.[19]

But as experience in Côte d'Ivoire, Botswana, Tanzania and Zambia shows, the influence of leadership goes both ways. In some cases where atrocities begin but are ended relatively early—as in the post-election violence in Kenya in 2007–8, or in the communal violence experienced in Kyrgyzstan's city of Osh in 2008—it is often political leadership that has been effective in changing course away from violence. As the next section demonstrates, there are numerous examples where leaders have helped curb mass violence and de-escalate risk. Knowing how these different scenarios unfold is crucial in developing our understanding as we continue to seek greater clarity on why, as Ban Ki-moon observed during his time as the UN's Secretary-General, 'some states have taken one path and other states a different path'.[20]

What does this mean for how we ought to think about the prevention of mass atrocities? Surprisingly, perhaps, given the voluminous historical literature on the role of individual leaders, emerging practices, policies and theories for atrocity prevention pay scant regard to understanding the role of leaders and leadership, the importance of their decision-making, or the manner in which influence might be effectively wielded. Indeed, thus far deliberations have tended to focus on the importance of ensuring the legal accountability of leaders in the event of mass violence, without much in the way of longitudinal or case specific evidence that accountability factors into the decisions leaders make. Thus, for example, the landmark International Commission on Intervention and State Sovereignty (ICISS) report on the Responsibility to Protect (R2P) acknowledged that the systematic targeting of victims was the product of a failure of both 'leadership and institutions' and observed that in cases where such targeting was occurring, sanctions that targeted leadership groups were

---

[19] Neil J Kressel, *Mass Hate: The Global Rise of Genocide and Terror* (Cambridge, MA: Westview Press, 2002), 171; David Hamburg, *Preventing Genocide: Practical Steps Toward Early Detection and Effective Action* (Boulder: Paradigm, 2008), 34; Daniel Jonah Goldhagen, *Worse than War: Genocide, Eliminationism, and the Ongoing Assault on Humanity* (New York: Public Affairs, 2009), 76.

[20] Ban Ki-moon, *Implementing the Responsibility to Protect: Report of the Secretary-General*, A/63/677 (2009), 20.

more effective than general sanctions.²¹ Of course, mass atrocities are not 'failures' of leadership but the product of wilful choices made by leadership, the means by which leaders try to get what they want. Echoing the scholarly literature on the causes of genocide and other mass atrocities, the report identified 'leadership' as a key causal factor but this did not translate into guidance about how this might be addressed. The report's discussion of strategies of prevention focussed heavily on institutions such as human rights reform, improving the rule of law and the promotion of dialogue and reconciliation, but said nothing about leadership.²² In effect, then, leaders disappear from the equation when it comes to preventive policies and strategies, as if institutional reform is driven by invisible hands rather than existing political leaders.

The wider roles of leadership received more oxygen in Ban Ki-moon's first report on the R2P principle in 2009. In it, the Secretary-General observed that atrocity crimes are the results of the actions of political leaders who make deliberate political decisions aimed at manipulating pre-existing social divisions and weak institutions.²³ Ban Ki-moon went on to point out that often weak leadership lies at the heart of mass atrocity crimes, in response to which he recommends international programmes that seek to 'build leadership capacity', such as work done by the UNDP and the Woodrow Wilson Centre.²⁴ The Secretary-General broke new ground by observing that 'farsighted leadership' can play critical roles in preventing ethnic violence, pointing explicitly to the example of the former Yugoslav Republic of Macedonia in the early 1990s, which avoided mass violence as its neighbours Kosovo, Bosnia and Croatia burned. The Secretary-General also highlighted the importance that successive generations of leaders (in at-risk societies) have in preventing the kinds of 'fissures and frustrations' that lead to mass atrocity crimes.²⁵

Clearly, therefore, the UN's inaugural report on R2P laid out the importance of understanding the crucial role of leadership, both in the path to the perpetration of mass atrocities and in managing risk of such violence. Yet the precise role of leadership, in terms of mass atrocity prevention, is not clear. Indeed, the report acknowledged that: ' ... more research and analysis is needed on why one society plunges into mass violence while its neighbours remain relatively stable ... '²⁶ Little was known about why many at-risk societies *do not* experience mass atrocities, let alone the role that individual leaders might have played in risk de-escalation.

---

[21] International Commission on Intervention and State Sovereignty, The Responsibility to Protect (Ottawa: International Development Research Centre, 2001), 2.
[22] The Responsibility, 19.
[23] Ki-moon, *Implementing R2P*, 12.
[24] Ibid., 16.
[25] Ibid., 21.
[26] Ibid., 10–11.

The Secretary-General began to fill this void in a 2013 report that explored the domestic-level actors and strategies that made countries more (and less) resilient to mass atrocity risk—the first formal report on atrocity prevention to project a focus on the role that domestic actors play in avoiding mass violence. Ki-moon identified six key national sources of resilience that inhibited escalation towards mass atrocities—including constitutional protections, systems of democracy and accountability, measures addressing inequality and the criminalisation of atrocity crimes—but again opted to focus on institutional capacities and factors rather than individual agency. Indeed, none of the six sources of resilience identified individual agency and leadership as being important inhibiting factors in risk de-escalation and atrocity prevention.[27]

Subsequent United Nations reports on atrocity prevention and R2P have continued to gloss over the role of leadership. While there are passing references to the importance of leaders as prevention actors, they tend to articulate the importance of leadership in four ways: the preventive role of local leaders;[28] the importance of international leadership in responding to impending or unfolding atrocities around the world;[29] military leadership;[30] and the need for strong leadership at all levels (local, national and international).[31] The role of religious leaders has also emerged as a key focus thanks to the efforts of the Secretary-General's Special Adviser on the Prevention of Genocide, Adama Dieng. Nonetheless, though the idea of national leadership playing an important role in steering countries towards or away from upheaval and mass atrocities was acknowledged in the 2009 report on R2P, thinking about this important question has not advanced since.

In what remains of this essay, we want to suggest a more systematic way of thinking about this question that focuses on three critical contexts:

1. The role that leaders play in creating or inhibiting the risk of mass atrocities within societies;

---

[27] Ban Ki-moon, *Responsibility to Protect: State Responsibility and Prevention*, A/67/929-S/2013/399 (2013), 8–11.

[28] Ban Ki-moon, *A Vital and Enduring Commitment: Implementing the Responsibility to Protect*, A/69/981-S/2015/500 (2015), 8, 11, 20; Ban Ki-moon, *Mobilizing Collective Action: The Next Decade of the Responsibility to Protect*, A/70/999-S/2016/1620, 10, 14; António Guterres, *Implementing the Responsibility to Protect: Accountability for Protection*, A/71/1016-S/2017/556, 15; António Guterres, *Responsibility to Protect: From Early Warning to Early Action*, A/72/884-S/2018/525, 3, 4, 11, 14.

[29] A/69/981-S/2015/500, 13; /70/999-S/2016/1620, 14.

[30] A/69/981-S/2015/500, 11.

[31] A/70/999-S/2016/1620, 10, 18; A/72/884-S/2018/525, 7.

2. The role that leaders play in driving societies 'over the brink' into mass atrocities and why some leaders are effective in steering countries away from mass atrocities during times of upheaval and heightened risk; and
3. Why and how some leaders put a halt to mass atrocities early.

The fateful decisions leaders make can either inhibit mass atrocities or push states and societies towards—and over—the brink, as shown in the table below. In what follows, we will examine these different roles in more detail.

	Atrocity accelerator	Atrocity inhibitor
Context	*Risk makers* • Assads in Syria, Milošević in Serbia	*Risk breakers* • East Asian governments
Crisis	*Drivers* • Suharto in Indonesia	*Preventers* • Gligorov in Macedonia, Mandela in South Africa
Resolution	*Prolongers* • Government and opposition in Syria	*Terminators* • Kibaki and Odinga in Kenya

The role and impact of leaders

Risk makers and risk breakers

Social contexts—the stuff of atrocity risk factors measured by early warning frameworks—do not appear out of nowhere. Sometimes, as in the case of Hitler and Stalin and Pol Pot too, they are driven by ideology, the murderous intent there from the start, and an end in itself. More often, though—and this is something missed by our focus on the demagogic core—leaders create risk almost unknowingly, as a by-product of their efforts to simply cling to power in settings where most of their people would rather that they did not. A good recent example of this takes us back to where we started: Syria's Assad family.

The Assads, father Hafez and son Bashar, played a key role in creating the conditions for mass atrocities, building a corrupt minority-led state that maintained order through the ruthless and arbitrary application of extreme violence, including killing, torture and detention. Internally divided and externally threatened, it is unsurprising that post-independence Syrian domestic politics were anything but stable. After a failed attempt at parliamentary democracy and a series of coups and counter-coups, the Ba'athists seized control of the government in 1963. Arab nationalist and determinedly socialist in orientation, the Ba'ath Party appealed to Syrian society's outsiders, such as the religious minorities and rural poor.³² The new government, led by Salah Jadid, embarked on a radical programme of socialist reform. Behind the scenes, Hafez al-Assad, an ambitious army officer from the minority Alawite sect, consolidated his control over the military. In November 1970, a dispute over policy on the Palestinian issue came to a head. Jadid tried to dismiss Hafez, who then led a successful coup and claimed power.

Survival was the principal goal of Hafez's new government. Hafez al-Assad proved to be a supremely gifted, if ruthless, political tactician. But he lacked a compelling strategic vision beyond survival itself.³³ His ambition was to establish a strong Ba'athist state and mass party based on socialist principles that would marshal economic development, reform the social order and empower previously marginalised groups.³⁴ The reality rarely matched the ambition and Syria lurched from crisis to crisis, the government almost permanently in crisis mode. Hafez's 'was a government which grew out of seven years of bloody struggle, and its foundations were and would remain the army, the security services, and the party and government machinery'.³⁵ Trusted loyalists, most of them Alawites, were placed in the key command positions. The security sector was purged of non-Ba'athists and of any whose loyalty to Hafez al-Assad was questioned. Thus, the new president came to rely heavily on a close network of trusted personal followers, many of them kin, for leadership of the military and security forces.³⁶ While his government's legitimacy depended on a broader coalition of allies, those outside his almost exclusively Alawi inner circle were kept well away from positions that could be used to challenge the leader's supremacy.³⁷ According to one estimate, 90 per cent of the commanders of major military formations were Alawites.³⁸ Economic benefits were given

---

[32] John McHugo, *Syria: A Recent History* (London: Saqi Books, 2001), 118–22.

[33] Central argument made by Eyal Zisser, *Assad's Legacy: Syria in Transition* (New York: New York University Press, 2001), 190–91.

[34] Raymond Hinnebusch, *Authoritarian Power and State Formation in Ba'athist Syria: Army, Party and Peasant* (Boulder: Westview Press, 1990), 2; also Patrick Seale, *Assad: The Struggle for the Middle East* (Oakland: University of California Press, 1988).

[35] Seale, *Assad*, 178.

[36] Raymond Hinnebusch, *Syria: Revolution from Above* (London: Routledge, 2002), 67.

[37] Compare Hinnebusch, *Authoritarian Power* with Steven Heydemann, *Authoritarianism in Syria: Institutions and Social Conflict: 1946–1970* (Ithaca: Cornell University Press, 1999), and Andrew Rathmell, 'Syria's Intelligence Services: Origins and Development', *Journal of Conflict Studies* 16, no. 2 (1996): 75–96.

[38] Eyal Zisser, 'Appearance and Reality: Syria's Decision-Making Structure', *Middle East Review of International Affairs* 2, no. 2 (1998): 29–41.

to key allies, part of a highly corrupt patronage network designed to keep the Assads in power.

This was all part of the government's attempt to 'coup-proof' itself. To this, Hafez added a complex system of multiple overlapping security agencies, including the military, the secret police, six intelligence agencies (five of which focused primarily on 'internal' threats) and government militia—known collectively as the *mukhabarat*.[39] The feared *mukhabarat* enjoyed complete impunity and autonomy, and were responsible for policing Syrian society as well as each other. Their activities were governed by an 'emergency law' first enacted in 1963 and still in force at the beginning of 2011, which allowed the security forces to detain, try and sentence people—in secret—under the rubric of 'protecting the state'.[40] Numbering between 50,000 and 70,000 officers, these agencies supported operations overseas and extensive activities at home. Each agency also operated its own prisons and interrogation centres that enjoyed almost complete independence and faced little in the way of oversight or scrutiny.[41] *Mukhabarat* members enjoyed immunity from prosecution for any actions undertaken in the service of the state. Together, the security services maintained a dense network of surveillance and regularly used arrests, imprisonment, torture and extra-judicial killings to intimidate or eliminate actual or suspected opponents. In 1982, the security forces brutally repressed an uprising in Hama, killing 30,000 in the process. A demonstration of what the security forces were willing to do to keep the Assads in power, and a portent of worse to come.

Bashar al-Assad's ascendancy to the presidency in 2000 was greeted with optimism. The new leader promised reforms but the hope was short lived. The *mukhabarat* state prevailed. Indeed, if anything, the *mukhabarat* became a more visible part of daily life in Syria. According to a 2010 report by Human Rights Watch, 'Syria's security agencies … detain people without arrest warrants and torture with complete impunity'.[42] In 2003 there were an estimated 1,000 political prisoners.[43]

Thus, on the eve of the 'Arab Spring', Syria was a society on the brink, put there largely by the policy choices of its own leaders. Resentments over past violence, the privations caused by the *mukhabarat* state and Bashar's failure to deliver on reform ran deep. Economic hardships had grown, displacing whole communities, and the government had failed to offer any respite. Most Syrians

---

[39] On the establishment of the security state in Syria see Heydemann, *Authoritarianism in*.

[40] Lesch, *Syria*, 71.

[41] Alan George, *Syria: Neither Bread nor Freedom* (London: Zed Press, 2003), 2.

[42] https://www.hrw.org/news/2010/07/16/syria-al-asads-decade-power-marked-repression.

[43] International Crisis Group, 'Syria Under Bashar (II): Domestic Policy Challenges', Feb. 11, 2005, 11.

were deeply dissatisfied with their government, many loathed it, and a large number wanted it overthrown.

But national leaders can choose different paths. It is instructive to compare the experience of different regions on this point. Etel Solingen did just that in a landmark study that compared post-colonial East Asia with the Middle East. Both had emerged from colonisation around the same time, both were plagued by territorial disputes and ideological fissures, and in the 1950s they had similar types of highly centralised authoritarian states. They both had societies dominated by conservative feudal lords and military elites. In some respects, the Middle East's starting position was better than East Asia's since it enjoyed a higher degree of cultural similarity and fewer sharp ideological divides. From that point on, however, the two regions took very different paths. Most East Asian states consciously prioritised economic development through industrialisation and trade. National resources and government energies were directed towards supporting industrialisation. Intra-regional trade grew strongly, creating its own demands for regional stability and establishing national elites with international interests. The region developed strong anti-war norms of non-interference that helped stabilise relations between states. Middle Eastern governments, on the other hand, preferred self-sufficiency over trade, state-led rather than state-supported entrepreneurship and privileged the military, the military–industrial complex and militarised conceptions of security over the civilian economy.[44] In the Middle East, war remained a persistent feature of political life. In East Asia, it declined dramatically. The incidence of armed conflict in the Middle East was some five times greater than in East Asia. The principal cause of this marked difference, Solingen found, was the prioritisation of economics by East Asian governments and the outward-looking and trade-focused path to development they embraced. The prioritisation of 'economic development' in East Asia, Rosemary Foot writes, 'reflects a widely held belief among many of the elites in these states that there is a reciprocal relationship between economic growth and the promotion of regime and state security'.[45]

Our point here is that East Asian governments *chose* to prioritise economic development rather than military spending. Ironically, East Asia's path away from mass atrocities was shaped by a country that had recently perpetrated massive atrocity crimes but that was now looking to turn its back on that past. The adoption of the developmental trading state model began in Japan immediately after World War Two. It did not take long for others in the region

---

[44] Etel Solingen, 'Pax Asiatica versus Belli Levantina: The Foundations of War and Peace in East Asia and the Middle East', *American Political Science Review* 101, no. 4 (2007): 758.

[45] Rosemary Foot, 'Social Boundaries in Flux: Secondary Regional Organizations as a Reflection of Regional International Society', in *Contesting International Society in East Asia*, eds. Barry Buzan and Yongjin Zhang (Cambridge: Cambridge University Press, 2014), 196.

to notice Japan's remarkable post-war economic growth and try to emulate it. Another war-stricken country, Taiwan—an island state built on the remnants of China's nationalist government—quickly adopted Japanese style priorities and policies, with similar results. Not every government intervention was effective, of course, but the cumulative prioritisation of economic development, building of public-private partnerships and promotion of foreign trade yielded positive results overall. Taiwan was followed by Singapore, Hong Kong and South Korea—the growth of an educated middle class in the latter eventually propelling political reform, as well as elites realising the economic costs of trying to hang on to authoritarian government. Then Malaysia and Thailand followed, as authoritarian governments in Indonesia and The Philippines also tried, and failed, to mimic the model, prompting relatively peaceful transitions to democracy there too. And, as national leaders came to prioritise economic growth at the expense of military growth, ideological crusades and sectarian division, so the incidence of mass atrocities and the risks associated with them declined. As a result of that, one of the most violent and atrocity-risk prone parts of the world became progressively more peaceful as the social context of risk receded.[46]

Our point here is that just as the Assads played an instrumental role in *creating* the risk of mass atrocities in Syria, and successive governments in Sudan and Rwanda did the same, a number of leaders in East Asia played pivotal roles in dampening risks and helping their countries navigate difficult challenges without mass violence. The key lesson in all this is that, as Scott Straus has argued in the context of post-independence Africa, we need to pay much more attention to the states and societies that leaders build and shape, and think more carefully about how to engage earlier to inhibit the drift towards atrocities. As Straus explains, 'the long-term best asset against the risk of genocide and mass categorical violence is to craft a political vision that incorporates a role for multiple identities as fundamental to the project of the state'.[47] The key to this, Straus argues, is for national leaders to 'articulat[e] a nationalist narrative of pluralism and inclusion [which] provides the greatest source of restraint'.[48] Whether or not they do matters a great deal.

Drivers and inhibitors

Even in situations of risk, political leaders have choices about the type of political, institutional and economic paths they want to take. These choices are not pre-determined, but they are immensely consequential. We know this because societies with similar structural conditions can experience wildly different

---

[46] The central argument of Bellamy, *East Asia's Other Miracle*.
[47] Straus, *Making and Unmaking*, 323.
[48] Ibid.

trajectories owing to the decisions their leaders make. To give one example, Zimbabwe from the early 2000s contained all the elements necessary for internal conflict and mass atrocities. That it has not suffered the same fate as many of its neighbours owes much to the conscious decision of opposition leader Morgan Tsangirai to keep peace.[49]

It is not difficult to see evidence of leaders driving a politics of fear that push societies to the brink. For example, we can see it in the current Hungarian government's rhetoric and policy of marginalisation and discrimination directed towards the country's Roma population and refugees. We see it also in the sectarian preferences exhibited by states across the Middle Eastern region—practices that sowed the seeds of resentment, violent conflict and mass atrocities.[50]

It is also clear to see leaders driving states and societies over the brink. In fact, as a wide range of studies have demonstrated, mass atrocities rarely happen in the absence of humane leadership.[51] Take for example the mass killing of alleged communists in Indonesia in 1965–66, long regarded as an example of organised frenzied violence. The famous anthropologist, Clifford Geertz, who was well aware of the killings, ascribed the violence to cultural factors, specifically 'popular savagery' driven by pent up frustrations.[52] But it is now clear that the atrocities were planned, instigated and organised by the Indonesian army that was led by the country's incoming president, Suharto.

In late September 1965, a small group of Indonesian military officers with putative ties to the Communist Party (PKI), kidnapped and killed six senior army officers in what is widely thought to have been an attempted coup in support of Indonesia's increasingly leftward leaning President, General Sukarno. The army, led by General Suharto, quickly suppressed the coup and killed the ringleaders. The army then initiated the PKI's violent destruction. Between October 1965 and March 1966, around 500,000–600,000 Indonesians were slaughtered by the army and allied militia, religious youth groups

---

[49] On which, see Stephen Chan, *Citizen of Zimbabwe: Conversations with Morgan Tsangirai* (Harare: Weaver Press, 2010).

[50] Daniel Byman, 'Sectarianism Afflicts the New Middle East', *Survival* 56, no. 1 (2014): 79–100 and Christopher Phillips, 'Sectarianism and Conflict in Syria', *Third World Quarterly* 36, no. 2 (2015): 357–76.

[51] The literature on this is extensive. For example, see Kuper, *Genocide*; Fein, *Accounting for*; Goldhagen, *Worse than*; and Jacques Semelin, *Purify and Destroy: The Political Uses of Massacre and Genocide* (London: Hurst and Co., 2014).

[52] Clifford Geertz, 'Afterword: The Politics of Meaning', in *Culture and Politics in Indonesia*, ed. Claire Holt (Ithaca: Cornell University Press, 1972), 282, and Clifford Geertz, *The Interpretation of Cultures* (New York: Basic Books, 1973), 332.

and zealous mobs.⁵³ The killing was remarkable for its speed and intensity. Suharto employed units with strong anti-communist credentials KOSTRAD (reservists under Suharto's command) and RPKAD (elite units, staunchly anti-communist) to spearhead the killings.⁵⁴ The campaign began in Central Java and moved quickly to East Java and other provinces, Suharto claiming the purge was an 'absolutely essential cleaning out' of communists.⁵⁵ The army encouraged the establishment of militias and offered them the political authority, training, arms and logistical support they needed to conduct mass killings.⁵⁶

Although much of the killing was not done by the military, in most cases militias, youth groups and mobs did not start committing atrocities until elite military units arrived to direct, encourage and enable violence by instructing and arming the groups. In October 1965, the army worked hard to whip up a 'near hysterical anti-communist pogrom'.⁵⁷ Killing was typically initiated by the military and then continued by others at the military's urging.⁵⁸ The massacres were planned and orchestrated by the army with the intention of

---

⁵³ An army fact-finding commission put the figure at 78,500, but this has widely been criticised as being too low. Some estimates put the death toll at 2 million. Another official report, by KOPKAMTIB, estimated that 800,000 had been killed in central and eastern Java, and another 100,000 in both Bali and Sumatra, putting the total at 1 million. See Robert Cribb, 'Problems in the Historiography of the Killings in Indonesia', in *The Indonesian Killings 1965–1966: Studies From Java and Bali*, ed. Robert Cribb (Melbourne: Centre of Southeast Asian Studies, Monash, 1990), 7, and Arnold C. Brackman, *The Communist Collapse in Indonesia* (New York: W. W. Norton, 1969), 115. Today the figure of 400,000–500,000 is generally accepted by the Indonesian government.

⁵⁴ John Hughes, *Indonesian Upheaval* (New York: David McKay Co., 1967), 132.

⁵⁵ Brackman, *The Communist*, 119; Robert Cribb and Colin Brown, *Modern Indonesia: A History Since 1945 (The Postwar World)* (New York: Longman, 1995), 100. The actual complicity of the PKI remains a question of considerable doubt.

⁵⁶ Cribb, 'Problems in', 21.

⁵⁷ Michael van Langenberg, 'Gestapu and State Power in Indonesia', in *The Indonesian Killings of 1965–1966: Studies From Java and Bali* (Melbourne: Centre of Southeast Asian Studies, Monash University, 1990), 49.

⁵⁸ For example, Kenneth Orr, 'Schooling and Village Politics in Central Java in the Time of Turbulence', in *The Indonesian Killings 1965–1966: Studies From Java and Bali*, ed. Robert Cribb (Melbourne: Centre of Southeast Asian Studies, Monash University, 1990), 182–91, and Robert Cribb, 'Bali', in *The Indonesian Killings 1965–1966: Studies From Java and Bali*, ed. Robert Cribb (Melbourne: Centre of Southeast Asian Studies, Monash University, 1990), 182–91.

eliminating the PKI.⁵⁹ As Julie Southwood and Patrick Flanagan note: 'The Indonesian massacre was essentially a project of systematically indiscriminate killing. A project connotes aims, means and responsibility. It was systematic in that the military leadership clearly defined the set of victims: the PKI and its sympathisers. It was indiscriminate in that within the category of victims specified, all members were to be killed regardless of age, sex, guilt or any other criteria'.⁶⁰ By March 1966, the atrocities had achieved the army's objective of eliminating the PKI and it moved to end the killing and restore order.⁶¹ The deal was sealed by the elevation of General Suharto to the presidency.

There is abundant evidence that the military's senior leadership wilfully drove their country over the edge into mass atrocities. General Nasution, one of the survivors of the coup, instructed that, 'all of their [PKI] followers and sympathisers should be eliminated, otherwise the incident will recur'. The PKI, he argued, should be exterminated 'down to its very roots'.⁶² Nasution insisted that 'they must be immediately smashed' because 'they have committed treason'.⁶³ Army propagandists insisted that 'the sword cannot be met by the Koran ... but must be met by the sword. The Koran says that whoever opposes you should be opposed as they oppose you'.⁶⁴ The army forced or simply fabricated confessions from PKI leaders that intimated a deep plot to take over the country and impose communism.⁶⁵ In addition, the army concocted lurid stories about the torture, humiliation and mutilation of the six general who were killed and claimed that naked female communists danced over the generals' bodies. Images portraying these horrific scenes were frequently broadcast on television.⁶⁶ The communist assault on Indonesia's way of life and their perverted brutality required a thorough 'cleansing' and the killing was often described

---

[59] Julie Southwood and Patrick Flanagan, *Indonesia: Law, Propaganda and Terror* (London: Zed Press, 1983), 73.

[60] Southwood and Flanagan, *Indonesia: Law*, 73.

[61] Robert Cribb, 'Nation: Making Indonesia', in *Indonesia Beyond Suharto: Polity, Economy, Society, Transition*, ed. Donald K. Emmerson (Armonk: ME Sharpe, 1999), 33. As one officer put it, 'the people regained confidence in the government as a result of its positive actions to restore security and order'.

[62] Cited by Brackman, *The Communist*, 117.

[63] Cited by Hughes, *Indonesian Upheaval*, 189.

[64] Geoffrey Robinson, 'The Post-Coup Massacre in Bali', in *Making Indonesia: Essays on Modern Indonesia in Honour of George McT. Kahin*, eds. Daniel S. Lev and Ruth McVey (Ithaca: Southeast Asian Program Publications, Cornell University), 124.

[65] Dinas Sejarah, 'TNI—Angkatan Darat—Crushing the G30S/PKI in Central Java', in *The Indonesian Killings 1965-1966: Studies From Java and Bali*, ed. Robert Cribb (Melbourne: Centre of Southeast Asian Studies, Monash, 1990), 165.

[66] Rex Mortimer, *Indonesian Communism under Sukarno: Ideology and Politics, 1959-1965* (Ithaca: Cornell University Press, 1974), 389.

in this way by the army and its allies.⁶⁷ The army made a point of portraying the communists as denigrating traditional Indonesian beliefs, be they Islamic, Buddhist, Hindu, Christian or nationalist.⁶⁸

But leaders can also be proactive in introducing policies and strategies to confront escalating tensions even in the midst of crisis. In the early 1990s, as the Former Republic of Yugoslavia was fragmenting amid tension and conflict, the newly independent Republic of Macedonia stood at a crossroad. With minority Serbs and Albanians raising grievances, and Serbia threatening military action against Macedonia's recent secession, the country appeared to be on the brink of war. That Macedonia avoided the conflict and mass atrocities that unfolded in Croatia and then Bosnia, was largely due to its new president, Kiro Gligorov, but also other political and ethnic leaders.

Gligorov succeeded in negotiating an agreement with Serbia that was instrumental in defusing tensions between Skopje and Belgrade. Macedonia's declaration of independence in September 1991, took place in a climate of high tension. Secessions in Slovenia and Croatia earlier in the year had triggered violent clashes in both states with the Yugoslav National Army (JNA). JNA units were still stationed throughout Macedonia, making military reprisal a real possibility.⁶⁹ Gligorov negotiated with the Serbian government on the removal of all JNA units, securing an agreement in early February 1992. The agreement guaranteed the total withdrawal of JNA troops, while leaving behind some military equipment. The departure of the JNA decreased the likelihood of Serbian military interference in the nascent state of Macedonia.

Yet this move did not affect the possibility of internal identity-based tensions from escalating. There were two chief fault lines along which problems could potentially arise—between ethnic Serbs and ethnic Macedonians; and between Albanians and ethnic Macedonians. Leaders in the Macedonian government chose a path of accommodation and dialogue with the leaders of the largest Serbian political party, the Democratic Party of Serbs in Macedonia (DPSM). This led to an agreement that leaders on both sides signed in mid-1993, the terms of which included constitutional recognition of Serbs, greater media access and greater resources for Serbian language education. In return, the DPSM agreed to put an end to their opposition to Macedonia's statehood. As Ackerman points out, following the agreement, major confrontations between Serbs and Macedonian authorities ceased.⁷⁰

Accommodation and dialogue between leaders lay at the heart of managing tensions between ethnic Albanians and Slavic Macedonians. Prior to independence, the Macedonian government allowed ethnic Albanian political parties to be established, facilitating a range of voices and demands from the

---

⁶⁷ Cribb, 'Problems', 24, 30.
⁶⁸ See Robinson, 'The Post-Coup', 124.
⁶⁹ Alice Ackermann, *Making Peace Prevail: Preventing Violent Conflict in Macedonia* (Syracuse: Syracuse University Press, 2000), 82.
⁷⁰ Ackermann, *Making Peace*, 87.

Albanian community. While tensions remained high in the first couple of years of independence, the Macedonian government took political inclusion a step further by introducing power sharing measures. Five Albanians were elevated to ministers between 1990 and 1994, and following this, the number was four.[71] The government also agreed to include Albanian language programmes on the state-run television channels and radio stations and supported the daily publication of an Albanian language newspaper.[72] While these measures were still not regarded as sufficient by many in the Albanian community, grievances—particularly in the first few years of independence—were mostly aired in non-violent ways. Most Albanian leaders did not advocate the use of violence in their push for greater recognition.[73] Indeed, they themselves were measured in how far they would push their specific agendas for more autonomy within the newly independent state.[74] In an effort to place limits on Macedonian nationalism, Gligorov and other ministers were proactive in constructing a national identity that was broad based and inclusive. They did this by downplaying myths and avoiding extremist nationalist rhetoric in a variety of public forums and political debates.[75]

Finally, Gligorov was aware that the departure of the JNA left Macedonia vulnerable to potential outside military threats. In an effort to avoid the possibility of the descent into violence that occurred in other newly independent states from the Former Republic of Yugoslavia, Gligorov made a personal appeal to the United Nations for military assistance. The UN Preventive Deployment Force (UNPREDEP)[76] was authorised at the end of 1992. Gligorov first flagged the idea for a preventive deployment in December 1991 in a meeting with Cyrus Vance, UN special envoy at the time. He then made an official appeal in November 1992, as the conflict in Bosnia was rapidly escalating, amidst growing concerns that violence would spill over into Macedonia. In a letter to Secretary-General Boutros Boutros-Ghali, Gligorov proposed a 'preventive mission', which then led to the authorisation of UNPROFOR's deployment along Macedonia's borders. This then evolved into UNPREDEP in 1995. UNPREDEP is broadly credited with playing a key role in preventing war from spilling over into Macedonia.[77] Gligorov, along with other political leaders in Macedonia, were instrumental in preventing identity-based violence in

---

[71] Ackermann, *Making Peace*, 90.
[72] Ibid., 91.
[73] Ibid., 94.
[74] Stefan Troebst, 'An Ethnic War that Did Not Take Place: Macedonia, its Minorities and its Neighbours in the 1990s', in *War and Ethnicity: Global Connections and Local Violence*, ed. David Turton (San Francisco: Boydell Press, 1997), 90–91.
[75] Ackermann, *Making Peace*, 95.
[76] UNPREDEP was part of the larger UN Protection Force in the Former Yugoslavia (UNPROFOR).
[77] Ackermann, *Making Peace*, 84; Raimo Väryrynen, 'Challenges to Preventive Action: The Cases of Kosovo and Macedonia', in *Conflict Prevention: Path to*

the early years of the country's independence. Their strategies anticipated and targeted multiple flashpoints, which meant that preventive strategies they instigated included accommodation of and dialogue with the country's minority groups; the effective negotiating of the JNA's departure; and the facilitation of an international military presence, which helped to plug the gap in the nascent country's security capacity during an extremely volatile period.

Mediation, compromise and public appeals based on inclusive ideas also lay at the heart of South Africa's transformation from Apartheid state to universal enfranchisement, steered by Nelson Mandela and F. W. de Klerk. The avoidance of mass atrocities during this transition in the early 1990s was a product of de Klerk's commitment to dismantling Apartheid, Mandela's willingness to shift away from some of the ANC's more radical objectives, and the readiness of both to consult and compromise. These factors ensured that South Africa's transformation had widespread support. They were also instrumental in preventing extremist groups on both sides of the political divide from provoking widespread conflict. Yet, the transition away from Apartheid took place in a context of rising inter-group tension and violence, and widespread mistrust. The challenges, on de Klerk's part, of managing rogue elements within the security establishment, and on Mandela's part of dampening tensions between Inkatha Freedom Party supporters and ANC supporters, made the prospect of a peaceful transition insurmountable at times. However, both leaders were instrumental in navigating the country to peaceful elections in 1994.

Two moments stand out. The first was a speech made by de Klerk on 2 February 1990, when he announced the lifting of the ban on previously illegal opposition parties, the repeal of the 1953 Separate Amenities Act and the immediate and unconditional release of Mandela.[78] This sudden and dramatic change heralded the instant end of the Apartheid system, and belied de Klerk's record as a solid advocate of National Party policies to that point. However, upon becoming president in 1989, he concluded that a continuation of the status quo would place the country on an irreversibly destructive path.[79] In his opening speech to parliament, he prefaced the rescinding of Apartheid policies by stating that 'only a negotiated understanding among the representative leaders of the entire population is able to ensure lasting peace. The alternative is growing violence, tension and conflict'.[80] With a single speech, de Klerk announced to the country a radical change of direction. Far from alienating the white population, the

---

Peace or Grand Illusion?, eds. David Carment and Albrecht Schabe (Tokyo: United Nations University Press, 2003), 50–53.

[78] Betty Glad and Robert Banton, 'F.W. de Klerk and Nelson Mandela: A Study in Cooperative Transformational Leadership', *Presidential Studies Quarterly* 27, no. 3 (1997): 565–90, 567.

[79] Betty Glad, 'Passing the Baton: Transformative Political Leadership from Gorbachev to Yeltsin; From de Klerk to Mandela', *Political Psychology* 17, no. 1 (1996), 1–28: 3.

[80] F.W. de Klerk, 'Address by the State President, F. W. de Klerk, DMS, at the Opening of the Second Session of the Ninth Parliament of the Republic of

speech won the support of most South Africans, including the white population. According to one journalist, people 'were propelled by the sheer excitement of a journey undertaken at last'.[81] A referendum conducted two years later confirmed that two thirds of the white population were indeed in favour of these reforms.[82] It was de Klerk's decisive public announcement that marked the end of Apartheid, and won widespread support, both among the minority white and broader South African population.

The second moment was Mandela's commitment to diffusing inter-ethnic tensions in the year leading up to the election in 1994. Between 1990 and 1994, inter-group tensions grew increasingly violent and threatened to derail the transition to democracy. This provoked tensions on two fronts—between supporters of the Inkatha Freedom Party (IFP) and the ANC, but also between Mandela and de Klerk.[83] In this four-year period, the IFP perpetrated thousands of human rights violations, including the Boipatong massacre, which resulted in forty-five deaths, prompting the ANC to temporarily halt transition talks with the South African government and other groups.[84] In the wake of this, Mandela faced calls from his own supporters to abandon peaceful strategies and resume an armed struggle. His public response to such calls was emphatic and uncompromising, using his own position to drive home a path of peace: 'If you have no discipline, you are not a freedom fighter. If you are going to kill innocent people, you don't belong to the ANC. Your task is reconciliation'.[85] Violence escalated again in 1993, with the assassination of Chris Hani, leader of the South African Communist Party and head of the ANC's armed wing, *Umkhontu we Sizwe*, by a white nationalist. This triggered widespread riots that threatened to escalate to full blown war. Again, Mandela publicly diffused tensions and steered public rhetoric away from calls for retribution.[86] Mandela's determination to transition away from Apartheid through negotiation and not

---

South Africa, Cape Town, February 2, 1990', https://www.politicsweb.co.za/documents/fw-de-klerks-address-of-february-2-1990.

[81] Journalist Bill Keller, quoted in Glad and Banton, 'F.W. de Klerk and Mandela', 567.

[82] Glad and Banton, 'F.W. de Klerk and Mandela', 570.

[83] The tensions between Mandela and de Klerk increased partly due to the South African security establishment's covert support of IFP's militant activities, though de Klerk later claimed that he had knowledge of government involvement in such violence. See Tom Lodge, *Mandela: A Critical Life* (Oxford: Oxford University Press, 2006), 170.

[84] Truth and Reconciliation Commission, *Truth and Reconciliation Commission of South Africa Report, Volume 2*, 1998, http://www.justice.gov.za/trc/report/finalreport/Volume%202.pdf, 583–84.

[85] Nelson Mandela, quoted in Martin Meredith, *Mandela: A Biography* (London: Simon & Schuster, 2014), 495.

[86] Lodge, *Mandela*, 180–82.

violence, and his calls for supporters to refrain from responding violently to inter-group violence provoked by both the IFP and security forces, were instrumental in navigating the country back from the brink of conflict in 1993 and the final months leading up to the elections in April 1994.

Thus, Gligorov and Mandela chose a path different to Suharto, Nasution and their allies, and managed political transitions without mass bloodshed. And while Indonesia pressed on into a bloody war of aggression in Timor Leste and civil war in Aceh that were resolved only decades later with Suharto's forced removal from office, both Macedonia and South Africa emerged from their transitions into a period free from mass killing, both avoiding the very real potential for civil war. Understanding why Gligorov and Mandela chose this path, setting out precisely how both they and their countries benefitted immensely from their actions, and figuring out how others might be encouraged to follow suit, ought to become central avenues of research for those concerned with preventing future violence.

Prolongers and terminators

Once mass killing erupts, leaders make choices about whether to prolong the violence in the hope of getting themselves a better outcome or to prioritise the lives of their people by looking for ways out of the violence. Of course, the choices leaders make are influenced and constrained by their context, ideology and the situation around them, but nevertheless there is ample evidence to suggest that national leaders often do have the room to change their mind if they so choose. Even leaders who for a time drive their societies over the brink are capable of walking them back. In 1995, for example, Slobodan Milošević, the architect and chief prolonger of war, mass atrocities and genocide in former Yugoslavia, decided to abandon the Bosnian Serbs in order to protect his own domestic position.

We can return to the Syrian tragedy for an example of leaders choosing to prolong rather than terminate atrocities, calculating that they could get a better deal by killing more people. In 2012, a plan put forward by former UN Secretary-General Kofi Annan seemed to offer a chance for peace. Yet by all indications, despite enjoying the UN Security Council's formal support, the plan seemed doomed to failure from the beginning. Why?

Most commentators acknowledge that the Annan plan's failure was caused by forces beyond Annan's control, principally that neither the government nor the opposition was wholly committed to it and that the major powers were deeply divided about it.[87] Annan explained that 'without serious, purposeful

---

[87] Julien Barnes-Dacey, 'West Should Give Annan Plan another Chance', *CNN*, July 31, 2012, http://globalpublicsquare.blogs.cnn.com/2012/07/31/west-should-give-annan-plan-another-chance/.

and united international pressure, including from the powers in the region, it is impossible for me, or anyone, to compel the Syrian government in the first place, and also the opposition, to take the steps necessary to begin a political process'.[88]

First, the Syrian government was never committed to the peace process and likely never intended to entertain a political process that would result in it having to share power or lose power altogether. Russian support for the April 12 ceasefire persuaded Damascus to accept the plan and even to restrain its use of heavy weapons, but, Annan argues, 'sustained international support did not follow'. As the ceasefire unravelled, 'the government, realizing that there would be no consequences if it returned to an overt military campaign, reverted to using heavy weapons in towns'. Then, having tried to reinvigorate the process by securing an agreement in Geneva on the need for a political transition, no pressure was brought to bear to force Assad to accept it.[89] Likewise, the armed opposition—emboldened by international support and convinced that Assad's days were numbered—viewed the initiative as a means to the end of removing Assad. Annan's deputies, al-Qudwa and Martin Griffiths, engaged with the opposition but found them uncompromising. One UN official, for example, visited the Free Syrian Army and found that the Army believed that NATO was poised to intervene as it had in Libya and this this was only a matter of time.[90] That belief, combined with the influx of weapons from outside, made the opposition think that victory was inevitable. As such, they had few incentives to compromise, and instead looked only to use the process for their advantage. What is more, even had the SNC, for example, been more fully committed, the opposition lacked sufficient unity and coherence to hold the ceasefire together.

Second, Annan could only paper over the deep international fissures for so long. It was immediately clear that the Geneva Communiqué had done little to alleviate the problem. Governments offered wildly different interpretations of what had been agreed. Ultimately, international support for Annan was lukewarm at best, and in some quarters actively hostile. No state was prepared to prioritise the peace plan above their own positions on Syria's future. Ultimately, while the Kremlin was prepared to urge Damascus to accept Annan's six-point plan, it had no intention of allowing material pressure to be brought against it. When Moscow reached the limits of its influence, it chose to protect the regime. Russia was adamant that the armed opposition was as much to blame as the

---

[88] Cited in Rick Gladstone, 'Annan Steps Down as Peace Envoy and Cites Barriers in Syria and the United Nations', *New York Times*, Aug. 3, 2012, A6.

[89] Kofi Annan, 'My Departing Advice on How to Save Syria', *Financial Times*, Aug. 3, 2012, https://www.ft.com/content/b00b6ed4-dbc9-11e1-8d78-00144feab49a.

[90] Raymond Hinnebusch and I William Zartman, *UN Mediation in the Syrian Crisis: From Kofi Annan to Lakhdar Brahimi*, New York Peace Institute, Mar., 2016, 11.

government for the breakdown of the ceasefire, arguing that the opposition had tried to exploit the ceasefire in order to gain territory. On the other side, Turkey, Qatar and Saudi Arabia voiced disquiet about the process before it had even begun, Saudi Arabia for example criticising Annan for even engaging with Assad.[91] All three continued to supply or facilitate the supply of arms to the opposition during (albeit not at the levels seen after the process collapsed), and none used their influence over the opposition to encourage it to comply with the ceasefire. All gave the impression that the process was but a stepping stone towards more robust military support for the opposition. The opposition, then, saw little reason to compromise.

Third, there was a pronounced gap between the glacial pace of political negotiations and the deteriorating situation on the ground. The Syrian leadership negotiated while simultaneously stepping up its military actions. As violence escalated, it was clear that the non-coercive approach was not working. Indeed, many in the West worried that the process itself was providing cover for the continuation of violence and that the Russians were stalling in order to buy time for Damascus. There was little point persisting with a failing strategy, they argued, but there was little idea of what could replace it. The peace process collapsed and Syria's war entered a new, even deadlier, phase. At the time of writing, more than 500,000 Syrians had been killed and 6.5 million forced out of the country.

But it does not have to be like this. The ethnic violence that erupted in the aftermath of the disputed 30 December 2007 elections in Kenya was quickly stemmed by both sides of the political divide who agreed to negotiate a compromise that left neither with everything they wanted, but which saved their country from the fate that befell Syria.[92] While up to 1,500 people were killed and 300,000 displaced, a coordinated diplomatic effort by a troika of eminent persons mandated by the African Union (AU), spearheaded by Kofi Annan and supported by the UN Secretary-General, persuaded the country's president, Mwai Kibaki and main opponent, Raila Odinga, to conclude a power-sharing agreement and rein in the violent mobs. This prevented what many feared could have been the beginning of a much worse campaign of mass atrocities.

---

[91] Emile Hokayem, *Syria's Uprising and the Fracturing of the Levant* (New York: Routledge, 2013), 161.

[92] For example, Gareth Evans, *Responsibility to Protect: Ending Mass Atrocities Once and For All* (Washington, DC: Brookings Institute Press, 2009), 106; Desmond Tutu, 'Taking the Responsibility to Protect', *New York Times*, Nov. 9, 2008, https://www.nytimes.com/2008/02/19/opinion/19iht-edtutu.1.10186157.html; Donald Steinberg, 'Responsibility to Protect: Coming of Age?', *Global Responsibility to Protect* 1, no. 4 (2009): 432–41. For the most comprehensive account to date see Elizabeth Lindenmayer and Josie Lianna Kaye, *A Choice for Peace? The Story of Forty-One Days of Mediation in Kenya*, International Peace Institute, Aug., 2009.

When genocide and mass atrocities erupt, the degree to which global actors can make a difference depends on whether local and national leaders are willing to reach compromises and pull their followers back from violence. Do they believe, for instance, that their reputations and futures could be adversely affected by escalating violence? When they do not care what others think, have very different value systems, see their choices in existential terms and/or are highly resentful of external interference, the range of options for international action narrows markedly. Very often, decisions about whether to prolong or terminate atrocities are driven by domestic politics and personal ambitions. In practice, political leaders tend to be swayed more by what their political allies and financial backers are telling them than by the protests of outsiders. If major trading, economic, political or security partners are capable of making—and are prepared to make—perpetrators pay a significant price for bad behaviour, they will weigh their options differently. Such partners can, of course, act as spoilers instead. Whatever focus we take, more attention needs to be paid to how and why leaders choose to prolong or terminate mass atrocities.

Conclusion

When it comes to understanding mass atrocities and their prevention, leadership and individual responsibility are crucial. The intent and receptiveness of national leaders is of uttermost importance. Intransigent leaders can incite and perpetuate violence, block international action, refuse to implement agreements, stir up distrust and animosity towards the United Nations. Consensual preventive measures tend to have limited effect when leaders are intransigent. Receptive leaders, however, can negotiate and peacefully resolve crises, are open to persuasion, and are more likely to implement agreements.

In this essay we have begun to sketch out a typology of the roles that leaders can play as a first step towards a more detailed understanding of leadership and, critically, of how leadership can be used to support the prevention of mass atrocities. Our central argument is that the emerging field of atrocity prevention must pay far greater attention to questions of human agency than it hitherto has. As this avenue of enquiry develops, three critical sets of questions will need to be addressed.

First, we will need to develop more comprehensive accounts of the relationship between leaders' agency and the social, historical, institutional and normative structures they inhabit. We have proposed here that leaders typically have sufficient agency to make fateful choices but clearly the degree of agency they have is bounded by context. To better understand the extent of agency that leaders enjoy, we will need a more differentiated account of how different contexts impact and shape agency. We have also suggested that leaders are not passive recipients of social context, but often play a determining role in shaping that context. Once again though, greater specificity is needed to understand the different roles that different sorts of leaders play.

Second, and following on from this, we will need to develop frameworks for better understanding different leadership types, drivers and causal influences to afford us sharper analytical and predictive tools.[93]

Third, we might also look for leadership in different places. For example, in 2013–14, the Nobel Prize-winning Tunisian National Dialogue Quartet comprising civil society organisations representing organised labour, the private sector, the legal profession and human rights advocates, navigated the country peacefully through a political transition that contained all the portents of violence and atrocities. Similarly, in 2013, KEPSA—a Kenyan Private Sector Alliance—played a pivotal role in supporting atrocity prevention activities that helped the country avoid a repeat of the violence resulting from elections from 2007 to 2008.

When it comes to understanding and preventing mass atrocities, leadership matters. In this essay we have explored some of the different ways in which it matters, but this is a field of exploration that has a long way yet to go.

---

[93] A useful start is Bruce W. Jentleson, *The Peacemakers: Leadership Lessons from Twentieth-century Statesmanship* (New York: W. W. Norton, 2018).

CHAPTER 2

Freedom of Religion in the Genocidal Process and Group Destruction in the Holocaust and Armenian and Cambodian Genocides

Melanie O'Brien

Human rights are freedoms that are inherent to all persons, which states are obligated to protect. The atrocities of World War Two, in particular the annihilation of Jews in the Holocaust, shocked the global community into the creation of today's human rights legal system. Traditionally, international law was concerned with the rights and regulations of states. Following the Holocaust however, other actors (including individuals) were included in international law, based on the idea that states should not be free to treat persons within their territory as they wish and, in particular, should not be free to persecute and kill. The sentiment was that people should be respected and accorded rights to be able to live with dignity and liberty, within a broader desire for democratic rule of law.[94] Dignity and freedom are the essence of human rights, and are to be enjoyed by all without discrimination as to race, gender, religion,

---

[94] J.S. Mill, *On Liberty and Other Essays* (Oxford: Oxford University Press, 1991).

How to cite this book chapter:
O'Brien, M. 2020. Freedom of Religion in the Genocidal Process and Group Destruction in the Holocaust and Armenian and Cambodian Genocides. In: Marczak, N. and Shields, K. (eds.) *Genocide Perspectives VI: The Process and the Personal Cost of Genocide*. Pp. 33–52. Sydney: UTS ePRESS. DOI: https://doi.org/10.5130/aaf.c. License: CC BY-NC-ND.

ethnicity, sexuality, nationality, language, political or other opinion, disability, or any other reason. This is the universality and inalienability of human rights: everyone, everywhere is entitled to human rights. Protection of human rights is fundamental.

Genocide is a process,[95] throughout which many human rights violations occur, usually on a mass scale. The process begins with violations such as restrictions on freedom of expression and freedom of movement, escalating to violations of rights to family and health, before intensifying to violations of right to freedom from torture and cruel, inhuman and degrading treatment, and right to life.[96] This chapter will consider one particular human rights violation in genocide: violation of the right to freedom of religion.

Genocide consists of multiple crimes, including non-physical-extermination crimes: causing serious bodily or mental harm to members of national, ethnical, racial, or religious groups; and forcibly transferring children of the group to another group. Such crimes are essential in determining genocide and must not be suppressed from deliberations over the definition of genocide or the prosecution of perpetrators. While genocidal crimes may manifest in many forms, this essay focuses on violations of freedom of religion, which amount to criminal conduct as they cause serious bodily or mental harm, and include forcible transfer of children (for religious conversion) and killing members of a group (religious leaders).

Some groups are targeted for genocide because of religion, and are subject to substantial violations of their right to freedom of religion. Nonetheless, as will

---

[95] On genocide as a process, see for example, Martin Shaw, *What is Genocide?* (Cambridge: Polity Press, 2015), 101–3; Sheri P Rosenberg, 'Genocide Is a Process, Not an Event', *Genocide Studies and Prevention* 7, no. 1 (2012): 17–23; Scott Straus, 'Contested Meanings and Conflicting Imperatives: A Conceptual Analysis of Genocide', *Journal of Genocide Research* 3, no. 3 (2001): 349–75; Sheri P Rosenberg and Everita Silina, 'Genocide by Attrition: Silent and Efficient', in *Genocide Matters: Ongoing Issues and Emerging Perspectives*, eds. Joyce Apsel and Ernesto Verdeja (Abingdon: Routledge, 1999), 106–26; Helen Fein, 'Genocide by Attrition 1939–1993: The Warsaw Ghetto, Cambodia, and Sudan: Links Between Human Rights, Health, and Mass Death', *Health and Human Rights* 2, no. 2 (1997): 14; Leo Kuper, *Genocide: Its Political Use in the Twentieth Century* (New Haven: Yale University Press, 1982); Helen Fein, *Accounting for Genocide: National Responses and Jewish Victimization During the Holocaust* (New York: Free Press, 1979), 60; 'The 8 Stages of Genocide', Genocide Watch, 1998, http://www.genocidewatch.org/aboutgenocide/8stagesofgenocide.html; 'The Ten Stages of Genocide', Genocide Watch, 2016, http://genocidewatch.net/genocide-2/8-stages-of-genocide/.

[96] These violations are somewhat linear, but there are also many overlapping stages.

be demonstrated by the case studies in this chapter, even if a group is targeted for their nationality, race, or ethnicity, genocidal regimes have a tendency to fixate on destruction of religion as they execute genocide. This chapter examines the specific targeting of religion itself; how genocidal regimes breach the human right of freedom of religion as part of the destruction of that group as a social structure. Analysis will be offered of violations of freedom of religion as carried out by the Nazis, Committee of Union and Progress (CUP or Young Turks), and Khmer Rouge respectively in the Holocaust, and the Armenian and Cambodian genocides. The chapter will demonstrate how this particular human rights violation contributes to genocide, regardless of whether the group targeted for destruction is categorised as a religious group. This essay will conclude with what can be appropriated from these case studies for prevention and punishment of genocide.

Right to freedom of religion

The right to freedom of religion is enshrined in the Universal Declaration of Human Rights (article 18) and the International Covenant on Civil and Political Rights (article 18). It is considered a 'far-reaching and profound' human right, as it is part of the sweeping human right to thought, conscience and religion.[97] It protects theistic, non-theistic, and atheistic beliefs, and religions of any age or group size. Also included is the right not to profess any religion or belief.[98]

The right protects freedom to manifest religion or belief in worship, observance, practice, and teaching. This is an inclusive freedom covering: ritual and ceremonial acts; building of places of worship; use of ritual formulae and objects; display of symbols; observance of holidays and days of rest; dietary requirements; wearing of distinctive clothing or head coverings; participation in rituals associated with certain stages of life; use of a particular language customarily spoken by a group; choice of religious leaders, priests, and teachers; establishment of seminaries or religious schools; and preparation and distribution of religious texts or publications.[99] It is prohibited to coerce or impair the right to have or adopt a religion or belief, or to restrict access to services (medical, education, and etcetera) based on religion.[100]

---

[97] Human Rights Committee General Comment No. 22, UN Doc. CCPR/C/21/Rev.1/Add.4, 27 Sept. 1993, para. 1.
[98] Ibid., para. 2.
[99] Ibid., para. 4.
[100] Ibid., para. 5; Heiner Bielefeldt, Nazila Ghanea, and Michael Wiener, *Freedom of Religion or Belief: An International Law Commentary*, Oxford Scholarly Authorities on International Law (Oxford: Oxford University Press, 2016), 56.

Limitations on the right to freedom of religion are permitted. However, as with the general rule on limitations on human rights, such limitations are only permissible when prescribed by law and when necessary to protect public safety, order, health, or morals. No limitation is authorised with regards to the prohibition on coercion of religion and on religious education. This equates the prohibition on coercion and education with the prohibitions on slavery and torture, from which derogations are also not authorised, in order to ensure human dignity (an underlying principle of human rights). Even more specifically, '[r]estrictions may not be imposed for discriminatory purposes or applied in a discriminatory manner'.[101]

Minority religions are not to be discriminated against. The terminology used by the United Nations Human Rights Committee indicates that violation of freedom of religion is inherently linked to discrimination, persecution, and even violence:

> In particular, certain measures discriminating against [adherents of minority religions or non-believers], such as measures restricting eligibility for government service to members of the predominant religion or giving economic privileges to them or imposing special restrictions on the practice of other faiths, are not in accordance with the prohibition of discrimination based on religion or belief and the guarantee of equal protection under article 26.[102]

Freedom of religion is a human right that, while granted to the individual, has inherent communal and social aspects. Bielefeld et al. suggest that '[h]uman rights have a strong positive bearing on communities, since they are always exercised in a social context'.[103] Religion is an individual choice, but is often practiced communally and seen as very significant socially. It exists in many cultures as a defining element of that culture, of that group, even if that group is considered national, ethnical, or racial. Therefore, violation of the right to freedom of religion can lead to communal and social disintegration.

Writing of his experience in the Holocaust, Jean Améry described the violation of human rights during the genocide process as a destruction of his society and community: 'The functionary of an authoritarian system who beats me arbitrarily, does not merely violate my body; he rips apart ... the social contract within whose limits any human conduct, across all societal roles and situations, must always remain'.[104] Améry noted that 'dignity can be bestowed only

---

[101] HRC GC No. 22, para. 8.
[102] HRC GC No. 22, para. 9.
[103] Bielefeldt, Ghanea, and Wiener, *Freedom of Religion*, 69.
[104] Améry speaks specifically of this struggle: Jean Améry, *Jenseits von Schuld und Sühne: Bewältigungsversuche eines Überwältigten* (Stuttgart:

by society', and that dignity is connected to trust in the world and the social contract.¹⁰⁵ Freedom of religion is part of the fundamental right to human dignity, and part of the social contract. Destruction of dignity and social binds is a substantial element of the destruction of a group in genocide; one that survivors struggle to reclaim and to deal with.¹⁰⁶

Violations during the Armenian Genocide

The Ottoman Empire was a fairly tolerant pluralistic empire. A variety of groups of different ethnicities and religions co-existed without being persecuted. However, this did not mean that all groups—particularly minority groups—had equality. Armenians were a distinct minority group in the Ottoman Empire: they were Christian in a Muslim majority.¹⁰⁷ Moreover, Armenians were a distinctive group, with their own religion, language, and culture. They were a *millet*, a religious community within the Empire, with well-defined statuses, duties, and obligations, and a great deal of autonomy, including the right to practice their religion.¹⁰⁸ Yet this status also resulted in legalised discrimination in certain areas of life, such as multiple taxes and exclusion from military service.¹⁰⁹ As Melson explains, 'This was the explicit agreement that dhimmis [people of the scripture] were never to consider themselves the equals of Muslims. The Ottoman state considered Muslim superiority to be both just and natural, and the necessary if not merely sufficient condition for its continued tolerance of inferior minorities'.¹¹⁰ Christians were second-class citizens due to their religion. Muslims referred to them as *Gavur* (or *Kafir*)—unbeliever or 'infidel', a word with emotional and derogatory overtones.

Klett-Cotta, 1977), 64, cited in Bielefeldt, Ghanea, and Wiener, *Freedom of Religion*, 80.

¹⁰⁵ Jean Améry, *At the Mind's Limits: Contemplations By a Survivor on Auschwitz and Its Realities* (Bloomington: Indiana University Press, 1980), 28, 89.

¹⁰⁶ Ibid.

¹⁰⁷ The Armenians were not the only Christian group to be targeted for destruction by the Ottoman leaders. Others such as the Assyrian and Greek Christians were also victims of persecution and massacres; Benny Morris and Dror Ze'evi, *The Thirty-Year Genocide: Turkey's Destruction of Its Christian Minorities, 1894–1924* (Cambridge: Harvard University Press, 2019).

¹⁰⁸ Robert Melson, *Revolution and Genocide: On the Origins of the Armenian Genocide and the Holocaust* (Chicago: University of Chicago Press, 1992), 54.

¹⁰⁹ Ibid.

¹¹⁰ Ibid., 56.

In the 1800s, despite anti-Christian sentiment, Armenians were granted rights such as taxation rights.[111] However, these rights did not materialise. Consequently, Armenians began to push for implementation of these rights. When the Young Turks came to power in 1908, the Armenian campaign for rights coincided with a loss of territory for the Ottoman Empire. Consequently, the Young Turks linked the Armenian push for rights to the idea that Armenians were seeking independence and collaborating with Russia. This was part of the justification provided for what became the genocide of the Armenians. In doing this, the Armenians were targeted as an ethnic (or national) and religious group. Principally, their Christianity held them apart and sculpted them as outsiders in an empire that was to become today's nation of Turkey. The success of the Armenian minority 'gave the appearance that it was challenging a traditional and hierarchical, Muslim and imperial, religious and political order'.[112]

Officially, the Armenian Genocide began on 24 April 1915. However, there were massacres and human rights violations preceding this, from the 1890s. From 1894–96, massacres were carried out under Sultan Abdul Hamid II against Armenians and other Christian minorities of the Ottoman Empire.[113] Up to 300,000 Armenians were killed in the Hamidian massacres.[114] As part of these pogroms, forced Islamisation also took place, with approximately 40,000–100,000 Christians forcibly converted. Churches and monasteries were pillaged, profaned, and demolished; churches were converted into mosques; priests and vicars[115] were killed.[116] The Christianity of these groups was used against them: 'Ittihadists, like Sultan Abdul Hamid, employed religion as an instrument of propaganda to mobilise the Muslim masses'.[117]

---

[111] Ruben Safrastyan, *Ottoman Empire: The Genesis of the Program of Genocide (1876-1920)* (Yerevan: National Academy of Sciences, 2011), 32–99.

[112] Melson, *Revolution and*, 53.

[113] Anahit Khosroeva, 'The Assyrian Genocide in the Ottoman Empire and Adjacent Territories', in *The Armenian Genocide: Cultural and Ethical Legacies*, ed. Richard G. Hovannisian (New Brunswick: Transaction Publishers, 2007), 26; Deborah Mayersen, *On the Path to Genocide: Armenia and Rwanda Reexamined* (New York: Berghahn Books, 2014), 40–60.

[114] Melson, *Revolution and*, 47.

[115] 'Vicar' translated from '*desservant*' in French texts (author's translation).

[116] Mayersen, *On the Path*, 49; Armenian National Archives document, 'Liste abrégée, relatant exclusivement les profanations d'églizes, les conversions forcées et les assassinats d'ecclésiastiques, qui ont eu lieu lors des massacres commis dans les provinces de la Turquie habitées par les Arméniens, depuis les derniers jours du mois de septembre 1895', undated, with handwritten notations dated 1895/6.

[117] Simon Payaslian, 'The Destruction of the Armenian Church during the Genocide', *Genocide Studies and Prevention* 1, no. 2 (2006): 156. Ittihadists were the Committee of Union and Progress; initially a secret society

The anti-Christian sentiment grew under the Young Turks, for whom priority was Turkification of the empire, including Islamisation.[118] Discrimination against Christians grew. No clocks were permitted on church towers, and only wooden bells were allowed. Church towers could not be higher than mosque minarets; Christians were prohibited from having houses higher than Muslim houses.

From April 1915 onwards, the Armenians were subject to a significant range of well-organised crimes. As part of this, freedom of religion was specifically targeted. Supreme religious leaders were deported as part of the deconstruction of the Armenian Church as an entity.[119] Priests and other religious leaders were specifically targeted in massacres. Unlike the killings of ordinary people, religious leaders were often tortured publicly before being killed. Survivor testimony demonstrates that '[t]he clergy were treated with particular severity, priests were killed through brutal torturing, their beards were torn out or singed, eyes blinded, tongues and noses cut off and so on'.[120] One survivor recounted:

> From their stories I learned that our priest (Ter Yeghiazar) and the primate (Ter Yeghishe), and all prominent Armenians were on the kaymakam's order to be slaughtered. And cut into pieces with daggers. Before murdering them, their beards would be removed by flaying their skin and displayed on the market wall as an ornament.[121]

Another described the beating to death of a priest with sticks, after which '[t]hey filled his mouth with rubbish and threw him in the river'.[122]

In addition to targeting religious leaders, religious buildings and icons were also specifically attacked. Churches were ransacked, particularly for valuable religious icons; less valuable artefacts were destroyed. Churches were often profaned, for the specific objective of humiliating the religion and the religious. Further, churches were converted into stables, which resulted in profanation

---

formed in 1889, the CUP later became a political party that merged with the Young Turks.

[118] Melson, *Revolution and*, 138; Raymond Kévorkian, *The Armenian Genocide: A Complete History* (London: I.B. Tauris, 2011), 189–200.

[119] Payaslian, 'The Destruction', 160–61.

[120] National Archives of Armenia, *Armenian Genocide by Ottoman Turkey 1915: Testimony of Survivors-Collection of Documents* (Yerevant: Zangak Publishing House, 2013), 19.

[121] No. 23 Mkrtich Alsanian on massacre of township of Akants-Archesh in Archesh District of Van, (testimony taken 23 Aug. 1916, Oshakan), in Armenia, *Testimony of Survivors*, 72.

[122] No. 17 Sanam Vardanian; Hamlet of Berkri in Berkri District of Van (testimony taken 6 Aug. 1916, Mazra), in Armenia, *Testimony of Survivors*, 72.

by cattle or sheep. Destroyed Armenian churches can still be found in Eastern Turkey in use as stables.[123]

The forcible conversion of women and children, with forced marriages of girls and young women to Muslim men, formed a fundamental component of the genocide and demonstrates how the removal of freedom of religion can be used as a genocidal act.[124] Those who refused to convert were raped and/or killed.[125] After deportations of Armenians in later stages of the genocide to what is now northern Syria, many women and children were forcibly converted; some women were converted by Kurds and subsequently compelled to have their faces and hands tattooed as per local tradition ('*deq*').

The Armenian Genocide left behind up to 200,000 orphans:[126] 'At wars end, Western aid officials and the Armenian ecclesiastical leadership estimated that the numbers of non-Muslim children housed in Ottoman State orphanages or in Muslim households was at least sixty thousand', with no attempt made to find and reunite children with living relatives.[127] These orphans ended up in orphanages in Armenia or other countries; some were adopted. Those adopted by non-Armenian families were thus not raised within the Armenian Church.[128]

Violations during the Holocaust

In Nazi Germany, Jews were targeted not as a religious group, but as a racial group. Jews were considered 'non-Aryan', and Aryan was regarded as a race.

---

[123] Such as the St Karapet Church at Avarabank Monastery.

[124] Or an 'offering' to convert for 'safety'; Kévorkian, *The Armenian*, 296; Vahakn N. Dadrian, 'Children as Victims of Genocide: The Armenian Case', *Journal of Genocide Research* 5, no. 3 (2003): 422–35; Taner Akçam, 'Deportation and Massacres in the Cipher Telegrams of the Interior Ministry in the Prime Ministerial Archive (Başbakanlık Arşivi)', *Genocide Studies and Prevention* 1, no. 3 (2006): 310–11; Keith David Watenpaugh, '"The League of Nations" Rescue of Armenian Genocide Survivors and the Making of Modern Humanitarianism, 1920–1927', *The American Historical Review* 115, no. 5 (2010): 1324–26; Lorne Shirinian, 'Orphans of the Armenian Genocide with Special Reference to the Georgetown Boys and Girls in Canada', in *The Armenian Genocide Legacy*, ed. Alexis Demirdjian (London: Palgrave, 2016), 46.

[125] See for example, No. 37 Sara Muradian [F] on massacre at village of Boghanis in Gyavash District (testimony taken 1916, Baku), in Armenia, *Testimony of Survivors*, 92. Many other testimonies recorded mention forced conversions to Islam (often with the subsequent enslavement of the women).

[126] Shirinian, 'Orphans of', 45.

[127] Keith David Watenpaugh, ' "Are There Any Children for Sale?": Genocide and the Transfer of Armenian Children (1915–1922)', *Journal of Human Rights* 12, no. 3 (2013): 292; Watenpaugh, 'Rescue of Armenian', 37–39.

[128] Watenpaugh, 'Transfer of Armenian', 294.

Nazis were motivated by decades of changing theory about 'race' and the idea of preserving German 'racial purity'.[129] Law and decrees passed in Nazi Germany and occupied territories used the terms 'race' and 'non-Aryan' when implementing anti-Jewish laws and policies.[130]

Due to Nazi infatuation with 'race', the Jewish religion experienced relative freedom under Nazi rule. In ghettos, religion continued to be a major part of life for the Jews therein. Religious ceremonies were still undertaken, such as evening services and weddings. Sabbath and Jewish holy days were observed, Torah study took place, and religious education for children took place.[131] Some ghettos had synagogues. Continuation of religious rituals served to help ghetto inhabitants retain some element of normality, routine, and community.

Religion was not necessarily restricted or even banned in concentration and death camps. Prisoners in Belzec had prayer shawls and *tefillin*, and prayed in their barracks at night.[132] In Treblinka, evening services were held, with SS guards listening to the melodic voice of the Kapo who ran the service. Treblinka prisoners also had shawls and *tefillin*, along with prayer books, and were permitted morning and evening prayers. *Minyan* was permitted in the carpentry workshop in the morning and evening before and after work. In bitter irony, the SS also permitted funerals in some instances, including erection of headstones. Weddings were even held, *matzot* baked for Passover, and the *Kol Nidre* service

---

[129] Karl A. Schleunes, *The Twisted Road to Auschwitz: Nazi Policy Towards German Jews 1933–139* (Urbana and Chicago: University of Illinois Press, 1990), 15–35.

[130] See, for example, Germany: Harry Reicher, *Law and the Holocaust: Cases and Materials*, 4th ed. (Philadelphia: University of Pennsylvania Law School, 2001); Janos Pelle, *Sowing the Seeds of Hatred: Anti-Jewish Laws and Hungarian Public Opinion, 1938–1944* (Boulder: East European Monographs, 2004); Vera Ranki, *The Politics of Inclusion and Exclusion: Jews and Nationalism in Hungary* (St Leonards: Allen and Unwin, 1999); Nathaniel Katzburg, 'Anti-Jewish Legislation in Hungary 1940–1941', *Annual of Bar-Ilan University Studies in Judaica and the Humanities XVI–XVII* (1979): 86–87. Italy: Liliana Picciotto Fargion, 'The Anti-Jewish Policy of the Italian Social Republic (1943–1945)', *Yad Vashem Studies* 17 (1986): 17; Renzo De Felice, *The Jews in Fascist Italy: A History* (New York: Enigma Books, 2001), 337. Ironically, under French law 26 Apr. 1941 *Troisième Ordonnance relative aux mesures contre les juifs*, race was defined by religion: a person was considered *ipso jure* as pure Jewish if one grand-parent was part of the Jewish religious community; Philippe Héraclès, *La Loi Nazie en France* (Paris: Guy Authier Editeur, 1974), 180–81; J. Lubetzki, *La Condition des Juifs en France sous L'Occupation Allemande 1940–1944* (Paris: CDJC, 1945), 137–38, 58–61, 65–70.

[131] Yitzhak Arad, *The Pictorial History of the Holocaust* (Jerusalem: Yad Vashem, 1990), 124, 26–27.

[132] Yitzhak Arad, *Belzec, Sobibor, Treblinka: The Operation Reinhardt Death Camps* (Bloomington and Indianapolis: Indiana University Press, 1987), 217.

held for Yom Kippur.¹³³ The *Kaddish* was very commonly and frequently recited in camps, given the high number and daily occurrence of deaths.¹³⁴ In one incident at Auschwitz, 2,000 prisoners recited the *Viddui* with no reaction from SS guards watching.¹³⁵ Auschwitz prisoners were able to access prayer books and *tefillin*.¹³⁶

It should be noted, though, that the permissiveness of the Nazis towards Jewish religious practice was not based on any mercy or concession, but rather because the Nazis assumed the Jews would be killed anyway. The ultimate goal was to eradicate not only the Jewish people but the entire existence of Jewish history, culture, and religion. Thus, individual Jews or groups of Jews practicing religious tradition was irrelevant because they were going to be completely annihilated, including their religion.

Regardless of the fact that Jews were not targeted specifically as a religious group and were still permitted to conduct religious rituals, freedom of religion was nonetheless impeded. Jewish markers such as beards on religious men were often cut or pulled off as an act of humiliation. Jewish religious monuments and property were destroyed. Synagogues were prime targets for destruction. During the 9–10 November 1938 *Reichspogromnacht* (or *Kristallnacht*), in addition to Jewish houses and businesses, synagogues were attacked, with windows broken and many set on fire, under orders of Josef Goebbels.¹³⁷ An estimated 1,400 synagogues and prayer rooms throughout the German Reich were destroyed or burned.¹³⁸ Religious icons such as Torah scrolls were desecrated and furniture smashed. Synagogues in the Polish city of Łódź, for example, were dismantled and burned early on under Nazi occupation (1939 and 1940).¹³⁹

In ghettos, Sabbath and holy days were observed where possible, however the Germans did not honour these festivals and rituals. Indeed, ghetto inhabitants

---

[133] Arad, *Belzec, Sobibor*, 216–17.

[134] Arad, *Belzec, Sobibor*; Filip Müller, *Eyewitness Auschwitz: Three Years in the Gas Chambers* (Chicago: Ivan R. Dee, 1979), 48. Recounts one incident in Auschwitz when another inmate recited the Kaddish as they cremated Müller's own father.

[135] Ibid., 70–71. Prayer and song permission may have been allowed in order to calm victims before their deaths.

[136] Ibid., 35.

[137] Saul Friedländer, *Nazi Germany and the Jews 1933–1939: The Years of Persecution* (London: Phoenix, 1997), 272–74.

[138] Arad, *Pictorial History*, 54–59.

[139] Shimon Huberband, 'The Destruction of the Synagogues in Łódź', in *Łódź Ghetto: Inside a Community Under Siege*, eds. Alan Adelson and Robert Lapides (New York: Viking, 1989), 70–71. See also photographic evidence as taken by Henryk Ross such as Henryk Ross, 'Ruins of a Destroyed Synagogue on Wolborska Street, Which was Blown up by the German Authorities', United States Holocaust Memorial Museum, https://collections.ushmm.org/search/catalog/pa1054357.

were forced to work on these holy days, and at times *Aktionen* were carried out specifically on these days, as a way of deliberately disrupting Jewish life and community.[140]

In addition to these overt acts, in some circumstances children had to suppress their Jewish identity,[141] even converting to other religions such as Catholicism.[142] For example, in France, children were hidden with families or in convents and converted to Catholicism, either during the war or afterwards when their families did not return. Some children did not even know they were Jewish, and discovering this led to identity crises for those who had been raised in a Catholic family or convent; some even rejected their Jewishness for fear of persecution.[143] Moreover, some children as sole survivors of their family lived with non-Jewish families, into which they were adopted after the war. Through no fault of their own or the families they ended up living with, the children were unaware of their Jewish heritage and grew up under a different or no religion.[144] The numbers of these children is unknown, but, like the Armenian Genocide, this demonstrates the long-term impact that genocide can have on freedom of religion, even after killing has stopped.

Violations during the Cambodian Genocide

Under the Khmer Rouge regime from 1975 to 1979, 1.7 million people died.[145] While it has been argued that the Khmer Rouge killings did not amount to

---

[140] Arad, *Pictorial History*, 124.

[141] Vicki Gordon, 'The Experience of Being a Hidden Child Survivor of the Holocaust' (Doctor of Philosophy University of Melbourne, 2002), 140–41, http://hdl.handle.net/11343/39539.

[142] One of Gordon's interview subjects, D, notes that in Budapest, Hungary, she and her sister took classes to convert to Christianity, to save themselves; and that even the Chief Rabbi had an honorary conversion. D did not want to continue the classes, even though she risked her own survival; Ibid., 242. Another subject, P, notes that 'a great number of Hungarians became Catholic'; Ibid., 325.

[143] Ibid., 155–57.

[144] Gordon's interview subject, P, took conversion classes later in life, to relearn about Judaism; Ibid., 325. The author of this chapter interviewed a child survivor of the Holocaust (including camps) who was ultimately adopted by a Jewish family in the USA. However, she had almost been adopted by a Christian family in Sweden where she was in a refugee camp. It was only by luck that she was raised in her original faith. Interview with Rina, Jerusalem, Jan. 2013.

[145] Sliwinski's study estimates a death toll of 24 per cent to 25.6 per cent of the early 1975 population by 1979, the majority of whom died through execution or famine/exhaustion, or disappeared; Marek Sliwinski, *Le Génocide Khmer Rouge: une analyse démographique* (Paris: l'Harmattan, 1995), 60.

genocide,¹⁴⁶ this article takes the view that genocide did take place under the Khmer Rouge, with the intent being to destroy in part the Khmer people,¹⁴⁷ in addition to destruction of certain minority groups, including Vietnamese, ethnic Chinese, and Muslim Cham.¹⁴⁸

The dominant religion in Cambodia was Buddhism. The main group of people targeted by the Khmer Rouge were 'city people', or intellectuals. However, religious and minority nationality groups were also marked groups. Khmer Rouge communist ideals excluded religion completely. Consequently, freedom of religion was almost completely and at times violently restricted, with a goal to eliminate religion.¹⁴⁹

'Reactionary' religions were banned under the Constitution of Democratic Kampuchea.¹⁵⁰ Buddhism was seen as a reactionary religion because it had passivity and lacked interest in collective construction of the country. However,

---

Kiernan estimates the death toll at 21 per cent; Ben Kiernan, *The Pol Pot Regime: Race, Power, and Genocide in Cambodia Under the Khmer Rouge, 1975–79*, 3rd ed. (New Haven: Yale University Press, 2008), 458.

[146] For example, William A Schabas, 'Problems of International Codification: Were the Atrocities in Cambodia and Kosovo Genocide?' *New England Law Review* 35, no. 2 (2001): 287–302; William A Schabas, 'Cambodia: Was it Really Genocide?' *Human Rights Quarterly* 23, no. 2 (2001): 470–77.

[147] For discussion of the composition of the partial group, see Marcelo Ferreira, 'Genocide, and its Definition as the "Partial Elimination of a National Group"', *Genocide Studies and Prevention* 8, no. 1 (2013): 14–16.

[148] For example, Kiernan, *Pol Pot Regime*, 460–63; Ysa Osman, *The Cham Rebellion* (Phnom Penh: Documentation Center of Cambodia, 2006), 119. The Extraordinary Chambers in the Courts of Cambodia convicted Khieu Samphan and Nuon Chea of charges of genocide with regards to the minority groups, the Muslim Cham and Vietnamese, in Case 002/02 Judgement (16 Nov. 2018). For specific reference to the genocide of the Khmer in part, see Ben Kiernan, 'The Cambodian Genocide, 1975–1979', in *Centuries of Genocide: Essays and Eyewitness Accounts*, eds. Samuel Totten, and William S. Parsons (New York: Routledge, 2012), 325. Also note that while religious persons/leaders were particularly targeted for annihilation under the Khmer Rouge, foreign religious leaders were permitted to flee. Ponchaud describes the separation of Khmer Catholic monks and nuns from foreign (mostly French) ones, the latter being rescued by the French embassy; François Ponchaud, *La Cathédrale De La Rizière: Histoire De L'église Au Cambodge* (Paris: CLD éditions, 2000), 205.

[149] Kiernan, 'The Cambodian', 322.

[150] Article 20 'Every citizen of Kampuchea has the right to worship according to any religion and the right not to worship according to any religion. Reactionary religions which are detrimental to Democratic Kampuchea and Kampuchean people are absolutely forbidden'.

Buddhism was also a significant source of power in Khmer culture, with village life revolving around the temple(s). It was a source of authority and power that could threaten the authority of *Angkar* ('the Organisation', as the Khmer Rouge termed itself).[151]

Consequently, Buddhist monks were de-robed; those who refused to do so were tortured and killed.[152] Monks who de-robed undertook forced labour with the rest of the population.[153] Religious practice was banned, in particular funerals and giving alms. However, some ceremonies still took place. These were the ceremonies involving the donation of money, the majority of which was afterwards stolen by Khmer Rouge cadres.[154] There are instances of the practice of secret rites where possible, but these activities were rare due to the danger of carrying them out.

Forced marriage took place under the Khmer Rouge. These 'marriages' were not carried out according to Khmer Buddhist tradition, but rather a group 'marriage' pledging allegiance to *Angkar*. Survivors who were forced into these 'marriages' consistently note their distress at the fact the marriage was not carried out according to traditional rites with family present.[155]

Temples were ransacked and repurposed, with valuable statues stolen and temples converted into military offices, rice storage, or pigsties, or dismantled

---

[151] François Ponchaud, *Cambodge année zéro* (Paris: Editions Kailash, 2012), 146, 269–70. This is despite the fact that, ironically, the Khmer Rouge initially incorporated Buddhist concepts into their ideology in order to win over the Khmer people; Ibid., 276, 277.

[152] Kiernan, 'The Cambodian', 323. 'The Khmer Rouge didn't believe in Buddhism and wanted to eliminate it. They didn't need monks and didn't want people to celebrate any festivals. One monk in our village refused to disrobe, so they came in the middle of the night, tied him to a banana tree, and killed him', Eng Sam Ol in Wynne Cougill with Pang Pivoine, Ra Chhayran, and Sim Sopheak, *Stilled Lives: Photographs from the Cambodian Genocide*, trans. by Chy Terith (Phnom Penh: Documentation Center of Cambodia, 2004), 31; see also other testimonies at 72–73, 76. Ian Harris, *Buddhism Under Pol Pot* (Phnom Penh: Documentation Center of Cambodia, 2007), 122–27, 34–35; Chanthou Boua, 'Genocide of a Religious Group: Pol Pot and Cambodia's Buddhist Monks', in *State Organized Terror: The Case of Violent Internal Repression*, ed. P. Timothy Bushnell (Westview Press, 1991), 232–5.

[153] Ponchaud, *Cambodge année*, 147–9; Harris, *Buddhism Under*, 114–6; Boua, 'Genocide of', 236–37.

[154] Harris, *Buddhism Under*, 145–50.

[155] See for example, testimonies before the Extraordinary Chambers in the Courts of Cambodia, Case 002/02, transcript, Witness 2-TCCP-274, 22 and 23 Aug. 2016; Witness 2-TCCP-224, 23 and 24 Aug. 2016; Witness 2-TCCP-286, 30 Aug. 2016; Witness 2-TCCP-1064, 24 Oct. 2016.

for other use.¹⁵⁶ Non-valuable religious objects such as statues, books, and manuscript were destroyed, including book burnings.¹⁵⁷ Propaganda expounded Buddhist monks as leeches and imperialists.¹⁵⁸

Islam was specifically targeted too, considered a 'polluted and inferior religion'.¹⁵⁹ Profanation of mosques and graves took place; sacred texts were destroyed.¹⁶⁰ Muslims were forced to change their names to ones that were 'less Muslim sounding' and to eat pork (refusal for which resulted in arrest, torture, and death).¹⁶¹ Religious books such as the Qur'an were destroyed, Qur'anic schools closed down, and religious practices such as visiting shrines or Qur'anic recitation forbidden.¹⁶² As with Buddhist practices, some people prayed in secret, despite the significant risk.¹⁶³ The destruction of Muslim identity 'was abrupt, brutal and widespread'.¹⁶⁴

Catholic and Christian churches were not immune: many were razed to the ground; for example, the Phnom Penh cathedral was blown up and replaced with a garden.¹⁶⁵ In Battambang, the cemetery was also destroyed.¹⁶⁶ All Catholic Church leaders and eleven evangelical pastors were executed or died from starvation or fatigue.¹⁶⁷

All persons of faith and religious leaders were subject to forced de-conversion. They were made to wear secular clothing (the typical all-black attire of the regime), and to have their hair cut according to regime regulations.¹⁶⁸

Religious leaders of all faiths were tortured and killed, including Buddhist monks, Muslim leaders, and Islamic teachers.¹⁶⁹ Marek Sliwinski estimates the

---

156 Ponchaud, *Cambodge année*, 151; Harris, *Buddhism Under*, 154–67
157 Harris, *Buddhism Under*, 162–69.
158 Ponchaud, *Cambodge année*, 149–51.
159 Farina So, *The Hijab of Cambodia: Memories of Cham Muslim Women after the Khmer Rouge* (Phnom Penh: Documentation Center of Cambodia, 2011), 55.
160 François Ponchaud, *La Cathédrale de la Rizière: Histoire de l'Eglise au Cambodge*, 2nd ed. (Paris: CLD éditions, 2006), 271; So, *Hijab of*, 54–55.
161 Kiernan, *Pol Pot Regime*, 461; Ponchaud, *La Cathédrale*, 271; Osman, *The Cham Rebellion*, 115. Changing names was either to another Cham Muslim name, to a Khmer name, or by shortening the original name, to hide identity; So, *Hijab of*, 61–62.
162 So, *Hijab of*, 54–55, 57.
163 Ibid., 59–61.
164 Ibid., 64.
165 Ponchaud, *La Cathédrale*, 239.
166 Ibid., 240, 60.
167 Ibid., 239, 65.
168 So, *Hijab of*, 61–62.
169 Ben Kiernan, 'Genocidal Targeting: Two Groups of Victims in Pol Pot's Cambodia', in *State Organized Terror: The Case of Violent Internal Repression*,

mortality rate at 29.8 per cent for Buddhists, 40.6 per cent for Muslim Cham, and 48.6 per cent for Catholics.[170] In 1975, 0.18 per cent of Cambodians had a religious profession; this was reduced to only 0.03 per cent by 1976.[171] Chanthou Boua estimates that fewer than 2,000 of Cambodia's 65,000–70,000 monks survived.[172]

Destruction of Buddhism was particularly significant in Cambodia, where the essence of Khmer culture was Buddhism. François Ponchaud writes: 'Until April 1975, "race" and "religion" were expressed using the same word, and in the everyday language, saying "khmer" meant "Buddhist" … it is at the temple where Khmers rediscover their *khméritude*'.[173] In capturing the minds of young Khmer people, Buddhism was lost to the younger generation, who embraced the violence of the communist revolution and not the values of Buddhism. In eliminating Buddhism, *Angkar* sought to eliminate the Khmer as they existed, creating a completely new Khmer nation by radically transforming their culture.[174]

Freedom of religion and genocide: definition and prevention

These case studies show clear violation of multiple aspects of the right to freedom of religion. All three regimes restricted or prohibited the right to manifest religion or belief through worship, observance, practice, and teaching, through destruction of buildings, banning of religious rites and rituals, closure of religious education, and killing of religious leaders. The absolute right to not be coerced was violated in the Armenian and Cambodian genocides, through forcible conversion. Under the Nazis, people converted to Christian religions as a means of saving themselves; this is also coercion, conversion out of desperation rather than true choice.[175] All restrictions on religion in the Armenian Genocide and the Holocaust were carried out as discrimination against minorities.

---

ed. P. Timothy Bushnell (Westview Press, 1991), 223; Harris, *Buddhism Under*, 131–33; So, *Hijab of*, 54.
[170] Compared with an estimated overall death rate of 21–24 per cent of the general population. Sliwinski, *Le Génocide*, 76–77. Ponchaud provides numbers from specific communities, with some losing up to two-thirds of their Catholic population; Ponchaud, *La Cathédrale*, 259–65.
[171] Sliwinski, *Le Génocide*, 92.
[172] Boua, 'Genocide of', 239.
[173] Ponchaud, *Cambodge année*, 145–271 (author's translation).
[174] For discussion on the inherent connection between nationalism and Buddhism in Cambodia, see John Marston and Elizabeth Guthrie, eds., *History, Buddhism and New Religious Movements in Cambodia* (Honolulu: University of Hawai'i Press, 2004).
[175] Of course, if their true identity was discovered, conversion did not save the converted Jews, because Jewishness was in the 'blood' and had to be destroyed.

In the Cambodian Genocide, Buddhists were the majority group but minority religions such as Islam and Catholicism were discriminated against. These restrictions were not implemented as legitimate limitations for public safety, order, health or morals;[176] rather to specifically discriminate and destroy.

Raphael Lemkin delineated 'religious techniques' as a specific part of genocide, along with political, cultural, economic, biological, physical, and moral.[177] Steven Leonard Jacobs found '"religion" is all too often overlooked as an important factor in contributing to either the implementation and perpetuation of genocide, or as a foundational underpinning and rationalization for such collective acts'.[178] Leo Kuper has written of this distinct role of religion in the dehumanisation process within genocide:

> It is striking that the cases of genocide discussed [in this book], with a few exceptions … are marked by religious differences between the killers and the victims. This suggests that religious values (even among those who are not devout and in conflicts quite unrelated to matters of faith) may be ideologically significant at a different level, shaping sentiments of exclusion, and derogatory stereotypes of the followers of other religions. And it suggests too that we underestimate the contemporary significance of religion in genocide.[179]

More recently, Kate Temoney examined the role of religion in genocide, focusing on Rwanda and Bosnia.[180] She categorised four broad roles of religion in genocide: a religious group being targeted; use of religionised language by perpetrators; the condonation of genocide explicitly or implicitly by religious leaders; and the role of religious groups in preventing or interrupting genocide. Temoney determined: 'although religious belief is rarely the only driving factor in genocide, it is not merely ancillary to genocide but potentiates genocide in

---

[176] Such limitations or derogations are permissible under human rights law during public emergency; see, for example, Article 4 of the International Covenant on Civil and Political Rights; and Olivier de Schutter, *International Human Rights Law: Cases, Materials, Commentary*, 2nd ed. (Cambridge: Cambridge University Press, 2014), 339–426.

[177] Raphael Lemkin, *Axis Rule in Occupied Europe* (Washington DC: Carnegie Endowment for International Peace, 1944), 89.

[178] Steven Leonard Jacobs, 'Introduction: Genocide in the Name of God: Thoughts on Religion and Genocide', in *Confronting Genocide: Judaism, Christianity, Islam*, ed. Steven Leonard Jacobs (New York: Lexington Books, 2009), ix.

[179] Kuper, *Genocide*, 90.

[180] Kate Temoney, 'Religion and Genocide Nexuses: Bosnia as Case Study', *Religions* 8, vol. 6 (2017), 112–25; Kate Temoney, 'The 1994 Rwandan Genocide: The Religion/Genocide Nexus, Sexual Violence, and the Future of Genocide Studies', *Genocide Studies and Prevention* 10, no. 3 (2016): 3–24.

a particular manner'.¹⁸¹ Religion thus becomes an inherent and critical part of the 'othering' aspect of genocide. I would add to Temoney's list a fifth broad role of religion in genocide: religion as a specific target of discrimination and rights violations (occurring even when a group is not targeted as a religious group).

Preservation of religious rituals in targeted groups continued where possible for normality and routine, but also as a form of resistance.¹⁸² Safeguarding culture and rituals was a means of survival through perpetuation of that group's existence as it is existed as a separate and distinct cultural entity. While not all members of the targeted group may have been religious, the particular religion of their group was a significant component of their group as it existed culturally and whether defined as nation, race or ethnicity.

The example of the Cambodian Genocide is particularly noteworthy, where we see Buddhism targeted separately from 'urban people', both part of Khmer society. To destroy Buddhism was to destroy Khmer, and part of the reparation of Khmer society post-1979 was rehabilitation of the ritual life of their community. This rehabilitation was also necessary for Armenians and Jews.

Thus, destroying religion was part and parcel of destroying a group, in whole or in part: destroying that group as a social structure. Religion and the freedom to practice are substantial elements of this social structure or figuration, and thus require elimination if a group is to be extinguished. When genocide is committed, it is done so for the purpose of destruction (in whole or in part) of a group of people based on their nationality, ethnicity, race, or religion.¹⁸³ As Christopher Powell noted, destroying *a group* is not killing multiple individuals, but rather eradicating 'something more than or other than the sum of the individuals who belong to it ... genocide is the killing or destruction of that "something more"'.¹⁸⁴ That is, the '*genos*' in genocide 'must connote a type of social figuration. The collective object ... must ... have the general property of being a dynamic relational network formed through practical social interactions in historical time'.¹⁸⁵ Daniel Feierstein has referred to genocide as 'a specific technology of power for destroying and reorganizing social relations', observing that it 'is impossible to commit genocide without first building models of identity and Otherness'.¹⁸⁶

---

¹⁸¹ Temoney, 'Religion and', 3.
¹⁸² Stanislav Zámečník, *That Was Dachau 1933–1945* (Brussels: Comité International de Dachau, 2004), 307.
¹⁸³ For a discussion of 'groups' in the purview of genocide, see William A Schabas, *Genocide in International Law*, 2nd ed. (Cambridge: Cambridge University Press, 2009), 117–71.
¹⁸⁴ Christopher Powell, 'What do Genocides Kill? A Relational Concept of Genocide', *Journal of Genocide Research* 9, no. 4 (2007): 524
¹⁸⁵ Ibid., 538.
¹⁸⁶ Daniel Feierstein, *Genocide as Social Practice* (New Brunswick: Rutgers University Press, 2014), 205–09.

Claudia Card describes genocide as social death, different from simply killing large number of people through, for example, terrorism, or war.[187] Social death comes through annihilation of social vitality, which only exists through relationships, including those mediated through social institutions such as religion.[188] Members of the group lose their context and identity that shapes their lives.[189] Card notes:

> In genocides, survivors experience a social death, to a degree and for a time. Some later become revitalised in new ways; others do not. Descendants of genocide survivors, like descendants of slaves who were kidnapped, may be "natally alienated," no longer able to pass along and build upon the traditions, cultural developments (including languages), and projects of earlier generations.[190]

The International Criminal Tribunal for the former Yugoslavia Appeals Chamber specifically noted that the goal of génocidaires is 'to deprive humanity of the manifold richness its nationalities, races, ethnicities and religions provide'; in other words, it is the group as a cultural concept, a social structure that génocidaires seek to eliminate.[191] Lemkin created the term genocide as a word to capture 'the destruction of essential foundations of the life of national groups', however did not necessarily see killing as the crucial component of that destruction. Instead, he saw the plan of destruction as encompassing 'the disintegration of political and social institutions, of culture, language, national feelings, religion, and the economic existence of national groups, and the destruction of the personal security, liberty, health, dignity, and even the lives of the individuals belonging to such groups'.[192] Lemkin considered loss of life as the extreme end of genocide, but not the point around which the other crimes pivoted.[193] His focus was the social structure of the targeted communities, the

---

[187] Claudia Card, *Confronting Evils: Terrorism, Torture, Genocide* (Cambridge: Cambridge University Press, 2010).

[188] Card, *Confronting Evils*, 237.

[189] Ibid., 254.

[190] Ibid., 262. See also Shmuel Lederman, 'A Nation Destroyed: An Existential Approach to the Distinctive Harm of Genocide', *Journal of Genocide Research* 19, no. 1 (2017): 112–32.

[191] *Prosecutor v Krstić*, IT-98-33-A, Appeals Judgement (19 Apr. 2004), 12, para. 36.

[192] Lemkin, *Axis Rule*, 79; Schabas, *Genocide in*, 30.

[193] Lemkin framed the social, cultural and economic aspects of genocide and the 'biological aspect', which was 'physical decline and even destruction of the population involved'; Lemkin, *Axis Rule*, 80. In addition to these aspects, he also included religious and moral genocide techniques; Ibid., 82–90.

removal of rights from that group, and 'the imposition of the national pattern of the oppressor' on the oppressed group.[194]

Considering the specific fixation on the religion of a group, regardless of how the perpetrator categorises that group designated for destruction, enables adoption of a broader interpretation of the definition of genocide. Rather than a separate concept of 'cultural genocide', the essential destruction of *a group* includes destruction of identity, not just physical elimination. Indeed, to fall under the ambit of the Genocide Convention, a group is required to have a perspicuous *identity*. 'Genocide not only intentionally strips individuals of the ability to participate in social relationships, activities, and traditions, it aims to destroy the possibility of those particular kinds of relationships, activities, and traditions for others in the future'.[195] For survivors, there is alienation, deracination, from their people—their *group*.

Genocide is defined as acts committed with intent to destroy a group in whole or in part. The Genocide Convention and ICC definition requires acts be committed 'with intent to destroy'. One of the crimes of genocide is infliction of conditions of life calculated to bring about 'the physical destruction in whole or in part' of the group. The fact that the umbrella definition does not include the word 'physical' but one of the specific crimes does, indicates that interpretation of 'intent to destroy' can be broader than simply physical destruction.[196] International and domestic case law has referred to the bonds of group members as a defining element of the group, 'as well as such aspects of the group as its members' culture and beliefs', hence the 'intent to destroy' 'cannot sensibly be regarded as reducible to an intent to destroy the group physically or biologically'.[197]

Violations of freedom of religion are genocidal crimes: causing serious bodily or mental harm, forcible transfer of children, and killing members of the group. Most violations are the former—impediments to exercising freedom of religion result in or constitute serious bodily or mental harm, destroying the social structure of that group. For example, tattooing of Armenian Christian women amounts to serious bodily and mental harm; destruction of religious buildings and icons generates serious mental harm; forced conversion creates serious mental harm; and cessation of religious rites and rituals also results in

---

[194] Lemkin, *Axis Rule*, 79.

[195] Card, *Confronting Evils*, 265.

[196] For further discussion on treaty interpretation in the context of the crime of genocide, see Elisa Novic, "Physical-biological or Socio-cultural 'Destruction' in Genocide? Unravelling the Legal Underpinnings of Conflicting Interpretations," *Journal of Genocide Research* 17, no. 1 (2015): 70–73.

[197] *Prosecutor v Krajišnik*, IT-00-39-T, Trial Judgement (27 Sept. 2006), 302, para. 854, fn. 1701. See also John Quigley, *The Genocide Convention: An International Law Analysis* (Aldershot: Ashgate, 2006), 103–05.

serious mental harm. Forcible transfer of children sometimes occurs specifically for the purposes of forced conversion (as in the Armenian Genocide).

Taking a more expansive interpretation of the crime of genocide will enable international criminal courts and tribunals to prosecute more perpetrators of genocide, reducing impunity of perpetrators for these significant and enduring crimes. Attentiveness to violations of freedom of religion in the context of genocide is crucial, where perpetrators can be punished for causing serious bodily or mental harm for crimes committed that are also rights violations. There is a compelling obligation to look beyond torture and killing in genocide, to human rights violations amounting to genocide crimes that have frequently been neglected for prosecution in favour of prosecuting crimes of torture and killing. Focus on physical destruction in prosecutions ignores the seriousness of crimes that destroy the very fabric of a group, crimes that are 'a deliberate attempt to change the identity of the survivors by modifying relationships within a given society'.[198]

Recognition of the role of religious freedom in the genocide process also has repercussions for genocide prevention. The case studies assessed here demonstrate violations of the right to freedom of religion take place in genocides even if the targeted group is not exclusively a religious group, and well before killing begins. There are distinct similarities in the way that freedom of religion is violated in the genocide process: destruction of religious icons, buildings, and texts; restriction of or complete banning of religious rites, rituals, and ceremonies; prohibition of religious education; forced conversion; and specific targeting of religious leaders for torture and killing. These consistent patterns position the right to freedom of religion as a potentially significant genocide indicator/risk factor (within the broader context of human rights violations more generally).

There is a need for specific scrutiny of violations of religious rights in assessing genocide risk factors. These rights violations can also be used to deepen interpretations of the definition of genocide by international criminal courts and tribunals. Violations of freedom of religion thus have the potential to play a significant role in prevention and punishment of genocide. The importance of this particular rights violation should not be underestimated, and therefore freedom of religion should be staunchly and consistently protected at domestic and international levels.

---

[198] Feierstein, *Genocide as*, 12.

CHAPTER 3

Post-memory and Artefacts
The Gelber/Altschul Collection[199]

Katharine Gelber

At around the age of 10 I was told that, as a boy aged 12, my father had been put on a *Kindertransport* out of Vienna in late 1938, taken to a camp in England, fostered by an (unnamed) English headmaster and his wife, and then evacuated to Yorkshire where he was boarded at a school until the end of the war. To say this story is brief is an understatement. The details of it were not discussed, and as a child I gleaned these few memories and this truncated version of the story from my father only once, and at the direct urging of my mother.

Yet after my father died in 2017 I discovered a trove of objects, artefacts of a life I knew almost nothing about but which he had had in his possession for decades. These artefacts—books, photographs, letters, and other documents[200]—had survived World War Two and the bombing of the flat in which his family had once lived in Vienna. But I do not, and will never, know

---

[199] I presented an earlier version of this at the *Yom HaShoah* (Holocaust Memorial Day) commemoration, The University of Queensland, 1 May 2019.

[200] All the artefacts referred to in this essay were donated to the Sydney Jewish Museum in 2019 under the name 'The Gelber/Altschul Collection'.

How to cite this book chapter:
Gelber, K. 2020. Post-memory and Artefacts: The Gelber/Altschul Collection. In: Marczak, N. and Shields, K. (eds.) *Genocide Perspectives VI: The Process and the Personal Cost of Genocide.* Pp. 53–68. Sydney: UTS ePRESS. DOI: https://doi.org/10.5130/aaf.d. License: CC BY-NC-ND.

how they survived. I just found them in his filing cabinet and on his bookshelves. Having discovered the artefacts I felt driven to explore their meaning and so embarked on two years of detective work to identify the people whose stories I tell here. Among the artefacts were original photographs, many 100 years old. There were also original letters, postcards, documents, school reports, published books, certificates, and my father's notes. It turned out that he had travelled to Vienna, and further to Eastern Europe, in search of elements of his family history. Again, I knew nothing substantive of this until after he died. His notes were, typically, written in a stream-of-consciousness manner, interpolating a detailed description of the cake he had eaten for afternoon tea in between critical pieces of family history. These notes, too, took a long time to decipher. All of the historically important items I have now donated to the Sydney Jewish Museum as the Gelber/Altschul Collection.

The obligation of second generation storytelling

Having done the preliminary work of identifying people and stories, I was confronted with the deeper question of why I felt compelled to explore these materials. This led me to contemplate the status of being a 'second generation'[201] storyteller. Eva Hoffman famously discusses the importance of guardianship of the Holocaust through the transmission of stories to and by the second generation, the 'hinge generation in which received, transferred knowledge of events is being transmuted into history, or into myth'.[202] She has posited that second generation stories of Holocaust survival help us to grapple with the horrors of that event, even as we instinctively recoil from them.[203]

Efraim Sicher conceptualises the idea of a second generation, to whom have fallen the obligation and the difficulties of telling such stories, as broadly as possible, including any who choose to write about the un-writeable.[204] As the daughter of a survivor, I am a second generation writer. But even more saliently, Sicher emphasises the obligation of storytelling in the context of the ongoing risks of racism and antisemitism, what he described in 1998 as the 'new

---

[201] Efraim Sicher, ed., *Breaking Crystal: Writing and Memory After Auschwitz* (Chicago: University of Illinois Press, 1998).

[202] Eva Hoffman, *After Such Knowledge: Memory, History, and the Legacy of the Holocaust* (New York: Public Affairs, 2004), cited in Marianne Hirsch, *The Generation of Postmemory: Writing and Visual Culture after the Holocaust* (New York: Cambridge University Press, 2012), 1.

[203] Ibid.

[204] Efraim Sicher, 'Introduction', in *Breaking Crystal: Writing and Memory After Auschwitz*, ed. E Sicher (Chicago: University of Illinois Press, 1998), 7.

legitimacy of racist discourse in Europe'.[205] Twenty years on his warning is even more prescient as racism and antisemitism are on the rise globally.

I am a scholar and researcher focussed on the justifiability of the regulation of hate speech, and the harms of hate speech. I have dedicated my academic career to understanding the power of words to do material harm.[206] The obligation to tell these stories has, then, a source both internal in my family history and external in my life's work combatting racism and antisemitism.

I am the daughter of a parent who chose 'silence'[207] as his preferred mechanism for dealing with his past. Silence on the part of some survivors was not at all unusual and could reflect a fear of stigma, or simply the unspeakability of their experiences, resulting in an 'inexpressibility' of survivors' anguish.[208] I have, therefore, had to glean the information that follows from the artefacts themselves, his disorganised notes, and my own research. I have traced the identities and stories of the strangers whose photographs I discovered. Marianne Hirsch talks of how photographs can be used to help new audiences understand the Holocaust; they can help structure 'post-memory', memories of the second generation of an event they did not experience first-hand but which are embedded in their lived worlds. More than that, she suggests photographs can be a way of reconstituting the family you did not have,[209] a means to 'uncover and restore experiences and life stories that might otherwise remain absent from the historical archive'.[210]

There may be errors in the detail, but this is as much of the personal stories as I have been able to recover.[211] In the pages that follow I restore life stories to those whose lives were cut short or significantly altered by the Holocaust. In doing so, I interpolate myself into the story, uncover tales that were otherwise untold, seek to preserve the memory of those who have been lost, and reconstitute a family I did not know enough about.

---

[205] Efraim Sicher, 'The Burden of Memory: The Writing of the Post-Holocaust Generation', in *Breaking Crystal: Writing and Memory After Auschwitz*, ed. E Sicher (Chicago: University of Illinois Press, 1998), 19.

[206] For example Katharine Gelber, 'Differentiating Hate Speech: A Systemic Discrimination Approach', *Critical Review of International Social and Political Philosophy* (2019), https://doi.org/10.1080/13698230.2019.1576006; Katharine Gelber and Luke McNamara, 'Evidencing the Harms of Hate Speech', *Social Identities* 22, no. 1–3 (2016): 324–41; Katharine Gelber, 'Freedom of Political Speech, Hate Speech and the Argument from Democracy: the Transformative Contribution of Capabilities Theory', *Contemporary Political Theory* 9, no. 3 (2010): 304–24.

[207] Sicher, 'The Burden', 24.

[208] Hoffman, *After Such*, 46–47.

[209] Hirsch, *The Generation*, 13.

[210] Ibid., 15.

[211] Sicher, 'Introduction', 6.

My father and his parents

My father was born in Vienna in 1926 and in the 1930s moved to Paris with his parents where he lived in the Rue Botzaris in the 16th *arrondisement*. He spoke fluent French all his life as a result. His family also spent some time in Troppau in then Czechoslovakia, before moving back to Vienna in 1937. They lived in a flat in the *Wollzeile*, which was bombed in November 1944. By then the only family member still living there was his Aunt Gretel, who spent the rest of the war in a flat belonging to the managing director of the Vienna Opera, Leopold Ludwig. After the war she transported her belongings back to the flat by handcart, including a tiny Hermes typewriter. She remained living there until she died in 2000. I never met her.

My father was the only child of middleclass parents. Among the artefacts I found were studio photographs, stylised images of my father as a very young child. He had a nanny called Minnie and a dog called Lumpi. Also among his papers I found this photograph (Figure 1), in which he looks about the age of 12. I imagine it was taken on my father's departure for England on the *Kindertransport*. He looks the right age and very unsure of himself.

Among the papers, I discovered stories my father had written down about his life in Vienna before he left. He remembered *Kristallnacht*: people of all ages being beaten, shops being wrecked and plundered. He remembered antisemitic signs scrawled on Jewish shops in Vienna ('Germans, don't buy here'), and old men made to wear a Star of David and on their knees in the street, forced to scrub cobblestones with a toothbrush while being jeered and spat at. He remembered that it was hard to leave as few countries were taking in refugees

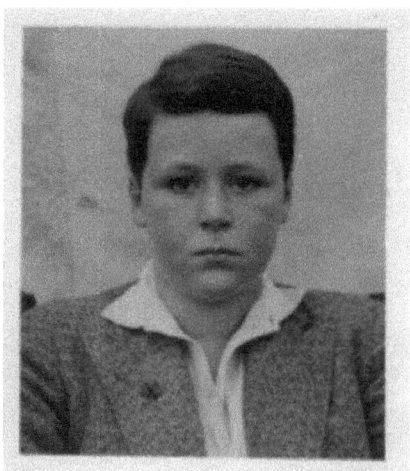

Figure 1: Harry Gregor Vladin Emil Gelber,[212] circa 1930s.

---

[212] Born 2 June 1926 Vienna, Austria, died 10 April 2017 Hobart, Australia.

and that debates in the house were frantic, fearful, and anxious. There was talk of destinations such as Sweden, Uruguay, or China. Obstacles, such as fees for exit permits, were put in place by the Nazi regime to make it difficult to leave. He remembered needing to walk softly and 'bite one's tongue', even at home. He remembered wearing a swastika in his buttonhole whenever he went out, and he even wore it on his journey to England.

He remembered in late 1938 that the Nazis had had a dispute with the Cardinal of Vienna, so one day a mob broke in to the Archbishop's residence opposite St Stephen's Cathedral, near where he lived, ransacked it, beat up priests, and threw furniture and books into the courtyard and burned them. The mob then marched down the street in which he lived, in serried ranks that filled the entire street from wall to wall, chanting threatening and menacing slogans. He and his family took care not to stand too close to the window, lest someone should see them and take it as provocation. His parents were terrified and he could smell their fear.

After he was evacuated to England he was housed in a camp, and from there he was taken in by Jean and Geoffrey Turberville—for the first time in my life, I know their names. Although my father had told me when I was a child that he had been evacuated, and that he was taken in by an English couple, I had not known their names. Apparently, after he left their house, my father never contacted them again. The Turbervilles had no children of their own and so were prepared to take in a refugee child. Geoffrey Turberville was headmaster of Eltham College, and the family lived in 'Tower House' across the road from the school. My father's first English words as they drove him home from Dovercourt Bay were, 'I'm hungry'. He remembered watching the Battle of Britain overhead. He remembered air raid warnings and having to clear the school grounds of shell splinters before playing outside. In 1942 Eltham was evacuated to Richmond, North Yorkshire, and Harry boarded at Richmond Grammar— I have no idea who paid for this. He joined the school cadet corps, and he remembered icicles in the winter outdoor showers at 6.30am every day.

After he left school, my father joined the army and was commissioned as a Second Lieutenant in the Northamptonshire Regiment (48th Foot). He was sent to India, then Kuala Lumpur, then Singapore. On his return to the United Kingdom he went to Downing College, Cambridge University, and after graduating obtained a position as a journalist for Reuters. Because he spoke German he was posted to Frankfurt, and then Berlin. There he met my mother, a photography student. After they married he was posted first to Bonn and then to Vienna. My mother told me, when I was about 30 years old, that while they were living in Vienna in 1955 they attended the first event held at the Vienna Opera since the war. My mother told me that an elderly gentleman had approached my father when he saw his nameplate on the table and asked, 'Are you the son of Dolf Gelber?' To which my father apparently answered 'No', and turned his back on him. When my mother asked, 'Why did you do that?' my father would not reply. I have never stopped wondering who the gentleman was and what connections he could have made for us.

My father's parents (Figure 2 and Figure 3) also fled Vienna. His mother had trained herself as a cook before leaving. Among my father's papers was an original letter written for his mother, Gertrude, dated May 1938 stating that she had to be dismissed from her voluntary employment in the kitchen at the Hotel Imperial, Vienna, 'due to the political events in Austria'. Gertrude made her way to England in 1938—I do not know how—and became a cook in a hotel, and then ran a 'British Restaurant' in Cloudesley Square, Islington, which also provided dinners for school children under the auspices of the London City Council. A collection of reference letters, all attesting to her diligence and hard work, was among the possessions I discovered that had been kept by my father.

Dolf was the last to leave Austria and he got out just before borders were closed in September 1939. In late August friends told him the security services were after him and he would be arrested the next day. Most of the frontiers had been warned of his departure, except the Dutch border where these friends would hold up notification about him for 24 hours or so. He slipped across the Dutch border at once, with (as he put it) only a toothbrush and made his way to England. He was interned on Alderney, a Channel Island, and then in South Wales. He joined the Pioneer Corps of the Army, repairing railways and digging latrines. He spent some time at Catterick, England's second largest military complex in North Yorkshire, and told a story that when the General in command wanted entertainment for dinner guests he summoned a string quartet from the pioneers, which typically included the former first violin of the Vienna Philharmonic or a flute player from the Leipzig orchestra. After some time, Dolf saw an advertisement for the Royal Navy wanting German speakers to work as

Figure 2: Dolf Otto Caesar Gelber.[213]   **Figure 3:** Gertrude Altschul.[214]

---

[213] Born 30 November 1900 Vienna, Austria, died 2 January 1976 London, United Kingdom.

[214] Born 2 January 1903 Vienna, Austria, died 28 January 1955 London, United Kingdom.

translators. In his interview, when asked why he wished to fight the Germans, he replied, 'because so many of my wife's family died in concentration camps'. He became a Leading Writer Special and translated intercepted U-boat communications. On D-Day he was on the HMS Eglinton off Normandy. Eventually both my father's parents were able to move to Yorkshire, presumably to live near him while he attended school. But he never lived with them again.

The Altschuls

My father's mother, Gertrude, came from the Altschul family. Her parents were Max Altschul, originally from Prague, and Bertha Knoepfelmacher (Figure 4).

In the collection of my father's papers I found documentation that he had evidently obtained from the Austrian archives at some point, confirming the confiscation of their family's assets under the Nazi occupation—first a leather factory, then personal belongings such as jewellery and silver tableware. At the time the family appealed because their pension was paid on the basis of their assets, and because their assets had been seized their pension was severely reduced, but of course this was of no use. In the later documentation, family members were forced to adopt the middle names 'Isaac' and 'Sarah', which was a legal way of identifying Jews.

Max and Bertha were deported from Vienna to Theresienstadt/Terezin on 22 July 1942. Bertha worked as a 'postmistress' at Theresienstadt/Terezin. They were transported from there to Auschwitz in May 1944. Max died in the train on the way there; Bertha died in Auschwitz in July 1944. Before being deported they had owned a six volume, nineteenth century edition of the collected works of Heinrich Heine. I know this because when I was in my thirties my father

Figure 4: Max Altschul[215] and Bertha Knoepfelmacher.[216]

---

[215] Born 24 September 1870 Prague, Czech Republic, died May 1944, Europe.
[216] Born 15 March 1878 Vienna, Austria, died 15 July 1944, Auschwitz, Poland.

Figure 5: Max Altschul's siblings.

gifted me these books, as I am the only one of his children who speaks fluent German. In the front cover of the first volume is an annotation: 'To my dear Harry, in memory of his grandparents Max and Bertha' and signed by them. I have no idea how these volumes survived.

Bertha had a brother, Gustav, who moved to Brazil. Among the documents I found were letters exchanged between Gustav's son Pedro, and my father, in which Pedro states that Gustav had identified at least 23 family members who were killed in concentration camps. Among them were siblings of Max Altschul (Figure 5: Top row l-r Marie Wehle, Ludwig Altschul, Moritz Altschul. Middle row l-r Emma Heller nee Altschul, Julie Altschul, Hugo Altschul. Bottom row l-r Emil Altschul, Max and Bertha Altschul, Otto and Ottilie Taussig).

Also among the documents I found in my father's possession was an original letter (Figure 6) typed on the flimsiest of blue paper, so thin that the full stops made by the typewriter had created holes in the parchment. It is dated 14 July 1945, and written by Kurt Wehle, a cousin of my family, after his liberation from Auschwitz. Kurt was a survivor of Theresienstadt/Terezin and Auschwitz, and moved to the United States of America in 1951. In the letter, Kurt details the fate of members of the family. He uses initials to describe both places and names—which I presume was an instinctive safety measure. He said, 'I am writing this first of my letters from S', saying he is 'conscious of being the only one of all the big family and I feel like crying like a child'. He goes on:

> The balance sheet of our family after these six years is horrible. E. and H. were deported to Lodz with the first Polish transport in October 1941. ... H. and H. died still in Prague. ... There is no news from R. who was in a Polish labour camp. She is certain not to be alive any more. ... H. O. and S. went to Terezin in summer 1942. H. went on to Poland, where she died. O. and S. died in Terezin. G. V. and their younger daughter Sonja were deported from Melnik to Terezin, and later on to Poland, where they most probably died. ... E. went in summer 1942 to Terezin and on to Poland, where she certainly died. P.H. was since November 1941 in Terezin and died there soon. My father went to Terezin in July 1942 and died there in October of the same year. A. W. and his wife H. were deported to Terezin in December 1942 and from there, in September 1943, to Oswiecim. They died in the gas chamber on 8.3.44 ...

The letter talks of 'Max and Berta' and outlines their fate:

> Max and Berta were deported to Terezin in summer 1942. Alice and I, my wife's parents and also A. supplied them with food, often did their cooking and later on, when Alice and I were ourselves in Terezin, we cared for them like for our own parents. Daily we took them food, supplied them with clothes, helped them to better quarters; we had Berta accommodated in the home for the aged, and saw to it that she had medical aid. They longed to see their children once again. Unfortunately, it came otherwise. In May 1944 they were taken from Terezin to Poland. Max died on the train, Berta came to Oswiecim. As I shall describe further down, Alice and I were in the same camp and did for her everything in our power. We got her medical aid, better treatment by overseers and superiors and took her food every day, so she did not go hungry. Around 15.7.44 she died.

He also describes his own circumstances:

> Alice and I were taken to Terezin on 10.7.42 and from there on 18.12.43 to Oswiecim, where we were together until 1.7.44. On this day I was taken away to the concentration camp of Oranienburg. From 19.4.45 I was on the evacuation march and arrived in Terezin on 8.5.45. The 10.5.45 I came to Prague. I have no news from Alice since 1.7.44 and always hope she will return. A week ago I learned that she was taken to

Stutthoff concentration camp and that she was, in August or September 1944, in so hopeless a physical and mental state, that she must be certainly dead by now. Can you imagine how I feel?

Only the first page of this letter survives.

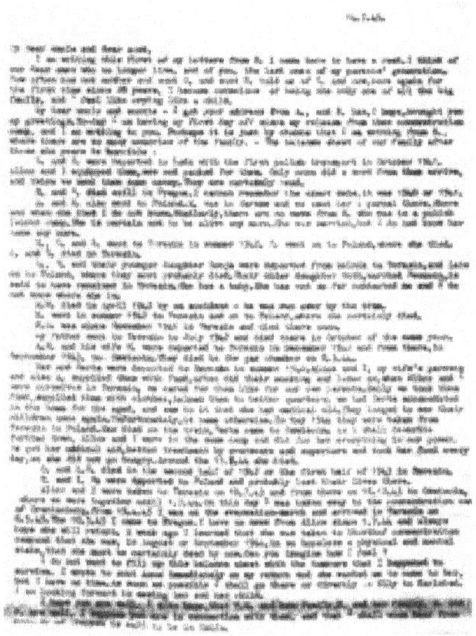

Figure 6: Letter written by Kurt Wehle.

The Gelbers

At the beginning of the twentieth century, Vienna was a melting pot of intellectuals and artists, and the parents of my father's father moved in those circles. My great grandfather was Adolf Gelber (Figure 7), a Jew who had originated from Podhajce in Eastern Europe. Podjajce was a once thriving Jewish town with a grand synagogue built in 1529 and scholar-rabbis, but it had also been subjected to antisemitic pogroms. It has been part of Poland, then the USSR, and is now in Ukraine. He was sent to boarding school in Lemberg (Lvóv, now Lviv) at a German high school, then on to the University of Czernowitz. He transferred to Vienna University to study law once the universities became open to Jews. By this time his father had lost his wealth and could no longer support him. His brothers Jacob Josef and Leisor/Ludwig joined him in Vienna and apparently the three brothers had one pair of trousers between them (the family made it a joke: *Das war eine arge Chose, drei Brueder und eine Hose* – That was a funny thing, three brothers and one pair of trousers).

Figure 7: Adolf Aron Abraham Gelber[217] (photograph from an original portrait by Rauchinger).

Adolf became a literary figure and lecturer with an interest in Shakespeare. His first book in this field was *Shakespearean Problems: Plan and Unity in Hamlet*, published in 1891 and influential in the staging of the play. This led to a highly successful production in Munich in 1896 and among the artefacts I found is a copy of this version of *Hamlet* with Adolf's hand-written notes and corrections in the margin for the theatre production (Figure 8). He interpreted Shakespeare's works for a modern and German-speaking audience.[218] His version of *Troilus and Cressida* was premiered at the Vienna Burgtheater in 1902 and was also staged by the Hungarian National Theatre. Adolf would often bring people home to lunch with no notice, and was described in his obituary as having an open, welcoming house. Among his friends were Karl May (author),[219] Otto Artbauer (author), Ferdinand Bonn (actor), and Josef Popper-Lynkeus (poet).[220]

---

[217] Born 13 or 15 May 1856, Podhajce, Ukraine, died 7 February 1923 Vienna, Austria.

[218] Adolf Gelber, *Dreihundert Jahre Shylock-Schimpf: Vortrag gehalten am 5. Jänner 1901 in der Österr. Israelit. Union* (Vienna: Österr. Israelitische Union, 1901).

[219] For further information on Karl May, see http://karl-may-wiki.de/index.php/Adolf_Gelber.

[220] Signed photographs of these three people are in The Gelber/Altschul Collection.

Figure 8: Hand annotated edition of *Hamlet* for production.

Adolf Gelber was also a journalist and editor of a newspaper (*Neues Wiener Tagblatt*) for 40 years, and a traveller. He visited Greece and wrote a book about it in 1912, for which he was rewarded with the Greek Order of the Redeemer (an original publication of this book, *Auf Griechischer Erde* [*On Greek Soil*] and the original certificate are in the Gelber/Altschul Collection). He wrote another book after travelling to Poland. [221] He wrote a book on *The Origins of the World War*,[222] an essay on 'Human Rights in our Culture',[223] and a treatise on the poetry of Josef Popper-Lynkeus.[224] I had known the bare bones of this story—that he was a newspaper editor and scholar—but not the details until I found the original books and papers in my father's possessions.

I also found a set of fairy tales on my father's bookshelf, published in the first two decades of the twentieth century and written by Adolf Gelber. I am ashamed to say that when I found them I had no idea what they were, and considered putting them in the trash. But thankfully I Googled them and discovered that Adolf Gelber was a well-known writer of fairy tales, some of which have been preserved in open source format.[225]

---

[221] Adolf Gelber, *Auf Polnischer Erde: der Sommer 1917 im Osten* (Vienna: Perles Signature, 1919).

[222] Adolf Gelber, *Die Urheber des Weltkrieges, Sonderdruck des Geleitwortes aus dem 'Heldenwerk 1914–1915'* (Vienna: Verlag des Heldenwerkes, 1915).

[223] Adolf Gelber, *Der Menschenwert in unserer Kultur* (Vienna: Der Verein zur Abwehr des Antisemitismus, 1911).

[224] Adolf Gelber, *Ueber den 'Weltangstschrei' und seinen Dichter Josef Popper (Lynkeus)* (Vienna: Wladarz, 1912).

[225] For further information on Adolf Gelber, see https://gutenberg.spiegel.de/autor/adolf-gelber-1430.

Figure 9: Illustration inside *Snow White's Christmas in the Forest*.

One is a Snow White story of his own invention[226] (Figure 9) and the others are folk tales from different ethnic communities—African,[227] Native American,[228] and the Kalmuck people.[229] I never knew these existed but I have now discovered that the Snow White story was reproduced in a recent edited collection, *The Most Beautiful Christmas Fairytales*.[230] Adolf Gelber also wrote a book about the Arabian Nights tales,[231] an interest that occupied him for 16 years. In my father's notes he said he remembered reading this four volume work as a child and that the books were destroyed when the flat was bombed in World War Two. But two volumes survived and are now in the Gelber/Altschul Collection.

Some of the actors, musicians, and writers among the friends of Adolf Gelber met their fate in the Holocaust. Although their photographs do not depict specific events from that time, they reveal people whose stories have otherwise become obscured by the fog of history and the chaos of war. My two years of detective work uncovering their identities from hand-written signatures produced a trove of connections.

---

[226] Adolf Gelber, *Schneewitchens Weihnachten im Walde* (Vienna: Carl Konegen Verlag, 1919).
[227] Adolf Gelber, *Negermaerchen. Aus Imanas Landen* (Vienna: Rikola Verlag, 1921).
[228] Adolf Gelber, *Indianer-Maerchen. Manito und seine Leute* (Vienna: Rikola Verlag, 1921).
[229] Adolf Gelber, *Kalmueckische Maerchen* (Vienna: Rikola Verlag, 1921).
[230] Adolf Gelber, 'Schneewittchens Weihnachten im Walde', in *Schoensten Maerchen zur Weihnachtszeit* (Frankfurt: Fischer Verlag, 2003).
[231] Adolf Gelber, *Tausend und Eine Nacht: der Sinn der Erzaehlungen der Scheherazade* (Vienna: Verlag von Moritz Perles, 1917).

Figure 10: Signed photograph of Conrad Veidt.

Figure 11: Annotated photograph of Edmund Eysler.

One is a signed photograph of Conrad Veidt (Figure 10), an actor (22 January 1893—3 April 1943), who with his wife was forced to leave Germany in 1933. He is best known for starring as Major Heinrich Strasser in the movie *Casablanca*.

Another is a signed photograph of composer Edmund Eysler (Figure 11), which is annotated 'To Mr and Mrs Dr A. Gelber, in devotion, January 1914'. Edmund Eysler composed hugely popular operettas in Vienna in the early part of the twentieth century. Between the end of World War One and the ban on his works introduced by the Nazi occupation of Vienna, he composed 24 stage works. During the war his works were banned and a plaque outside his birthplace was removed. He survived and, following the war, was welcomed back to Vienna with a return of the plaque.[232]

---

[232] For further information on Edmund Eysler, see https://forbiddenmusic.org/2016/02/03/the-heavy-loss-of-the-light-weight-edmund-eysler/.

Figure 12: Annotated photograph of Gisela Springer.

Figure 13: Annotated photograph of Thomas Edison.

Gisela Springer (Figure 12) was a solo pianist with the Vienna Symphony. Her photograph is annotated, 'To the lovely Family Gelber, with the wish that you hold me in as deep affection as I hold you! In true friendship, March 1916'. Gisela Springer moved to Berlin in the 1920s, where she remained until she was deported on 18 October 1941 to Lodz/Litzmannstadt, and then in May 1942 to Chelmno/Kulmhof where she was murdered on 8 May 1942.[233]

I even discovered a signed photograph (Figure 13) of Thomas Edison, inventor, annotated 'To Dr Adolf Gelber'.[234]

---

[233] For further information on Gisela Springer, see https://www.stolpersteine-berlin.de/de/biografie/8178.

[234] This item is in my private collection.

Reflections

The reconstruction of these stories has filled gaps in my own family history. Uncovering the stories of loss and tragedy evoked very strong emotions as I undertook this work. I hope that by writing this down, these peoples' memories will be preserved. It is interesting that my father kept all of these artefacts without putting them into a coherent narrative. Perhaps I have now been able to do what he wanted, but could not bring himself to do.

Eva Hoffman suggests that post-memory has profound effects on the children of Holocaust survivors, whether the events 'were spoken about or not'.[235] She suggests that the hinge generation moves through 'stages of understanding'[236] the events of the Holocaust and their ongoing impact on political, social, and family life. The photographs I discovered, while they do not depict suffering or harrowing events, tell stories that contribute to our understanding of what was lost. They document untold stories from my family that deserve to be told.

And although in my family the transmission of the details of the stories was sparse as we grew up, it may well have been that the transmission of trauma was not. It is impossible to know how much of my father's personality was a product of his being sent away from his family, to a new country, where he did not speak the language and at such a young age. I knew a man who aspired to identify as an English gentleman, and indeed he did this so successfully that many people with whom he worked and socialised did not know he had been born and raised in Vienna. He was also secretive, critical, and quick to anger. My mother once put a bright orange smiley face over the door of the living room, right opposite where he would sit and read at night in 'his' chair, in a forlorn bid to get him to smile more often.

So I also hope that the telling of these stories can help to heal the intergenerational trauma[237] transmitted to me and my siblings from my father. In the end, second generation stories are also stories of hope. Because those who survived became parents to second generation witnesses, many of whom (myself and my three siblings included) are thriving. That is an achievement of which he would be proud.

---

[235] Hoffman, *After Such*, xi.
[236] Ibid., xiv.
[237] Petra Fachinger, 'Poland and Post-Memory in Second-Generation German Jewish Fiction', *Shofar* 27, no. 4 (2009): 49–65.

CHAPTER 4

'If You're Different Are You the Same?'

The Nazi Genocide of Disabled People and Les Murray's *Fredy Neptune*

Amanda Tink

Before returning to academia I worked as an Education and Training Manager, organising events, reviewing disability action plans and conducting disability awareness training. The sessions I facilitated were for staff at any level of an arts organisation who wanted to increase the involvement of disabled people in the arts as artists, audience members and arts workers. Three years into my job I was at a point where I could still deliver an authentic performance, and participants' evaluations of my style and content remained consistently high, but I was becoming disheartened about the possibility for my training to achieve nuances in others' conceptions of disabled people that would last beyond our four hours together. Then, at the end of a session that seemed no different from any other, one of the participants came up to me after everyone else had left the room and said: 'I just want you to know that you have changed my life. For ten years I thought I was suffering from chronic pain, and now I know I'm not suffering, I'm living with it', and she began to cry. For the three years that I had been training people in the use of language, and all the years prior that I had been talking about it, it was not until that moment that I understood that words do not just affect us, they *are* us.

How to cite this book chapter:
Tink, A. 2020. 'If You're Different Are You the Same?': The Nazi Genocide of Disabled People and Les Murray's *Fredy Neptune*. In: Marczak, N. and Shields, K. (eds.) *Genocide Perspectives VI: The Process and the Personal Cost of Genocide.* Pp. 69–85. Sydney: UTS ePRESS. DOI: https://doi.org/10.5130/aaf.e. License: CC BY-NC-ND.

In turn, her telling me her story also changed my life: it renewed my faith in my work, and was one of the factors that led me to return to academia to research the influence of impairment and disability on Australian disabled writers and, consequently, to Les Murray. I was attracted to Murray's work not only because of his evident love of and care for words, but also because, like me, he was a disabled person who was continually and profoundly influenced by the Nazi genocide of disabled people.

Until recently, on the infrequent occasions when the genocide of disabled people by the Nazis is acknowledged in public discourse, it has been framed as a sidenote to the Holocaust. This suggests that little was done, for a short time, to few people. In fact, from July 1933 to the end of World War Two, 400,000 disabled people were forcibly sterilised as a result of Nazi policy.[238] Furthermore, as soon as Adolf Hitler had war to co-opt as a justification, the Nazis' euthanasia policies were rapidly implemented and regularly expanded. Since Nazi records of the murders of disabled people were often haphazardly kept and meticulously destroyed, the most conclusive thing that can be said about any estimate of the number of victims is that it is likely to be too low. In Suzanne Evans' thorough survey of the six Nazi euthanasia programmes targeting disabled people, she estimates the total number of disabled people murdered to be 750,000.[239]

I was born in Australia thirty years after the Nazi genocide ended, and therefore do not claim to know the terror experienced by my people in Germany, and around the world, at that time. However, I remain continually conscious that, as someone who was born totally blind, if I had been born in Germany or a Nazi-occupied country thirty years earlier I would at the very least have been sterilised, and my older autistic brother would have been murdered.

Les Murray was born in 1938 and thus was not distanced from the Nazi genocide by time, only by the much more precarious factor of country of birth. Though he did not explicitly identify as autistic until he was in his fifties, had he been born in Germany or a Nazi-occupied country, he too may have been murdered.[240] Someone close to Murray who probably would have been a victim of Nazi genocide if he had been born in Germany or a Nazi-occupied country before the end of World War Two, is Murray's fourth child, who was diagnosed as autistic when he was three.[241]

This consciousness drives a two-part commitment: one of those is to resist the sidelining of the Nazi genocide of disabled people, its victims and its

---

[238] Carol Poore, *Disability in Twentieth-Century German Culture* (Ann Arbor: University of Michigan Press, 2007), 78.

[239] Suzanne E. Evans, *Forgotten Crimes: The Holocaust and People with Disabilities* (Chicago: Ivan R Dee, 2004), 18.

[240] Peter F Alexander, *Les Murray: A Life in Progress* (South Melbourne: Oxford University Press, 2000), 25.

[241] Alexander, *Les Murray*, 215.

consequences. The other is to draw attention to the fact that the Nazi genocide of disabled people did not begin on 14 July 1933. As with all genocides, its roots are in language, and language around disability remains resolutely dehumanising even today. This, contrary to the popular belief that genocide is an event rather than an ongoing threat, raises questions about where the line between the genocide and non-genocide of disabled people is, and which side of the line our society is on. For example, when you say 'never again' do you have disabled people in mind?

Both of these commitments featured throughout Murray's 60-year writing career. He explicitly centred the victims and consequences of the Nazi genocide of disabled people in his poem 'Dog Fox Field', which he chose as the title poem for his book published in 1990.

'Dog Fox Field'

> The test for feeblemindedness was, they had to make up a sentence using the words dog, fox and field.
> Judgement at Nuremberg
>
> These were no leaders, but they were first
> into the dark on Dog Fox Field:
>
> Anna who rocked her head, and Paul
> who grew big and yet giggled small,
>
> Irma who looked Chinese, and Hans
> who knew his world as a fox knows a field.
>
> Hunted with needles, exposed, unfed,
> this time in their thousands they bore sad cuts
>
> for having gaped, and shuffled, and failed
> to field the lore of prey and hound
>
> they then had to thump and cry in the vans
> that ran while stopped in Dog Fox Field.
>
> Our sentries, whose holocaust does not end,
> they show us when we cross into Dog Fox Field.[242]

Although Murray is known for creating unusual and complex metaphors in his poetry, on this important topic he chooses to speak plainly: He lays bare the

---

[242] Les Murray, *Collected Poems* (Carlton: Black Inc, 2018), 325.

arbitrary and simplistic ways in which the Nazis determined who was 'feeble-minded'. He highlights the fact that disabled children were the first victims of the Nazi genocide, that eugenics, for all its theory, contains no complexity or humanity, and the variety of ways in which the children who failed the dog fox field test were murdered. Significantly, he emphasises that the Nazi genocide of disabled people was and is not an isolated incident—it is 'this time', implying that there were previous and successive times, and that crossing into dog fox field remains a matter of 'when' not if.

Murray explicitly centred his thesis on the roots of genocide in his second verse novel *Fredy Neptune*, which he wrote between 1993 and 1997. The book is the first person narrative of Fredy Boettcher, beginning in 1914 when he is 19-years-old, and covering the next 35 years of his life. Fredy is an autistic Australian man with German parents, who acquires a physical impairment when he is 20 as a result of witnessing mass murder during the Armenian Genocide. The novel also features a significant minor character called Hans, an intellectually impaired young man whom Fredy kidnaps in 1933 from Germany and brings back to Australia, so that Hans will not be forcibly sterilised by the Nazis. This paper identifies and explores the arguments advocated in *Fredy Neptune* with respect to the genocide of disabled people.

Impairment and disability

It is important to note that throughout this paper, the terms impairment and disability represent a social model of disability position, and not a traditional medical model of disability position.

While eugenics by name may have declined as a result of the Nazi genocide, eugenics by practice continues in the ways disabled people are segregated from and by society. One of the legacies of eugenics is the labelling of differences in human biology as 'defects' rather than 'variations', fostering the idea that a single measurement can sum up all that a whole human is or will be. According to eugenic thinking, disabled people never measure up, therefore their primary goal should be to do all they can to become 'normal'. Of course, this deliberately sets disabled people up to fail, because eugenics is predicated on the idea that a certain percentage of people are not 'normal'.

In 1975, the Union of the Physically Impaired Against Segregation (UPIAS) outlined 'The Fundamental Principles of Disability'.[243] Instead of continuing the eugenic tradition of labelling medical conditions as disability, the Union labelled them as impairment. Disability, it stated, is what happens to people with impairments when they are prevented from participating in society as

---

[243] Union of the Physically Impaired Against Segregation, Fundamental Principles of Disability (1975) www.disability.co.uk/fundamental-principles-disability.

equal citizens. This is now known as the 'social model of disability'.[244] Similar to other social movements of the time, UPIAS members recognised that it was not their biology preventing them from participating in society; rather, it was the attitudes of people who judged themselves to have better biology than someone with an impairment.

Silence and silencing

Before exploring the claims that Murray makes in *Fredy Neptune*, I want to consider the significant work this novel does in interrupting the silence and silencing on the Nazi genocide of disabled people. This silence began with how disabled victims of the Nazis were treated after World War Two. The victims of the forced sterilisation law, which was not declared unconstitutional until 2007, endured decades of negative treatment and lack of recognition. As Carol Poore describes:

> Having been told repeatedly that they were inferior and having been warned by Nazi authorities not to talk about sterilization, many of these victims remained silent for the rest of their lives. Forty years after the end of the war, for example, a West German organization of blind people issued a statement that read, 'Most of the blind who were sterilized at that time and who are still alive today met their fate in their youth. They were usually not at home but in an institution for the blind, where no one supported them and where they often had to endure the scorn and contempt of others. That affected them so deeply that they are still ashamed to talk about their sterilization today'.[245]

It was argued that since disabled people were not persecuted on racial grounds, they were ineligible for the compensation offered to other victims of Nazi genocides in 1953 (the Federal Law for the Compensation of the Victims of National Socialist Persecution).[246] As Evans notes: 'One reparations court declared that disabled victims were 'people below the level of ciphers.' Another court refused to punish those who acted in the euthanasia programme because euthanasia had its supporters before the Nazi era, therefore the act was not punishable as a specifically Nazi crime.'[247] In 2011, the German Government finally recognised

---

[244] Michael Oliver, *The Politics of Disablement* (London: Macmillan Education, 1990), 115.
[245] Poore, *Disability in*, 115.
[246] Susanne C. Knittel, *The Historical Uncanny: Disability, Ethnicity, and the Politics of Holocaust Memory* (New York: Fordham University, 2015), 14.
[247] Evans, *Forgotten Crimes*, 159.

disabled people equally with other victims of the Nazis, but this has not yet led to compensation.

Similarly, disabled people are marginalised in public remembrance of Nazi genocides. A memorial to the victims of the T4 programme was not opened until 2014 and was the last of the four Berlin memorials of the victims of Nazi genocides to be constructed. Access for disabled visitors to other memorials is not uniformly available, and has not even been a priority at the sites specifically commemorating disabled victims. At Grafeneck, for example, Susanne C. Knittel points out that:

> [i]t is surprising and puzzling to note that there are currently no special measures being taken to accommodate visitors with disabilities, beyond whatever structural features the site already has due to its function as a care facility. On average, 10 percent of all groups that visit Grafeneck include people with disabilities, and of the 400 groups, 20 to 30 consist entirely of people with disabilities or learning difficulties. The documentation center is wheelchair accessible and there are plans to create supplementary texts in simple language to accommodate visitors with mental disabilities and learning difficulties, but so far only a leaflet in simple language has been produced.[248]

Moreover, since Grafeneck is both a Holocaust memorial and a residential care centre for disabled people, the residents are limited in their own access to the memorial while playing a central role in nondisabled peoples' public remembering.[249]

Continuing this silence and silencing are researchers, journalists, critics, novelists and publishers who have rarely sought out the experiences of either the disabled victims of the Nazi genocide or, in the case of victims who were murdered, their families, friends or colleagues. Similarly, it is rare that accounts or discussions of the Holocaust mention disabled victims. There are, of course, exceptions but too often these mention the Nazi genocide of disabled people only to diminish its significance or excuse the perpetrators of their crimes. Giorgio Agamben, for example, says that there was a 'humanitarian' basis for the euthanasia programme.[250] As Knittel observes: 'it would be outrageous for anyone to make a similar claim regarding the "Humanitarian" motivations for the "final solution".[251]

Given the persistence of the silence and silencing on the Nazi genocide of disabled people, the existence of *Fredy Neptune* is significant in three equally

---

[248] Knittel, *Historical Uncanny*, 56.
[249] Ibid.
[250] Giorgio Agamben, *Homo Sacer: Sovereign Power and Bare Life* (California: Stanford University Press, 1998), 140.
[251] Knittel, *Historical Uncanny*, 133.

important ways. The first is that it locates the genocide of disabled people in the context of Nazi genocide more broadly, as well as the Armenian and Greek cases. Second, it highlights their relationships, while not subordinating nor devaluing the experiences of any of the victim groups. In addition, the main character, Fredy, and a significant minor character, Hans, are both disabled. So far as I have been able to find, prominent disabled characters have not been featured before in novels set during the Nazi era. Finally, the author is also a disabled person. This is rare but not unheard of in German literature on Nazi genocides but, as far as I can tell, had not occurred in English literature on Nazi genocides before *Fredy Neptune*. There are also four ways in which the text comments on the Nazi genocide of disabled people, which I now explore.

Dehumanising language

Critics often link, or, as Murray labels it, 'hogtie' *Fredy Neptune* to the epic tradition. However, classifying the novel in this way foregrounds Fredy's travels and diminishes the importance of his embodied experience. As Murray says about the novel: 'There is quite simply no other story that could be called The Man Who Lost His Sense of Touch. Or The Man Who Gave Up His Body Out of Shame'.[252]

Fredy's lack of sensation begins early in the novel when he witnesses, as part of the Armenian Genocide, a group of men pouring kerosene over a group of women and setting them on fire, burning them to death. His inability to mentally assimilate that one group of humans could be so cruel to another group of humans, coupled with his inability to prevent or halt this particular mass murder, cause in him trauma that manifests as physical numbness. To one degree or another, many critics have suggested that Murray employs Fredy's physical impairment throughout this novel purely for metaphorical purposes. Charles Lock, for example, in '*Fredy Neptune*: Metonymy and the Incarnate Preposition', emphatically states that the numbness 'is a poetic device, not a medical condition'. However, in 'How Fred and I wrote *Fredy Neptune*', Murray explains that Fredy's numbness is an impairment based in part on discussions with psychiatrists, but mostly on his personal experience: 'For most of the dissociative dimension, I could draw on things I knew from within myself. And because dissociation goes back in me to times before my conscious memory, I could put it into Fred's mouth in stumbling baby talk free from all analysis, the semi-articulate speech of innermost things'.[253] In other words, the character of Fredy both draws on and represents embodied experience.

---

[252] Les Murray, 'How Fred and I Wrote *Fredy Neptune*', in *The Best Australian Essays 1999*, ed. Peter Craven (Melbourne: Bookman Press, 1999), 365.
[253] Murray, 'How Fred', 369.

Furthermore, foundational to this text is objection to equating humans with anything other than humanness, since this practice is one of the places where mass murders, such as those witnessed by Fredy, originate. As Murray explains:

> I know a poet who is careful to flag his every image with 'like' or 'resembles' or some such. The surf doesn't fold its long green notes and cash them in foam-change on the beach, with him; rather, the waves of the surf are like long green folded notes cashed in foam on the beach. By the same strict token, no prime minister was ever a drover's dog. My colleague doesn't go beyond simile into the farther ranges of metaphor because to telescope statements overmuch is to lie. He is scrupulous not to let metaphor collapse into identity. This is very Protestant of him, though he is not Christian. It is also very responsible, because metaphor is dangerous stuff, the more so, perhaps, as it becomes worn and baggy with overuse and we forget it is metaphor.[254]

In summary, metaphorising humans and using human embodied experience as metaphor can both be dehumanising; a group that is frequently dehumanised in these ways is disabled people. The metaphorisation of the embodied experience of disabled people might be extremely common but its commonness does not make the practice ethical, and there is plenty of evidence, including the treatment of disabled people by the Nazis featured in 'Book IV' of *Fredy Neptune*, to demonstrate that the real world consequences of this practice for disabled people are devastating and ongoing.

One does not have to read far into *Fredy Neptune* to encounter careless metaphorisation of embodied experience. In the third verse Fredy says: 'That's how we came to be cooking alive that August, [1914] in Messina, plumy undertakers' city'. Here he is simply referring to the ship's crew's experience of the weather, but very soon, in Trabzon, as part of the Armenian Genocide, he witnesses people literally being burned to death:

> Their big loose dresses were sopping. Kerosene, you could smell it.
> The men were prancing, feeling them, poking at them to dance –
> then pouf! they were alight, the women, dark wicks to great orange flames, whooping and shrieking.[255]

Witnessing this atrocity and being unable to intervene causes in Fredy a condition that he first experiences as burning: 'I just curled up in my hammock, like a burnt thing myself, and turned my back. The POs couldn't scream me to work'.[256]

---

[254] Les Murray, *A Working Forest: Selected Prose* (Potts Point: Duffy & Snellgrove, 1997), 74.
[255] Les Murray, *Fredy Neptune* (Sydney: Duffy & Snellgrove, 1998), 15.
[256] Ibid.

Fredy's description of himself as 'like a burnt thing myself', although he does not realise it yet, connects his condition to the mass murder he has recently witnessed. Both echo his earlier careless 'cooking alive' metaphor, and together are the first of many instances that demonstrate the significant ways in which metaphor and embodied experience affect each other. There are a number of times throughout the novel when Fredy travels through or lives in high-temperature climates similar to Messina but, after witnessing the mass murder in Trabzon, this is the last time he uses the metaphor 'cooking alive' or anything similar.

Throughout the novel Fredy continues to encounter situations where the metaphorisation of a group of humans indicates that that group will soon be targeted for genocide. For example, four years later, when Fredy is travelling with a Turkish Colonel and they arrive in the town that the Turkish call Izmir and the Greeks call Smyrna, the Colonel refers to the Greeks as 'the dogs': 'The dogs, he said, call this Smyrna. They say it is part of Greece'. Fredy, pointing out the Colonel's dehumanisation of the Greeks asks 'what do the humans say?'[257] But the Colonel does not answer. Later that day Fredy meets Takis, a Greek man who assists Fredy to find work on a ship home to Australia. In return, Fredy gives Takis his suits, and later learns that Takis was wearing one of them when he was shot and killed two years later during attacks against the Greek community.

The Nazi genocides, too, are foreshadowed by the Nazis' deliberate use of dehumanising words to describe future victims. In early 1933, when Fredy is in Kassel, Germany, he sees SA (*Sturmabteilung*) officers chasing a man into a side alley and then hears a gunshot. The SA officers notice Fredy watching them and encourage him to 'Go and look! See how we treat trash'.[258] When he does, he realises they murdered the man for the specific purpose of indicating to the public how some of the disabled victims of Nazi genocide would be labelled:

> There was a cardboard placard
> hung round his neck, as he sat there dead in his blood:
> Congenital Criminal, it read. They must have been carrying it
> from where they'd meant to shoot him. They'd had no time
> to letter it there in the alley.[259]

Demonstrating that the line between target of genocide and free citizen is often blurred for disabled people, Hans, the intellectually impaired young man whom Fredy rescues from being forcibly sterilised by the Nazis, is routinely described using dehumanising labels. These include: 'cretin', 'dough-cock', 'zany', 'mad baby man', 'idiot', 'mental defective' and 'imbecile'. The people choosing to use

---

[257] Murray, *Fredy Neptune*, 54.
[258] Ibid., 196.
[259] Ibid.

these labels to refer to Hans are not Nazi officers but members of the public whom Hans encounters everywhere he goes.

The influence of metaphor is also demonstrated by the ways in which Fredy refers to his physical impairment. Initially he refers to it using a simile ('shedding like a gum tree'), but this becomes a metaphor three years later when he is mistaken for a spy, captured and tortured. Torture is traditionally a reliable method for dominating a person, but both Fredy and his torturers soon realise that Fredy has the upper hand. This is due to Fredy's numbness: 'They drew their truncheons, they started chopping a new me/ out of my trunk, not knowing it was dead timber'.[260] Ironically, this is a situation that frightens both of them: the torturers because it is unprecedented and gives them a story they want to tell, but that nobody else will believe; and Fredy because he knows the torturers would rather kill him than have to try to tell their story about him. However, Fredy soon becomes aware that the torturers have a second option of entertaining themselves by exhorting other prisoners to try to kill him. It is this fear that results in his first realisation about the advantages of his acquired impairment. He has already experienced one advantage—when he was able to save someone from burning to death, but not sense that his own skin was burning—but it has not yet occurred to him that this is an advantage.

Fredy's lack of sensation means he can not only endure but escape the torturers and their guards:

> I walked straight out of there
> past a sergeant blinded by his cap-peak who screamed HEY!
> I sat him flat on his bum, so fierce did I scream back!
> I was the wilder ape, and tottered like one out the door
> because this horse I rode inside of had started
> to float, and yaw.[261]

His metaphorical descriptions of his body change from being a tree, something with life, but not much agency in comparison with humans, to a Trojan horse, something that appears to others to have no life, but in fact has all the skills it needs to win the war. From then on, however, Fredy mostly refers to his physical impairment as 'the null', or 'the nothing'. It is not until he tells his best friend Sam about his impairment that this changes, due to Sam's response:

> If you told that to one of your moderns
> who think any name they can give to a phenomenon
> is its social superior, he finally told me, they'd snub it
> into line with a term like Shock or Reaction

---

[260] Murray, *Fredy Neptune*, 28.
[261] Ibid.

or Flight from Reality. To contain it and make it barren.
I think myself it's a story of law that you're carrying
for all places. You're wrong to call it the Nothing.
You should never accept any name for it, even from you.
Names don't last. When it ends, you'll have to tell it.[262]

Fredy takes Sam's advice, which creates the conditions for Fredy to be able to pray with a whole heart, and hence to be cured: 'I brooded, and the Nothing no-named inside me/ started to thin away. I had patches of feeling'.

Eugenic thinking and acting

The evidence for Murray's thesis that dehumanising language leads to dehumanising action is also demonstrated throughout the novel. In the case of the Nazi genocide of disabled people, the belief system used to justify it was eugenics. One of Murray's claims in *Fredy Neptune* is that eugenic thinking is pervasive, and in the case of disabled people, acting on that thinking is both common and limited only by what a person believes they can get away with. Fredy, as a disabled man, already knows this but the circumstances of his impairments mean that he does not have to engage deeply with some of the more frightening consequences of eugenic thinking. However, once Hans is part of Fredy's life, they are regularly confronted with the full reality of eugenic thinking and Fredy can no longer avoid acknowledging it.

As soon as Fredy's numbness develops, he quickly becomes aware of the need to hide it from other people due to their reactions. At work in particular, he learns that as soon as his colleagues are aware of his condition, they become suspicious of him:

a hatch-coaming dropped on my boot
was supposed to hurt. The blokes were looking at me.
Good, these steel toecaps, I thought to say, feeling nothing.
but hearing bones. I would have to learn quick, and practice
cracking normal, as I call it.[263]

He also soon learns that his impairment means he is the only one with the ability to avert many dangerous situations. On a ship he saves a boy from burning to death when the boy's clothes catch fire; after a car accident he lifts the car off the two people who are trapped under it; he stops a falling pole from crushing a work mate; and he rescues a child playing in water from being electrocuted by fallen electricity wires. In all these cases, even as the people involved are

---

[262] Murray, *Fredy Neptune*, 235.
[263] Ibid., 19.

grateful, they nevertheless react negatively to their awareness of Fredy's impairment. Consequently, they either throw Fredy out of where he is living or fire him from his job. There are also dozens of lower stake situations where people discover Fredy's impairment, either because he forgets to pretend to be nondisabled or because he sacrifices appearing nondisabled to help them. In almost all cases he is rejected by them afterwards.

The constant rejection Fredy experiences is a consequence of eugenic thinking—the idea that there is one correct way for humans to be, and that humans who do not measure up must be limited in all possible ways. Since most of the people Fredy encounters are not authorities in the eugenics system, and they discover he is a disabled person through a display of his strength, they feel frightened by him. Thus, the best they can do in limiting him is to remove him from his job or his house. Unsurprisingly though, there is one group of people who are not afraid of Fredy—those who have authority in the eugenics system, medical staff. For example, when Fredy visits Hans in the institution to which he has been committed in Australia and witnesses a nurse forcing another patient to cry, Fredy threatens the nurse, but the nurse is unconcerned:

> I was up and holding the window bars. That was a mongrel act,
> I said to the nurse fellow. He looked me up and down.
> Fuck you, squire, he said. I snapped the fastenings of the bars
> and dropped them out beside him. Now, care to say that again?
> But he was no coward. Come inside here and you'll be detained.
> As a patient, he said. We often see that strong-man stuff from them.
> We just sedate them; the padded cells soak up their flash.[264]

Unlike Fredy, Hans does not have superhuman strength. Hans also has an intellectual impairment, making him the epitome of everything eugenics stands against. Consequently, not only are people unafraid of him but they feel entitled, even justified, in victimising him. The frequency and degree to which other humans are willing to victimise Hans is something that Fredy tries to come to terms with from the moment they meet. For example, while Fredy and Hans are at the zoo, where Fredy has taken Hans while he considers how to prevent the forced sterilisation, Fredy thinks:

> What will I do with him? I'm asking myself. Next week
> He'll get another letter with maybe a cop to ensure
> he keeps his appointment this time. I'd have to keep him,
> kidnap him, get him out of Germany
> to where? No country would want him, they'd send him back
> to Germany and the doctors. Who were only doing what others
> didn't do, but agreed with.[265]

---

[264] Murray, *Fredy Neptune*, 248.
[265] Ibid., 204.

On the issue of compulsory sterilisation, Fredy's conclusion is incorrect. Other countries would certainly have sent Hans back to Germany, but other countries were also already sterilising their disabled citizens. Sterilisation policies and the resulting practices against disabled people had begun much earlier in the century and were becoming common around the world. Indiana, the first of the 29 US states to pass a law making the sterilisation of disabled people compulsory, did so in 1907. Over the next 20 years, many European countries followed suit. Adolf Hitler, in fact, based his 1933 law on a Swiss law passed in 1928.[266]

Fredy's incorrect conclusion is not an historical error, but a reflection of just how much Fredy is struggling with the knowledge that humans will willingly be cruel to other humans. It is the same type of reaction that Fredy experienced when he saw the Armenian women being burned alive, and it is Fredy's resistance to this knowledge that caused his physical impairment.

Fredy learns that his conclusion that no other country would sterilise Hans is incorrect eight years later, while still expressing his inability to accept just how far people who believe in eugenic thinking will go:

> I told their official what I'd rescued Hans from, and showed him
> what a Yank paper had reported: the T4 Programme,
> Tiergartenstrasse 4, for killing off cretins and incurables.
> We'd heard of the sterilization, of course, but this!
> You'd been in Berlin, Mr Beecher. Recently?
> Since you abducted Hans there? No? Castrating a defective
> guilty of sexual misconduct can be ordered here in some States.
> Let your Hans beware the Tasmanian Chief Secretary![267]

Most of the time however, in the company of Hans, Fredy's conclusions about the limits or lack thereof to eugenic thinking are quickly corrected. Putting the specific policy of sterilisation aside, the idea that people born with an impairment do not have the right to be in public space, or otherwise lead the kinds of lives that nondisabled people lead, is seen everywhere Hans goes. Hans is not just rejected, but harassed: at the castle where Fredy and Hans land while trying to escape by boat from Germany, one of the castle's servants torments Hans with a whip and then, later that day, a group of the servants convince Hans to masturbate in front of them; then, on the ship travelling to Australia, the cook tries to talk Hans into something similarly sexual and exploitative. In Australia, Hans cannot be anywhere in public without someone objecting to his presence, to the extent that Fredy and his wife Laura decide their family must move out to the bush for his safety. As soon as anyone feels they have the opportunity to push beyond harassment, they do. On the ship, the cook, who Fredy beats up for his behaviour towards Hans, then threatens to throw Hans overboard. Laura's mother takes advantage of Fredy serving in World War Two to have

---

[266] Evans, *Forgotten Crimes*, 107.
[267] Murray, *Fredy Neptune*, 130.

Hans committed to an institution. Then, at the institution, Hans is repeatedly raped by the staff.

Irreducible impairment

Another important point *Fredy Neptune* makes as a direct challenge to eugenic thinking is that impairment is dynamic and complex. A foundational principle of eugenic thinking is that all a person can or will be is a result of their heredity. This fallacy leads eugenicists to deduce two more principles: that a person who has an impairment has always had it; and that the capacities a person with an impairment has at the time when they are assessed by a medical professional is all they will ever have. Their consequent conclusion is that genocide of disabled people is justified.

In contrast to these ideas, Hans' and Fredy's experiences of impairment are complex and dynamic, and are primarily determined by their environment. Hans is declared by the Nazis to have a hereditary impairment. Although there is a possibility that this is true, there is no evidence of it for Hans, or indeed any disabled person targeted by the Nazis, because there was no way to prove heredity at that time. Also, there is no mention of Hans having any family members with the same condition, or even of Hans having had his impairment when he was born. While Hans does clearly and consistently have an intellectual impairment of some kind, this, true to reality, and in opposition to eugenic thinking, does not in any way limit his ability to learn, and thus increase his capacities. While Hans is living with his family who clearly have a limited conception of his capacities and future—including that Hans does not have the capacity to have a romantic relationship or have children—he is still able to travel independently and to ask strangers for assistance. Once Hans is living with Fredy and Laura, who have a much broader understanding of Hans' capacities and future, he acquires skills at an impressive rate. These include learning to swim, fish, speak English and shoot birds away from the vegetables the family are growing; as well as the tasks involved in a number of jobs including working on a ship, working on a truck, and fetching and carrying. By the end of the novel Hans is in a romantic relationship and there is nothing to suggest that he will not be successful at that relationship, or another relationship, or having children.

Fredy has a different experience of impairment, but one that is equally dynamic and complex. Many of the people who reject Fredy because of his acquired impairment do so with words such as 'unnatural' or 'freak', suggesting that they believe his impairment is something he was born with. However, Fredy's physical impairment developed when he was 20, and since he remembers his life without it and feels that he is missing out on opportunities because of it, he is constantly searching for a cure. Or thinks he is. In fact, soon after his numbness develops he also learns exactly what he needs to do to cure it, but he chooses not to until the very end of the novel. He knows that in giving up the numbness, he will also be giving up strengths and abilities that will not be available to him as a nondisabled person:

> I was coming home to my suspicion
> that the null had more strength in it, greatly more than I'd get
> just by not hurting. That it was the disguise of huge strength.[268]

Here the novel is making the point that not only do disabled people continue to develop capacities, but they also have capacities nondisabled people do not have. The other reason Fredy chooses not to cure his impairment until the end is that his impairment is the direct result of becoming aware of knowledge that he does not feel equipped to handle. Repeated exposure to that knowledge through how Hans is treated by other people, develops Fredy's capacity to cope. It also develops because Hans, as someone who constantly experiences this treatment while learning to live in a country that is completely unknown to him, represents for Fredy an example of incredible endurance.

Futures of worth

Another important point *Fredy Neptune* makes is that disabled people can have futures that are valuable and add value, challenging those who justified the Nazi genocide of disabled people at the time or have justified it since, on the basis that their own future is more valuable. Of course, eugenicists do not express their beliefs this way. They do not say their future is the future with the most value. They say the future of a particular category of people has the most value, and it just so happens that they belong to that category of people. Not belonging to that category is then justification for sterilising or murdering a person. At least 750,000 lives were taken, and at least 400,000 lives were severely damaged due to these beliefs. Hans would certainly have been sterilised, and may well have been murdered also, if Fredy had not kidnapped him. Therefore, Hans' life is an example of a life that any of the disabled victims of the Nazi genocide could have had. While Hans' life is still negatively affected by eugenic thinking, he has a job, a romantic relationship, the possibility of having children, and a life he enjoys, just as the other members of his Australian family do.

Consequential lines

Another important point that *Fredy Neptune* makes, in contexts that sometimes involve impairment and disability and sometimes do not, is that humans are always drawing lines between themselves and other humans. Given this, the

---

[268] Murray, *Fredy Neptune*, 102.

novel continually asks the reader to consider who they would or would not put on the opposite side of the line to them, and what consequences that decision has for both the reader and the other person.

The divisions that humans create and the consequences of those divisions, is raised directly in the text in discussions that Fredy (who has German parents) has with Sam, who has an Aboriginal father and a Jewish mother. Both men grow up in Australia and travel around the world. Fredy begins this exchange:

> How do you know so much, Sam? — We are studious people. —
> We Jews, or we blackfellows?—Both.—First you're one, then the other. —
> And I always will be. Surely you would know about division? —
> No. The world's divided. Not me. I won't shoot my left hand, nor my right. —
> True: both are white. Is a Jew white? Tell me, Fred. —[269]

This conversation continues when Fredy and Hans stay with Sam in France on their way to Australia. Beginning with Sam:

> You getting Hansel away equipped for Gretel is a start.
> Millions more need to go. Then he added I've also got some to leave your parents' Fatherland. Mad, though. Most Jews won't listen.
> Run, from that corporal? We're Germans too. It'll return to normal. —
> Aren't they really Germans, though? I asked. Are blackfellers Australian? Sam asked me. If you're different are you the same?[270]

Throughout the novel, as the characters continually draw lines between themselves and other people, the novel is asking the reader, 'Who would you put on the other side of the line to you?' Would that person be someone who saves another person from burning to death but does not notice that they themselves are burning, or someone who is half Jewish and half Aboriginal, or someone who is German or someone with an intellectual impairment? And once you have put them on the other side of the line to you, what is it that you would have happen to them? Would you take their job, take their house, make them move to another country, remove their testicles or murder them? Would you be willing to implement this yourself or would you have the government do it on your behalf? Would you do it on the government's behalf?

Fredy Neptune does not ask the reader to unthinkingly take a particular position but instead to consider that being on the other side of the line is continually difficult and often life threatening. As I have described, Fredy has either his job or his house taken from him every time a person discovers his physical impairment. This also happens to Fredy's parents in Australia during World War One because they are German. Further, being kidnapped by Fredy saves

---

[269] Murray, *Fredy Neptune*, 37.
[270] Ibid., 215.

Hans from sterilisation and probably murder, but even in Australia he is held in an institution for five years for no reason other than his intellectual impairment. Sam, after living abroad for the whole novel and helping many Jewish people escape Germany, travels by ship from China back to Australia, but kills himself just before he arrives. The novel is deliberately unclear about the specific reason for the suicide beyond the general toll on a person of the divisions between humans. The last time Sam and Fredy meet, Sam says:

> I feel like Noah, he said
> safe on the Ark while all his fellow humans were drowning.
> I've always felt that about my Dad's people. Now it's my mother's
> people too. Both my worlds.[271]

When Fredy is told that Sam has killed himself, he is also given a message from Sam:

> 'Tell Fred that Noah couldn't bear
> to look at the ground' or maybe 'to look at the drowned'.
> The sailor wasn't sure which, exactly.[272]

Conclusion

Given that the Nazi genocide of disabled people is often excused, minimised or completely unacknowledged, Murray's contribution to Holocaust literature is both vital and momentous. It can of course never be a substitute for the writing of disabled victims of the Nazis. However, as a novel on this topic written by a disabled author and featuring two significant disabled characters, *Fredy Neptune* is writing generated from lived experience that cannot be replaced by theory or research.

Fredy Neptune is an account of how words influence embodied experience, particularly for disabled people, since medicalised descriptions of us create 'suffering', and metaphors effect our lives, and deaths. It demonstrates how dehumanising language can lead to eugenic thinking, the influence of eugenic thinking on Nazi ideology and genocide more generally, and how eugenic thinking is still active in the minds of so many. Arguing against eugenic thinking, the novel presents impairment as continually changing and influenced by many factors, and people with impairments as capable, endurant and above all, human.

---

[271] Murray, *Fredy Neptune*, 235.
[272] Ibid., 263.

CHAPTER 5

Nursing in Nazi Germany and the 'Euthanasia' Programmes

Linda Shields and Susan Benedict

Nursing is one of the supposed 'caring professions'. The most widely recognised definition of nursing comes from Virginia Henderson, who said, '[t]he unique function of the nurse is to assist the individual, sick or well, in the performance of those activities contributing to health or its recovery (or to peaceful death) that he would perform unaided if he had the necessary strength, will or knowledge'.[273] Nursing bodies around the world have codes of ethics based on this definition and the main tenet is that ethical behaviour for all nurses centres on the human rights, well-being, dignity and autonomy of the patient, regardless of age, creed, race, culture, disability, sexual orientation, gender, nationality, class, politics.[274] These modern day principles reflect the morals that Florence Nightingale saw as necessary for nurses—'diligence, perseverance, observation, personal neatness, simplicity, carefulness, obedience, punctuality, honesty,

---

[273] Virginia Henderson, *The Nature of Nursing: A Definition and its Implications for Practice, Research, and Education* (New York: Macmillan, 1966), 15.
[274] 'The ICN Code of Ethics for Nurses', International Council of Nurses, 2012.

How to cite this book chapter:
Shields, L. and Benedict, S. 2020. Nursing in Nazi Germany and the 'Euthanasia' Programmes. In: Marczak, N. and Shields, K. (eds.) *Genocide Perspectives VI: The Process and the Personal Cost of Genocide*. Pp. 87–106. Sydney: UTS ePRESS. DOI: https://doi.org/10.5130/aaf.f. License: CC BY-NC-ND.

sobriety, and having a single eye to the patient's good',[275] and these, also, were the principles that Theodor Fliedner taught the women he trained as nurses in Germany before Nightingale.[276]

Nonetheless, nurses have been involved in crimes against humanity. These have ranged from nurses who killed patients suffering from mental illness, such as in Great Britain in 1991,[277] to active participation in large scale genocide, for example in Rwanda in 1994.[278] The aim of this essay is to examine the role of the nursing profession in Nazi 'euthanasia' programmes in Germany during the Third Reich. We describe nursing in Nazi Germany and explain its theoretical underpinnings, including how it became part of the racial hygiene machine. It is important to understand that only a minority of nurses became actively involved—most nurses at the time performed their duties as nurses by looking after the sick and providing care to those in need. It is equally important to understand that the nurses, although clearly influenced by Nazi propaganda, often participated in murder of their own free will. In some instances, if a nurse refused to participate, he or she was transferred to another ward or unit, or to another hospital, but suffered no more severe repercussions. Much is known about the role doctors played in the killings of patients, but the role of nurses, who made up the largest proportion of the workforce in any hospital, has not been well studied. It was only in the 1980s that a German nurse and historian, Hilde Steppe, began a discourse on nurses at Hadamar Psychiatric Hospital. Since then others have begun to examine how nurses became involved in the genocide of the disabled and mentally ill.

A framework for killing

In 1920, a book was published entitled *Die Freigabe der Vernichtung lebensunwerten Lebens* (*The Sanctioning of the Destruction of Lives Unworthy to be Lived*).[279] The authors, Alfred Hoche (1865–1943), Professor of Psychiatry at the University of Freiburg, and Karl Binding (1841–1920), a German judge and former president of the *Reichsagericht*, the highest criminal court in

---

[275] Stephanie Hoyt, 'Ethical Competence: An Integrative Review', *Nursing Ethics* 25, no. 6 (2016): 694–706.

[276] Thomas Foth, Jochen Kuhla, and Susan Benedict, 'Nursing during National Socialism' in *Nurses and Midwives in Nazi Germany: The 'Euthanasia' Program*, eds. Susan Benedict and Linda Shields (London: Routledge, 2014), 30.

[277] Cecil Clothier, *The Allitt Inquiry: Independent Inquiry Relating to Deaths and Injuries on the Children's Ward at Grantham and Kesteven General Hospital during the Period February to April 1991* (London: HMSO, 1994).

[278] *Rwanda: Not So Innocent: When Women Became Killers* (Kigali: African Rights, 1995), 128–29.

[279] Karl Binding and Alfred Hoche, *Die Freigabe der Vernichtung lebensunwerten Lebens* (Leipzig: Verlag von Felix Meiner, 1920).

Germany,[280] advocated the killing of people who were 'mentally ill or mentally defective'. They believed that the right to live should be earned and justifiable in light of contribution to humanity, and that those who had no capacity for human feeling were living lives not worth living. Hoche and Binding declared that it would be humane to kill such people.[281]

Soon after the publication of this book, at a Nazi party rally held in Nuremberg on 5 August 1929, Adolf Hitler stated the following and laid out his plans for the future:

> If Germany was to get a million children a year and was to remove 700,000–800,000 of the weakest people, then the final result might even be an increase in strength. ... As a result of our modern sentimental humanitarianism we are trying to maintain the weak at the expense of the healthy ... even cretins are able to procreate while more healthy people refrain from doing so. ... Criminals have the opportunity of procreating, degenerates are raised artificially and with difficulty. And in this way we are gradually breeding the weak and killing off the strong.[282]

People with mental or physical disabilities were viewed as detrimental to the health of the race. Propaganda posters portrayed the financial burden placed upon all Germans by the disabled. Films were shown in cinemas to promote 'euthanasia'.[283] These were intended to criminalise, degrade and dehumanise the mentally and physically disabled.[284] Such films were made for general consumption, always with the aim of socialising people into the acceptance of the killings as 'euthanasia'. Objections were raised by both Catholic and Protestant church leaders, some of whom tried to stop parishioners from seeing the films.[285]

Propaganda was wider than the cinema, however. Children's school exercise books contained examples of how much 'useless eaters' cost the nation; posters were displayed showing the 'burden' of caring for people with disabilities.[286]

---

[280] Jeremy Noakes and Geoffrey Pridham, eds., *Nazism 1919–1945, Volume 3: Foreign Policy, War and Racial Extermination: A Documentary Reader* (Exeter: University of Exeter Press, 1983).

[281] Robert Proctor, *Racial Hygiene: Medicine Under the Nazis* (Cambridge, Mass: Harvard University Press, 1988).

[282] Noakes and Pridham, *Nazism 1919–1945*, 1002.

[283] The term 'euthanasia' is a misnomer. The word means 'a good death' and there was nothing good about these Nazi programmes. Hence the convention—followed here—when discussing Nazi 'euthanasia', inverted commas are used.

[284] Michael Burleigh, *Death and Deliverance: 'Euthanasia' in Germany 1900–1945* (Cambridge: Cambridge University Press, 1994).

[285] Erwin Leiser, *Nazi Cinema*, trans. Gertrud Mander and David Wilson (New York: Collier Books, 1974).

[286] Burleigh, *Death and Deliverance*, 183.

Children were taken on school trips to institutions for the disabled. There they were told to observe the patients and see how much they were suffering, and to consider the benefits if Germany did not have to support such a burden. Adults could join guided excursions to psychiatric hospitals and this augmented public pity and loathing of those with mental disabilities.

It was not only those with mental illnesses, but also the elderly and people with serious illnesses who were considered a burden, and as the war progressed, even badly wounded soldiers were considered encumbrances on the state.[287]

In July 1933, the Law for the Prevention of Offspring with Hereditary Diseases was passed, stating, 'Any person suffering from a hereditary disease can be sterilised if medical knowledge indicates that his offspring will suffer from severe hereditary physical or mental damage'.[288] Among the stipulated conditions were 'feeblemindedness, schizophrenia, bipolar conditions, hereditary epilepsy, Huntington's chorea, hereditary blindness and deafness, severe hereditary physical deformity or severe alcoholism on a discretionary basis'.[289] Individuals who had one of these conditions could apply for sterilisation, or if they were inpatients or prisoners, the administrator of the facility could apply on their behalf.

Hereditary health courts were formed to hear the cases. The courts comprised one judge, one public health service physician and one physician with knowledge of genetics and heredity. If the court decided in favour, surgical sterilisation could be carried out without the consent of the individual.[290] Between 1934 and 1936, approximately 170,000 surgical sterilisations were undertaken with the greatest number being for 'feeblemindedness', a vague category that could apply to ever-greater numbers of victims.[291]

In September 1935, the Nuremberg Laws (Reich Citizenship Law, and the Law for the Protection of German Blood and German Honour) were enacted. The first law forbade Jews to marry or have sexual relations with non-Jews.[292] One month later, a similar law was passed against the disabled: the Law for the Protection of the Hereditary Health of the German Nation, or the so-called Marriage Health Law. This law required couples to obtain a Marriage Fitness Certificate indicating that there were no hereditary or contagious conditions.[293]

It soon became apparent to the Nazi administrators that limiting marriages and forcing sterilisations were insufficient to rid the Reich of the 'undesirable'

---

[287] Friedlander, *Origins of Nazi*, 81; *Trial Transcript of Hans Joachim Becker and Friedrich Robert Lorent, May 27 1970*, trans. Traute Lafrenz (Vienna: Dokumentationsarchiv des österreichischen Widerstandes), 716, 718.
[288] Friedlander, *Origins of Nazi*, 25, 26.
[289] Ibid., 26.
[290] Ibid.
[291] Ibid., 28.
[292] Ibid., 31.
[293] Ibid.

segments of the disabled and 'inferior' races. Thus, in September 1939, a plan to kill institutionalised disabled people was implemented under the name of 'euthanasia' and doctors were granted permission (though not required) to end the lives of their patients. It is also important to note that such acts were never passed into legislation.[294] Hitler was initially concerned about a possible backlash from church leaders and the community, and so did not publicly advocate killing the disabled until the war had begun, at which time he anticipated a change in community sentiment with the deaths of German soldiers. He could also promote the 'euthanasia' programme as saving valuable resources for the war effort.[295]

Eugenics and 'euthanasia'

Germany, like multiple other nations, embraced the pseudo-science of eugenics in the late 1800s and into the 1900s. Eugenics, or 'racial hygiene' as it was known in Germany, was based on the belief that many 'undesirable' characteristics could be eliminated from societies by the breeding of only healthy citizens. Against the backdrop of eugenics, the 'Aryan' race became the exemplar of a healthy German while those not fitting this model were viewed as 'inferior races'. Among these were the Jews, primarily, as well as Roma and Sinti ('Gypsies'), Blacks and Slavs.[296] Similarly, institutionalised people with disabilities were regarded as contaminants of race and an economic burden. They were labelled as 'useless eaters' and 'life unworthy of life',[297] draining resources from the already financially desperate Germany, and hazardous to the health of the German *Volk*. Approximately 300,000 people were murdered under the 'euthanasia' programmes,[298] 70,000 of whom were patients in psychiatric hospitals.[299] The Nazis' first programme of planned, industrialised killing was called *Aktion* T4 because its headquarters was

---

[294] Proctor, *Racial Hygiene*, 193.
[295] *Trial Transcript of Hans Joachim*, 719.
[296] Henry Friedlander, *The Origins of Nazi Genocide: From Euthanasia to the Final Solution* (Chapel Hill: University of North Carolina Press, 1995), 3, 10, 11.
[297] Michael Burleigh, *Death and Deliverance, Euthanasia in Germany 1900–1945* (London: Pan Books, 1994), 12–46.
[298] Heinz Faulstich, 'Die Zahl der 'Euthanasie'-Opfer', in *'Euthanasie' und die aktuelle Sterbehilfe-Debatte. Die historischen Hintergründe medizinischer Ethik*, eds. Andreas Frewer and Clemens Eickhoff (Frankfurt: 2000), 218–34; Zdisław Jaroszewski, *Die Ermordung der Geisteskranken in Polen 1939–1945* (Warsaw: Wydawnictwo Naukowne PWN, 1993).
[299] Linda Shields and Thomas Foth, 'Setting the Scene', in *Nurses and Midwives in Nazi Germany: The 'Euthanasia' Program*, eds. Susan Benedict and Linda Shields (London: Routledge, 2014), 7.

based at *Tiergartenstraße* 4 in Berlin. Disabled people, and those with mental illnesses, were killed in their hospitals and nursing homes. Protests from the public, led largely by Bishop Clemens August Graf von Galen, meant interruptions in the programmes,[300] yet they continued on an individual basis until well after World War Two ended, when disabled children continued to be murdered in special paediatric wards (*Kinderfachabteilungen*), 'hunger houses' (*Hungerhäuser*) and specialised asylums.[301] Across all programmes, nurses routinely assisted in killing their patients in their everyday practice.[302] Nurses actively and intentionally killed thousands of their most vulnerable patients.

Nurses were essential to the implementation of Nazi 'euthanasia'. Nurses often had a choice about whether or not to participate, although putative duress was indeed present. In a number of instances, some nurses who refused to take part were moved to another ward of the hospital, or simply were not asked by their supervisors to take part; there are also accounts of doctors and nurses who were coerced to carry out the killings despite repeatedly asking to be transferred.

Nurses were just as susceptible to Nazi propaganda as any other part of the German community, and nursing education included substantial teaching about those who were 'life unworthy of life', 'useless feeders' and the benefits of 'euthanasia'. While this cannot excuse those who murdered their patients, nor the bystanders, it perhaps goes some way to an understanding of how they came to believe that such intentional murder was, aside from being mandated by the government, humane and moral.

The children's 'euthanasia' programme

'Euthanasia' started with children. In early 1939, the father of a child named Gerhard Herbert Kretschmar who was born blind, missing one leg and part of an arm, and 'seemed to be an idiot',[303] wrote to Adolf Hitler to ask if his child could be killed in the interest of 'mercy'. Hitler ordered Dr Karl Brandt to inform the child's doctors, in Hitler's name, that they could 'euthanise' the boy,[304] making him the first known victim of the Nazi 'euthanasia' programme.[305]

---

[300] Susan Benedict, Alison O'Donnell, and Linda Shields, 'Children's 'Euthanasia' in Nazi Germany', *Journal of Paediatric Nursing* 24 (2009): 506–16.

[301] Heinz Faulstich, *Hungersterben in der Psychiatrie 1914–1949: Mit einer Topographie der NS-Psychiatrie* (Freiburg: Lambertus, 1998).

[302] Foth, Kuhla, and Benedict, 'Nursing during', 28.

[303] Ulf Schmidt, *Karl Brandt: The Nazi Doctor* (London: Hambledon Continuum, 2007), 117–23.

[304] Ibid.

[305] Patricia Heberer, '"Exitus Heute in Hadamar": The Hadamar Facility and "Euthanasia" in Nazi Germany' (PhD dissertation, University of Maryland, 2001).

Subsequent requests for 'euthanasia' were dealt with at the *Kanzlei des Führer* (Chancellery of the Führer) and kept secret in the interests of the state. Children's 'euthanasia' was hidden under the title of 'The Reich Committee for the Scientific Registration of Serious Hereditary-and Congenitally based Illnesses' (*Reichsausschuss zur wissenschaftlichen Erfassung von erb-und anlagebedingten schweren Leiden*), or 'Reich Committee'.[306] One of its goals was to find newborns with health conditions or developmental issues and to initiate their killing, as well as that of children with disabilities who were already institutionalised.[307] Community health nurses played a significant role in this phase of the children's 'euthanasia' programme.

Midwives as well as nurses became involved in 'euthanasia'. On 18 August 1939, the State Ministry of the Interior mandated that doctors and midwives report all newborn infants with physical and/or mental disabilities:

> RE: The duty to report deformed births etc.
> In order to clarify scientific questions in the field of congenital deformities and intellectual under-development, it is necessary to register the relevant cases as soon as possible … therefore instruct that the midwife who has assisted at the birth of a child—even in cases where a doctor has been called to the confinement—must make a report to the health Office nearest to the birth place on the enclosed form, which is available from Health Offices, in the event of the new-born child being suspected of suffering from the following congenital defects:
>
> i. Idiocy and Mongolism (particularly cases which involve blindness and deafness).
> ii. Microcephalie (sic) (an abnormally small skull).
> iii. Hydrocephalus of a serious or progressive nature (abnormally large skull caused by excessive fluid).
> iv. Deformities of every kind, in particular the absence of limbs, spina bifida etc.
> v. Paralysis including Little's disease (spastics).
>
> In addition, all doctors must report children who are suffering from one of the complaints in (i–v) and have not reached their third birthday in the event of the doctors becoming aware of such children in the course of their professional duties.
>
> The midwife will receive a fee of 2 *Reichmarks* in return for her trouble. The sum will be paid by the Health Office.[308]

---

[306] *Trial Transcript of Hans Joachim*, 721.
[307] *Hessisches hauptstaatsarchiv*. Wiesbaden, file 461/32061/23.
[308] Noakes and Pridham, *Nazism 1919–1945*, 1006–7.

Reports received from doctors and midwives were reviewed by medical examiners: Professor Hans Heinze (Director of the psychiatric facility at Brandenburg-Gorden), Professor Werner Catel (Director of the University Paediatrics Clinic in Leipzig) and Dr Ernst Wentzler (a paediatrician and director of a private clinic in Berlin). These doctors evaluated the infants' health purely from written reports and never examined the children themselves. If the child was to be killed, the doctor wrote a '+' on the form, or '-' if the child was to be allowed to live. Parents of disabled children were informed that paediatric units were being established and were persuaded to allow their children to be sent to the institutions, where, the parents were assured, the child would receive the very best of care. There were 22 of these institutions.[309] Parents could refuse, but had to sign a form stating that they took full responsibility for the child, no matter what their circumstances. If, for example, a mother was called away for war work and the father was already serving in the armed forces, the family had no choice but to place the child in one of the institutions,[310] thereby giving all responsibility to the state. It is unlikely that any of these children were ever returned to their homes or transferred to an ordinary hospital.[311]

Many disabled children removed from their homes became victims of Nazi medical experiments and research. Doctors and scientists performed experiments without consent or ethical considerations of any kind, and the effects could be immediately evaluated by killing the child and dissecting the child's body. Children exhibiting neurological disorders were murdered and their brains retained at institutions such as Am Spiegelgrund, even well into the twenty-first century.[312] Some children were starved to death while others were given drugs such as Luminal (phenobarbital), either mixed with their food or on their own. Others were killed by injections of morphine and scopolamine.[313] The nurses working in the wards where the killings took place received a supplemental payment of 25 *Reichmarks* per month, and the doctors could receive bonuses of 250 *Reichmarks* at Christmas.[314] Approximately 3,000 to 5,000 children were killed by nurses and doctors in the children's 'euthanasia' programme,[315] though accurate numbers are difficult to determine.

---

[309] Friedlander, *Origins of Nazi*, 47.
[310] Noakes and Pridham, *Nazism 1919–1945*, 1007.
[311] Gitta Sereny, *Into that Darkness: an Examination of Conscience* (New York: Vintage Books, 1974), 55.
[312] Paul Weindling, 'From Scientific Object to Commemorated Victim: The Children of the *Spiegelgrund*', *History and Philosophy of the Life Sciences* 3 (2013): 415–30.
[313] Burleigh, *Death and Deliverance*, 102.
[314] Ibid., 105.
[315] *Trial Transcript of Hans Joachim*, 721.

The adult 'euthanasia' programmes

In August 1939, Hitler ordered expansion of the 'euthanasia' programme to include adults with physical and/or mental conditions and illnesses, and the programme was to begin in secret.[316] The question of a written law permitting the killings arose among Nazi functionaries.[317] Viktor Brack reported that Hitler did not want the programmes enshrined in law in case it could be used as propaganda by his enemies.[318] However, as Führer and Reichschanceller, Hitler was able to issue 'Führer orders' ('*Führermanifest*'), which were similar in effect to laws. Several doctors continued to draft legislation permitting 'euthanasia'. Each draft was shown to Hitler and he eventually signed the following in October 1939, backdating it to coincide with the invasion of Poland and the start of the war:[319]

> Berlin 1 September 1939
> *Reichsleiter* Bouhler and Dr med. Brandt
> Are charged with the responsibility to extend the authorization of certain doctors designated by name in order to treat patients who must be considered incurable on the basis of human judgment, may be granted the mercy death after a critical evaluation of their illness.
> Signed: Adolf Hitler.[320]

During October 1939, psychiatric institutions and hospitals that cared for patients with epilepsy, developmental disabilities and other conditions, were required to complete questionnaires.[321] *Meldebogen* (questionnaire) I was used to describe individual patients, and *Meldebogen* II assessed the institution itself. *Meldebogen* I included, among other questions, the patient's diagnosis, probability of recovery, possibility of discharge, war-related injuries and work ability. Some questionnaires were incompletely filled out or were inaccurately completed because they were believed to be routine surveys. Other doctors were concerned that the purpose of the questionnaire was to remove patients capable of work and thus described patients as more disabled than they actually were. Some were rightly suspicious that the questionnaires would be used to inform a plan to kill the patients, and refused to complete the questionnaires.[322] The result was a commission of doctors sympathetic to the 'euthanasia' cause being sent to those hospitals whose compliance was lacking. Some institutional

---

[316] Noakes and Pridham, *Nazism 1919–1945*, 1007–9.
[317] *Trial Transcript of Hans Joachim*, 721.
[318] Ibid., 722.
[319] Burleigh, *Death and Deliverance*, 112.
[320] *Trial Transcript of Hans Joachim*, 722.
[321] Ibid., 730.
[322] Ibid., 734.

doctors and administrators resisted and complained about the competence of the commission. The Director of Neuendettelsau hospital, Dr Rudolf Boeckh, complained about the commission's visit on 7 November 1940:

> Contrary to the instructions of the Bavarian State Ministry, the commission completed several hundred of these forms and sent them off to Berlin without the presence of the senior doctor responsible for the asylums. ... The commission did not examine a single one of the 1,800 patients. The majority of the patients are not in Neuendettelsau but in branch asylums distributed all over northern Bavaria. Thus, the commission was incapable of forming its own judgment of the situation. ... Only the nurses were questioned ... and their objections were largely ignored. Indeed, it was even observed that the opposite of the true statements of the nursing personnel were recorded on the forms. The staff who composed the commission cannot really be blamed since the majority were medical students and typists who were completely incapable of properly assessing the statements of the nursing staff. The senior doctor on the commission, who worked in a separate room on his own, received the forms that had been completed by the assistants and then gave his judgment without any personal knowledge of the individual cases and without looking at the medical records.
>
> As the doctor responsible for the asylums I protest against this unprofessional method of working by the commission which goes against all the traditions of the medical profession. ... In view of the fact that the public is aware of the ultimate objectives of this registration of the patients, I have been burdened with a grave responsibility as the senior doctor responsible for these institutions.[323]

Completed questionnaires were sent to the T4 central office where they were recorded on a card register with copies sent to various functionaries in the system.[324] In the beginning, fewer than ten doctors evaluated the questionnaires, but as the workload grew, 30 to 40 were employed. The evaluators decided if the patient was to live or die and marked a red '+' if the patient was to die, a blue '–' to live, and a '?' or a 'Z' for undecided. These decisions were reviewed by the chief evaluators, Drs Heyde, Nitsche and Linden, who indicated a confirmation of the decision. Approximately 200,000 questionnaires were processed by August 1941.[325]

At a meeting held on 9 October 1939, the following calculation of the number of patients to eventually be killed was presented by Brack:

---

[323] Noakes and Pridham, *Nazism 1919–1945*, 1015–6.
[324] *Trial Transcript of Hans Joachim*, 735–36.
[325] Ibid., 736.

The number is arrived at through a calculation on the basis of a ratio of 1000:10:5:1. That means out of 1,000 people ten require psychiatric treatment; of these five in residential form. And, of these, one patient will come under the programme. If one applies this to the population of the Greater German Reich, then one must reckon with 65,000 to 75,000 cases.[326]

Much planning went into how the victims were to be killed. Several doctors were involved in discussions about the most efficient methods and how they would be operationalised.[327] Suggestions included substances such as morphine, scopolamine, prussic acid and carbon monoxide. A chemical engineer, Dr Widmann, suggested that carbon monoxide could be pumped into the wards while the patients slept.[328] Hermetically sealed vans into which exhaust gases were pumped, and gas chambers at selected psychiatric hospitals were eventually developed, becoming the prototype for the factory-style murders of the 'Final Solution of the Jewish Question'.[329] A complicated system of transfers and transport between institutions was set up to make the process less detectable.[330] During its initial phases, patients were taken by bus or train directly to a killing centre but in late 1940, patients were first transferred to intermediate institutions and then, within a few days, to a killing institution.[331] This phase of the 'euthanasia' programme was known as T4.[332]

Six institutions served as killing centres for adults although not all were operational at the same time. The first was located in an abandoned prison in Brandenburg, an hour from Berlin.[333] A tiled room measuring three by five metres and three metres high was built as a gas chamber. A pipe with small holes fed carbon monoxide from tanks into the room. Two crematoria were built to dispose of the bodies.[334] The first patient was killed on 4 January 1940. Nurses were an integral part of the system:

> For this first gassing, about 18–20 people were led into the 'shower room' by the nursing staff. These men had to undress in an anteroom until they were completely naked. The doors were shut behind them. These people went quietly into the room and showed no signs of being upset. Dr Widmann operated the gas. I could see through the peephole

---

[326] Noakes and Pridham, *Nazism 1919–1945*, 1010.
[327] *Trial Transcript of Hans Joachim*, 737.
[328] Noakes and Pridham, *Nazism 1919–1945*, 1919.
[329] Ibid., 1020.
[330] *Trial Transcript of Hans Joachim*, 740.
[331] Friedlander, *Origins of Nazi*, 108.
[332] Ibid., 68.
[333] Ibid., 88.
[334] Ibid., 87.

that after about a minute the people had collapsed or lay on the benches. There were no scenes and no disorder. After a further five minutes the room was ventilated. Specially assigned SS people collected the dead on special stretchers and took them to the crematoria. When I say special stretchers I mean stretchers specially constructed for this purpose. They could be placed directly in the ovens and the corpses could be pushed into the oven mechanically by means of a device without the people carrying them coming into contact with the corpse.[335]

Brandenburg was closed in September 1940 because of problems with body disposal and thereafter, patients were sent to Bernburg,[336] used as a killing site until spring of 1943. Brandenberg is still a major centre for the treatment of mental illnesses.

Grafeneck, a medieval castle of the Dukes of Württemberg, was a Protestant hospital for people with disabilities. It was closed and then re-opened as a state institution, and became a killing centre from January until December 1940. A coach house that was part of the castle complex was used for the killings.[337] Grafeneck was closed after the public became aware of the killings there,[338] and the patients transferred to another psychiatric hospital at Hadamar. In addition, the staff who were trained in the killing techniques moved to Hadamar.

Another killing centre opened at Hartheim, a Renaissance castle of the Prince of Starhemberg near Linz in Austria. It, too, was a hospital for the mentally ill.[339] Killings by gas occurred between May 1940 and December 1944.[340] Patients with disabilities came from Austria, Germany, Czechoslovakia and Yugoslavia, and because of its proximity to Mauthausen and Dachau, prisoners from these concentration camps who became too ill or debilitated to work were killed at Hartheim under the 14f13 programme.[341]

Aktion 14f13 or 'Sonderbehandlung' ('special treatment') was a particularly nefarious programme of specific killing of those already incarcerated in concentration camps who were sick, disabled or exhausted from overwork. The techniques and skills developed in T4 were employed in the gas chambers at Hartheim, Bernberg and Sonnenstein where the prisoners were sent for efficient disposal. This occurred between 1941 and 1944, by which time the T4 programme had officially ceased and the gas chambers were no longer in use (the patients continued to be killed using methods other than gas). Hartheim

---

[335] Noakes and Pridham, *Nazism 1919–1945*, 1019–20.
[336] Heberer, "'Exitus Heute'", 140.
[337] Ibid., 137.
[338] Friedlander, *Origins of Nazi*, 108.
[339] Heberer, "'Exitus Heute'", 137.
[340] Ibid., 138.
[341] Ibid.

was staffed by two doctors and 14 nurses (seven males and seven females).[342] There were some exemptions from the killings—those who were diagnosed as being senile, war veterans, mothers who had been awarded the *Mutterkreuz* (the Nazi medal awarded to mothers of more than four or more children), and relations of staff who worked in the T4 programme.[343]

Sonnenstein, near Dresden, also served as a T4 killing site from June 1940 and until mid-1943.[344] This was the only institution where other parts of the hospital operated simultaneously with the killing centre. The killing facility and living quarters for T4 staff were located in three buildings beside the perimeter of the hospital, while the other building was a functioning psychiatric hospital called Mariaheim.[345] Hadamar was the biggest of the killing institutions and is perhaps the best studied and understood. As with the other sites, it was a psychiatric hospital, and continues to be so today.

Nurses and adult 'euthanasia'

While nurses worked at all the killing centres, those employed at Hadamar were from two groups: some were already employed at Hadamar, while others were recruited to the work in the killing centre by the T4 central administration in Berlin. Many had been employed at Grafeneck from January until December 1940 and hence were experienced in the killing process.

Post-war trial interviews of the nurses reveal little pressure on them to participate in the killings. Nurses were usually referred by doctors or administrators to T4 as being potential candidates for the programme. Pauline Kneissler, a nurse from Grafeneck and Hadamar, described the process in which T4 administrators Werner Blankenburg and Gerhard Bohne informed a handful of young nurses that a new secret government programme was being initiated:

> [We were told that] every creature should be allowed a merciful death. This certainly made sense to me, although on the other hand, I was irritated that it should be I who was asked to do this. I would have preferred to act as a Red Cross nurse. ... I was asked if I wanted to participate. Whoever didn't agree could back out ... [346]

Kneissler felt that she was under a certain 'voluntary compulsion': 'We received a few minutes to think about things. Herr Blankenburg had left the room during this time. ... We didn't discuss the matter further amongst ourselves. No

---

[342] Sereny, *Into that Darkness*, 54.
[343] Ibid., 55.
[344] *Trial Transcript of Hans Joachim*, 738.
[345] Heberer, "'Exitus Heute'", 139.
[346] Ibid., 222–3.

one said that she couldn't do it'.³⁴⁷ The nurses were then sworn to an oath of silence and Blankenburg assured them that the doctors would be responsible for their actions; 'We didn't feel very good about it but had no moral reservations'.³⁴⁸

Initially, the nurses' work consisted of preparing the patients for transport and accompanying them on buses from their home institutions to the killing facility. When the buses arrived at the killing centre, nurses helped the patients undress, took them to be 'examined' by the doctor, to have photographs taken and then to the waiting room and finally the gas chamber.³⁴⁹

It was not just in psychiatric hospitals in Germany and Austria that the killing of mentally ill people occurred. Patients from institutions in Danzig, eastern Prussia, Upper Silesia, and Poland were shot by the Nazis as the army moved through Eastern Europe. Psychiatric hospitals were cleared of their patients and the hospitals used as barracks for soldiers. A Polish bulletin entitled *Biuletyn Glownej Komissji Badania Zbrodni Niemieckich w Polsce* describes:

> The patients were generally taken out of the institution, brought to an unpopulated area and there shot. All traces of the annihilation were carefully covered up. At other times the patients were gassed in special motorcars. In very few cases were they brought to an extermination camp.³⁵⁰

Trial documents reveal that a *Schutzstaffel* (SS) unit met trains carrying patients from psychiatric hospitals in Pomerania and took them to secluded woods where they were shot. Twelve Polish prisoners from Camp Stutthof were made to dig burial pits for the patients and they, in turn, were also shot.³⁵¹ Victims included elderly people who were considered a burden on the state. From testimony of the trial of Dr Georg Renno in 1962, Anna Stosik, a caregiver at a nursing home stated:

> I was sent to Tiegenhof [a town in Poland] (1942 or 1943). One day in Tiegenhof we admitted several older people from an old folks' home in Posen. They were not mentally ill, only old. After two or three weeks,

---

³⁴⁷ Antje Wettlaufer, "Die Beteiligung von Schwestern und Pflegern an den Morden in Hadamar" in *Psychiatrie in Faschismus: Der Anstalt Hadamar, 1933–1945*, eds. Dorothee Roer and Dieter Henkel (Bonn: Psychiatrie-Verlag, 1986), 283–330.

³⁴⁸ Ibid.

³⁴⁹ Heberer, "'Exitus Heute'", 236–7.

³⁵⁰ *Biuletyn Glownej Komissji Badania Zbrodni Niemieckich w Polsce* (Pozna-niu: Wydawn, Komisji, 1946–1949).

³⁵¹ 'Statement Against Grabowski, March 27, 1961' (Ludwigsburg: Zentrale Stelle der Landesjustizverwaltungen, 1961); A. Stosik, 1962. Statement. File no. 33.029/5. November 12. *Staatsarchiv München*. Munich, Germany.

they were picked up by the SS in special buses that were absolutely airtight. I asked one of the SS men why they were built that way. He asked why I was interested and I said I was a caregiver and just interested. He told me to mind my own business and that I had better get out of his sight. I still did not quite know what all this was about but I had a real bad feeling and from that day I tried to get away from my job as caregiver.

There was another group of patients picked up in these airtight vehicles. Maybe two more times but I cannot state how many patients and if they were severely ill or not. I remember that the patients fought and screamed when they were loaded on these buses.

I remember two older women from the home in Posen who went to a window saying, 'Come on, let us see God's sun one more time' before they were loaded on those buses. Did they know that this was a trip to their death?

For me it was now clear what would happen to those loaded into those buses. They were scantily dressed and without any provisions or luggage. There were no seats in the bus, only some straw on the floor. The first patients were bedded on the straw and the rest were just pushed in, falling or standing.[352]

Severely wounded soldiers were killed as well, sometimes by gassing. For example, a train returning soldiers wounded in Russia was stopped in a tunnel. According to Professor André Balser, a doctor from Switzerland:

The whole staff, conductors, nurses accompanying soldiers, etcetera, were summoned by the train commander, and were told to put on their gas masks and not to take them off before a special 'air clear' signal would be given.

… [When] Balser asked the commander, 'What about the wounded?' he was told 'Don't you know that they are in gas-proof compartments?'[353]

All the wounded men died. Rumours in Germany suggested that wounded soldiers were purposely being killed so they would not have to be transported home, but radio broadcasts tried to counteract such rumours.[354]

---

[352] A. Stosik. 1962. Statement. File no. 33.029/5. November 12. *Staatsarchiv München*. Munich, Germany.
[353] 'Wounded Nazis Fear Own Doctors Will Kill Them', *Evening Standard*, July 31, 1942.
[354] Ibid.

T4 was officially stopped in August 1941 due to public awareness and protests. Much of the resistance came from churches and clergy, such as the Catholic Bishop of Münster, August Claus von Galen, who spoke out about the Nazi 'euthanasia' programme.[355] Nonetheless, the killings continued on an individual basis (known as Wild or Decentralised 'Euthanasia'). Doctors ordered that disabled patients be murdered by means other than gassing, and nurses carried out their orders—giving drug overdoses, starving their patients to death and leaving them out in cold weather to die of hypothermia.

'Euthanasia' as a template for the Final Solution

At the end of 1941 and early 1942, some of the men who worked in T4, including male nurses and caregivers, were moved to Lublin.[356] These men were experienced in the killing techniques developed in T4; in particular, they had knowledge of the gassing method. In other words, T4 was the site of the development of prototypes of the mass murder techniques so effectively employed in the death camps. This programme was known as *Aktion Reinhard*. The men involved were in the SS or soon joined it—but they remained under the management of T4, and were able to take advantage of the many perks available to T4 employees, such as holidays in the 'euthanasia' programme's rest and recreation facilities at the Attersee Lake in Austria.[357] Many of the guards were Ukrainian, recruited into *Aktion Reinhard* by T4 personnel, and the SS staff numbered from 20 to 25 at each of the death camps.[358]

Only male nurses participated in *Aktion Reinhard*, although it is hard to find recorded reasons why women were excluded.[359] The work of nurses and caregivers in the death camps was the very antithesis of nursing care. Not only did they kill their patients, they did so under the most brutal and inhumane conditions with no recourse to the compassion that is supposed to predicate nursing. At least three of them, Karl Schluch and Heinrich Unverhau of Belzec, and Heinrich Arthur Matthes of Treblinka, returned to nursing after the war.[360]

Wild or decentralised 'euthanasia'

Under 'Wild Euthanasia', institutionalised patients were selected by doctors for death, largely based upon their ability to work, an essential part of psychiatric

---

[355] Burleigh, *Death and Deliverance*, 171.
[356] Yitzhak Arad, *Belzec, Sobibor, Treblinka: The Operation Reinhard Death Camps* (Bloomington: Indiana University Press, 1999), 12.
[357] Ibid., 17.
[358] Ibid., 193.
[359] Sereny, *Into that Darkness*, 86.
[360] www.deathcamps.org/treblinka/perpetrators.html.

care during that era. Psychiatric institutions were severely overcrowded and underfunded. They were expected to be largely self-sufficient by maintaining vegetable gardens, repairing their own clothing and linens and raising rabbits. Patients who were able to contribute even minimally to the ongoing labour of the institution were initially spared from 'wild euthanasia'. Patients who were totally dependent were the first to be killed in this phase of the 'euthanasia' programme.[361]

Unlike the T4 programme in which the nurses facilitated the process by escorting patients, nurses were active killers in the 'wild euthanasia' programme.[362] Doctors typically designated the patients to be killed, often with input from the nurses, but it was up to the nurses to murder the patients. These murders were done with lethal doses of oral sedatives such as Luminal or with injections of morphine and scopolamine, or a combination of all three. More patients were killed in the 'wild euthanasia' programme than in the T4 programme.[363]

A particularly egregious institution of the 'wild euthanasia' programme was Kaufbeuren in Bavaria, only 95 kilometres from Munich. Although the war had officially ended, the killings at Kaufbeuren continued less than half a mile from the US military police headquarters.[364] In April 1945, the American Army occupied Kaufbeuren, but the killings continued at the hospital for another 33 days.[365] In July 1945, the Americans heard that the hospital needed investigating, and two Public Health Section officers and 18 soldiers visited the institution, despite road signs in English saying the place was a 'lunatic asylum' and off-limits. Kaufbueren Hospital was large—it housed over 3,000 people in what was once a baroque monastery. On asking to see the doctor in charge the Americans were informed that he had suicided the previous day. The hospital morgue contained bodies of the most recently killed. The adult patients weighed between 26 and 33 kilograms; and a 10-year-old child weighed only 10 kilograms.[366] The distressed American personnel volunteered to serve on the squad which would, they felt, be needed to execute the hospital personnel.[367]

Documents from the 1965 trial of 14 nurses employed at one of the major 'wild euthanasia' hospitals, Meseritz-Obrawalde, and obtained from the

---

[361] Susan Benedict, 'Meseritz-Obrawalde: A Site for "Wild Euthanasia"', in *Nurses and Midwives in Nazi Germany: The 'Euthanasia' Program*, eds. Susan Benedict and Linda Shields (London: Routledge, 2014), 105.
[362] Ibid., 105–39.
[363] Friedlander, *Origins of Nazi*, 151.
[364] Susan Benedict, 'Klagenfurt: "She Killed As Part of Her Daily Duties"', in *Nurses and Midwives in Nazi Germany: The "Euthanasia" Program*, eds. Susan Benedict and Linda Shields (London: Routledge, 2014), 140–63.
[365] 'Special Statement of Fact', Headquarters, Regional Military Government, Bavaria. *US Army File*, 1945.
[366] Ibid.
[367] 'Murder Factory Found in Bavaria', *New York Times*, July 4, 1945.

archives in Munich, have provided extensive 'rationale' from nurses who killed their patients.[368] The word 'rationale' is in quotation marks because this testimony was provided a full 20 years after the killings, and of course there is never a 'rationale' for genocide. These 14 nurses not only had time to come to terms with their actions, but their lawyers had the benefit of knowing what testimonies had been effective in attaining acquittals in other 'euthanasia' cases. Susan Benedict and Jane Georges have explained how the characteristics so inherent in nursing philosophy at the time—duty and obedience—were factors that contributed to the nurses' actions.[369] Nonetheless, even though the nurses felt bound by the values of the day, they crossed boundaries that should never have been crossed when they saw killing their patients as a legitimate part of their caring role. Excuses used by defendants included: needing to keep her job because she was supporting her grandparents,[370] afraid of losing her job[371] and being obligated to follow the orders of superiors.[372]

The nurses involved in the programme came to be so by varying degrees of willingness. For the T4 gassings, nurses were selected, often by doctors, based upon perceived loyalty to the ideals of National Socialism.[373] These nurses were brought to the T4 Berlin headquarters, told they had been selected for a secret and important mission, informed of exactly what the mission was—the 'euthanasia' of the disabled in institutions—and then given a few minutes to decide.[374] These nurses were then assigned to one of the six killing centres and often transferred from one to another. Involvement of nurses in the later phase—'wild or decentralised euthanasia' occurred more subtly. It was often the hospital administrators who told staff that this '*aktion*' was to take place in their hospital, on particular units, and personnel assigned to those units were expected to carry out the mission.

---

[368] Susan Benedict, Arthur Caplan, and Traute Lafrenz Page, 'Duty and "Euthanasia": The Nurses of Meseritz-Obrawalde', *Nursing Ethics* 14 (2007): 781–94.

[369] Susan Benedict and Jane Georges, 'Nurses and the Sterilization Experiments of Auschwitz: A Postmodern Perspective', *Nursing Inquiry* 13 (2006): 277–88.

[370] M. Margarete. 1962. Testimony. File no. 33.029/4. *Staatsarchiv München*. Munich, Germany.

[371] G Anna. 1962. Testimony. File no. 33.029/2. *Staatsarchiv München*. Munich, Germany; W Martha. 1962. Testimony. File no. 33.029/2. *Staatsarchiv München*. Munich, Germany.

[372] B Edith. 1962. Testimony. File no. 33.029/4. *Staatsarchiv München*. Munich, Germany; D Erna. 1962. Testimony. File no. 33.029/2. *Staatsarchiv München*. Munich, Germany.

[373] Susan Benedict, 'The Medicalization of Murder: The 'Euthanasia' Programs', in *Nurses and Midwives in Nazi Germany: The 'Euthanasia' Program*, eds. Susan Benedict and Linda Shields (London: Routledge, 2014), 71–104.

[374] Ibid.

Some nurses were enthusiastic participants, whereas others were gradually drawn in. For example, a nurse's participation could have started by moving a patient into the 'killing room' or preparing the medication. Later the same nurse could have taken a more aggressive role, such as holding the patients and forcing them to drink the lethal medications. Little is known about nurses who refused to participate because they were not defendants in post-war trials. Some nurses requested transfers, some quit their jobs and others became pregnant so as to be excused from working.[375]

What happened to the nurses after the war?

Few nurses received maximum punishments for the killing of their patients. Helene Wieczorek, a nurse from the 'wild euthanasia' hospital Meseritz-Obrawalde, along with physician Hildegard Wernicke, were arrested soon after Meseritz-Obrawalde was discovered by the Russians in January 1945. They were sentenced to death in March 1946. The head female nurse from the same hospital, Amanda Ratajczak, was given a brief trial by the Russians during which she was made to re-enact one of the killings. She and the male head nurse, Hermann Guhlke, were shot by the Russians on 10 May 1945.[376]

There were two trials that involved some of the nurses from Hadamar: the first Hadamar trial concluded in October 1945 and two male nurses, Heinrich Ruoff and Karl Willig were sentenced to death by hanging. The head female nurse, Irmgard Huber, was sentenced to 25 years imprisonment. The second Hadamar trial occurred in 1947. Irmgard Huber received an additional sentence of eight years. Other Hadamar nurses were tried in the second trial and received sentences of two to five years.[377] Nurses from other hospitals including Grafeneck and the children's 'euthanasia' hospital, Am Spiegelgrund, received prison sentences for killing or assisting with killing their patients.[378] Anna Katschenka at Am Spiegelgrund was sentenced to eight years in prison and the loss of her government pension.

In 1965, 14 nurses from Meseritz-Obrawalde were tried and, despite their admission of guilt, acquitted.[379] The verdict in this trial is particularly baffling in that there was no doubt of the guilt of some of the defendants, yet the court declined to prosecute their crimes. The fact that 20 years had elapsed since the war and the general weariness of the post-Nazi era trials certainly coloured the judgment of the court when viewed in comparison with verdicts of earlier trials.

---

[375] Benedict, 'Meseritz-Obrawalde', 128.
[376] Ibid., 128–29.
[377] Susan Benedict, 'Killing While Caring: The Nurses of Hadamar', *Issues in Mental Health Nursing* 24, no. 1 (2003): 59–79.
[378] Benedict, 'The Medicalization', 83–85.
[379] Benedict, 'Meseritz-Obrawalde', 113.

Conclusion

While medicine as a profession has received much attention in relation to the actions of doctors in the 'euthanasia' programmes, genocide and the Final Solution, scholarship about nurses has been minimal. Many nurses actively killed their patients and the nursing profession was an integral part of the genocidal strategies used against both disabled people and Jews. At the T4 institutions, nurses helped with the transports of patients and led them to the gas chambers. Some of the T4 'euthanasia' nurses were subsequently transferred to the death camps to set up the gassing mechanisms for killing. In the 'special' paediatric units, nurses gave children overdoses of drugs, starved them or left them in the cold to die of hypothermia. In the 'wild euthanasia' programme, nurses became direct murderers of their patients. The reasons for their actions varied and cannot be fully and accurately judged by legal testimonies that were guided by lawyers whose interest was in gaining acquittals. In many cases, most notably the Meseritz-Obrawalde trial, so many years had elapsed that the defendants had plenty of time to develop a rationale of self-preservation and, similarly, their lawyers had ample time to prepare defences based upon the successful strategies of preceding 'euthanasia' trials. We cannot understand the horrific tortures endured by disabled patients during the Nazi era. Likewise, it is hard to understand, at this remove, how nurses could become so inculcated with the propaganda of the time about 'useless feeders', 'life unworthy of life' and subversion of the concept of 'a good death—euthanasia'—that they lost sight of right from wrong.

CHAPTER 6

Genocide and Suicide

Colin Tatz

'No one ever lacks a good reason for suicide'.

Cesare Pavese[380]

'Death crises occur more often for American Indians at an earlier age and, furthermore, the deaths of their ancestors (which came close to genocide) remains a powerful tribal memory. American Indians are aware of their isolation from mainstream culture. They are both isolated geographically and suffer from racism. ... Suicide by the American Indian, for example, may be seen as seeking freedom in death'.

David Lester[381]

Connections and disconnections

The killing of one and the killing of thousands or millions may seem a discordant relationship but there is a connection between suicide and genocide that calls for analysis. The connection can occur during genocide, as in the

---

[380] Pavese (1908–50) was a noted Italian poet, novelist, and literary critic.
[381] A British-American suicidologist and sociologist. See his *Suicide in American Indians* (New York: Nova Science Publications, 1997).

How to cite this book chapter:
Tatz, C. 2020. Genocide and Suicide. In: Marczak, N. and Shields, K. (eds.) *Genocide Perspectives VI: The Process and the Personal Cost of Genocide*. Pp. 107–127. Sydney: UTS ePRESS. DOI: https://doi.org/10.5130/aaf.g. License: CC BY-NC-ND.

Armenian and Jewish cases described in this essay; but it can occur *after* genocide, even generations after. This has been referred to as 'tribal memory' of victim groups: the legacy of history that is transmitted or osmosed over the generations and results in what is called transgenerational trauma.

The genocide experience and its legacy usually includes such factors as:

- experience of minority group status;
- separation from a mainstream society—politically, socially, physically and culturally;
- continuing wardship status of entire populations;
- a history of genocidal massacres or attacks of the kind that came to be called pogroms in the Jewish case but which befell other minorities in similar ways;
- forcible removal of children from parents, for long periods or for life;
- long-term institutionalisation of youth;
- radical geographic relocations;
- endemic and pervasive racism;
- early deaths, commonplace deaths and often violent deaths; and
- conscious efforts to escape such circumstances.

Many genocidal events warrant study for their connections to suicide, some a century old, others of much more recent times, but none more so than the experience of Indigenous peoples in Australia and North America. These two cases illustrate all of the above aspects and the legacy of genocide in current community experiences of suicide. In this essay I discuss both cases, while criticising current approaches to suicide and encouraging an approach of 'understanding' rather than 'explaining' and 'medicalising' the behaviour.

According to biomedicine, the very foundation of suicide resides in a 'mental health disorder' of some kind, usually 'depression' or a depletion of a hormone like serotonin, or a chemical imbalance in the brain.[382] The futile search is now on for a depression gene, even for a genetic marker that will explain *all* suicide. In *The Sealed Box of Suicide*, Simon Tatz and I analyse 33 categories of suicide, the majority of which have nothing to do with 'mental disorder', 'depression' or genes.[383] Among those who survive genocide, the biomedical equation ignores external contexts like history, geography, religion, sociology, philosophy and culture, and neglects the transmission of trauma from communal experiences such as genocide. These are the conditions or the circumstances that the father of modern suicide studies, Emil Durkheim, described in *Le Suicide* in 1897.

---

[382] Johann Hari, *Lost Connections: Uncovering the Real Causes of Depression—and the Unexpected Solutions* (London: Bloomsbury Circus, 2018).

[383] Colin Tatz and Simon Tatz, *The Sealed Box of Suicide: The Contexts of Self-Death* (Zug: Springer, 2019).

Defining the factors

Before it had a name, human beings understood what genocide is, and why and how rulers and states turn to biological solutions to solve social and political problems. We have known what suicide is since history began to find its written form. We have known a great deal about suicidal behaviour over millennia and tolerated it, even celebrated it in some cultures and historical eras. But in the twentieth century in particular, Western societies deemed suicide a scourge, a blight upon themselves, a rogue manifestation (much like smallpox or polio) that grows apace and needs prevention by some kind of pharmaceutical or therapeutic prophylaxis. 'Personality disorders' are rampant, we are told, and are being addressed by more and more funds in search of a possible vaccination.

But what is mental illness, a condition said to be suffered by one in five Australians? The Blackdog Institute, a major Australian agency in this field, insists that mental illness, especially among youth, is related to ADHD, anxiety disorder, major depressive disorder and conduct disorder, and its factsheets outline the genetic and biochemical factors in depression.[384] The *Diagnostic and Statistical Manual of Mental Disorders*,[385] now in its fifth edition and known as *DSM-V*, describes the hundreds of 'disorders' that bedevil us.

This 'bible of psychiatry' exercises an unparalleled influence on Western society. It has been much criticised, particularly by non-Americans, for telling us—amid the truly serious and verifiable brain diseases and lists of psychoses—that you have a 'mathematical deficit disorder' if you have trouble with arithmetic; that you suffer a 'communications disorder' if you wave your hands and point too much; that you have a 'substance use disorder' if you smoke cigarettes or gag for your morning coffee; and you exhibit a 'social phobia' if you are shy. An 'adjustment deficit disorder' arises where a stressor causes a great deal of worry in one's life—'like a wedding or buying a new home'. No matter how inane or banal the reaction, the emotion or the behaviour, once it has the label of disorder or a 'diagnosis' of 'a mental health issue', it becomes a significant social tattoo forever visible in the files of every institution. For much of the general public, 'deficit' and 'disorder' are characterised not just as 'disease' but as a socially pejorative disease, code for the once common (and now reviled) expressions of 'psycho' or 'nuts'. Contexts, external factors or a legacy of communal trauma have no place in the sovereign domain of this biomedical approach.

Increasingly, scholars and some practitioners embrace 'critical suicide studies', a movement that looks outside the insistent biomedical framework. These professionals examine history, the role of suicide in history and think outside 'the sealed box of suicide'. The title of Said Shahtahmasebi's book,

---

[384] See the website https://www.blackdoginstitute.org.au/docs/default-source/factsheets/causesofdepression.pdf?sfvrsn=2.
[385] *Diagnostic and Statistical Manual of Mental Disorders* (Arlington: American Psychiatric Association, 2013).

Suicide: The Broader View, sums up the movement's foundation. As a member of this group, I join those who look beyond, even way beyond the conventional 'at-risk' factors for suicide. Critical suicidologists compare suicide in diverse arenas; they try to *understand* rather than *explain* the place and impact of suicide in specific communities; they address more openly a taboo-laden topic and explore why it is that we, as a Western society, are so affronted by suicide, especially among the young.

For and *against* suicide

The Italian sociologist Marzio Barbagli posits two spurs to suicide: those who do it *for* self or *for* others, and those who take their lives as a form of revenge *against* others.[386] The Bologna professor does not mean honour or shame suicides (present in some cultures), nor does he include suicide bombers who, in intent and effect, are dedicated to killing others. Barbagli's dyad is based on the consciously rational perception that impels *for* and *against*. Another eminent Italian, Cesare Pavese, took his life—but he understood that reason has as much, if not more, of a role in suicide, as does unreason.

During at least two twentieth century genocides existed the simultaneous sister categories of *for* and *against* suicide: among the Armenians in Turkey from 1915 to 1923, and among the Jews in Nazi Germany in the 1930s and 1940s. The literature, albeit limited, on these two cases tells us something about rational, premeditated suicide. A few Holocaust scholars have talked about the need for new words to define the unprecedented events let loose on the world by nationalistic Turkey and then escalated to a more industrial scale by National Socialist Germany. *Die Endlösung der Judenfrage*—'the final solution to the Jewish question'—was the name the Nazis gave to their programme to eliminate both the physical being and the very concept of 'Jew'. For the American historian Lawrence Langer, what befell that victim group was 'facing choiceless choices'.[387] For Terrence des Pres—who analysed surviving a death camp—it was 'an excremental assault'.[388] From the viewpoint of one group of victims, those who suicided, we can look to the words of yet another American—this time the satirist and literary critic HL Mencken. In his inimitably acerbic way he declaimed that 'of all the escape mechanisms, death is the most efficient'.[389] Thus, while most people view suicide as resulting from 'disease of the mind',

---

[386] Marzio Barbagli, *Farewell to the World: A History of Suicide* (New Jersey: Wiley, 2015).
[387] Lawrence Langer, *Versions of Survival: The Holocaust and the Human Spirit* (New York: State University of New York Press, 1982), 72.
[388] Terrence des Pres, *The Survivor: The Anatomy of Life in a Death Camp* (Oxford: Oxford University Press, 1980).
[389] HL Mencken, *A Book of Burlesques* (New York: Alfred J Knopf, 1916).

for those imperilled by grotesque circumstances, self-destruction was, and is indeed, the best way out, the effective 'ultimate refuge'.

Apart from the Nazi invention of specific-purpose death factories, the Turkish nationalists set most of the precedents for the Holocaust a quarter of a century earlier. They articulated a formal ideological, sociological, anthropological and linguistic presentation of a superior civilisation confronted by an enemy within, with an ill-fitting, pernicious minority, a fifth-column and an 'abscess' in the midst of a burgeoning nationalistic state. They initiated deportations, population transfers and the confiscation and transfer of property; they rounded-up men, disarmed Armenian civilians and soldiers and created slave labour camps. The genocide involved the desecration of churches and cemeteries; sexual violence, trafficking and forced marriage of women; abduction and forced Turkification of women and children; elementary gas chambers; medical experiments; drownings and burnings; and large-scale death marches—all of which led to the annihilation of up to 1.5 million Armenians.

One major difference between the Armenian and Jewish cases was that Armenian children could be 'saved' by conversion and Turkification; and in some instances women could live, but only as trafficked objects or forced wives, completely cut off from their own community. While their physical life may have been saved, this programme of forced assimilation was a central part of the genocide of Armenians.

Sexual violence against Armenian women was common and systematic. Many survivor and witness testimonies mention suicides by women and girls, sometimes carried out collectively. Gendered notions of morality (that is, it was preferable to die than to be raped or abducted by the enemy), seem to have influenced at least some of these suicides. In addition, the way the suicides are remembered and narrated present the women as heroes for having done so. Raymond Kévorkian, a noted historian of the genocide, commented on one Armenian response to the events:

> Suicides were also quite frequent. If the main reason for this was simply despair, many of those who took their own lives were young women, who chose to throw themselves into the Euphrates rather than submit to rape. Mothers also frequently refused to submit to the will of their torturers, killing themselves and their children instead.[390]

Two scholars of the Armenian Genocide, Donald and Lorna Touryan Miller, have addressed the responses of Armenian women and children during the onslaught.[391] They note numerous references to suicide when interviewing

---

[390] Raymond Kévorkian, *The Armenian Genocide: A Complete History* (London: I.B. Taurus, 2011), 407.

[391] Donald Miller and Lorna Touryan Miller, 'Women and Children of the Armenian Genocide', in *The Armenian Genocide: History, Politics, Ethics*, ed. Richard Hovanissian (New York: St Martin's Press, 1992), 152–72.

survivors. Their conclusions are of particular interest, given that few suicide scholars have attempted to frame differing categories of suicide, something essential if we are to make any progress in alleviating or mitigating the 'problem'. The Millers posit three acts: *altruistic suicide, despairing suicide* and, significant for this analysis of suicides undertaken when a community is persecuted, *defiant suicide*. Thus, grandmothers and mothers who sacrificed themselves by giving their food rations to children were performing acts of altruism in dying *for* others. Grandmothers staying behind so that younger relatives could walk away faster was another example. The despairing ones were those who could physically walk on, but chose to stay behind and die; and those who were mentally exhausted and whose support structure had collapsed.

The *defiant* category is important: it fits Barbagli's dyad of both *for* and *against*. Some Armenian women took their lives rather than submit to the commonplace torture and sexual abuse by their Turkish oppressors. The Armenian Apostolic Church regards suicide as a grievous sin, placing the suicide as beyond salvation and beyond burial by the church (except where mental illness is evident). These women defied both biological instinct and Church doctrine. Yet in April 2015, the hundredth anniversary of the start of the genocide, the Apostolic Church sanctified *all* who died as martyrs—including those who suicided.

Most people made aware of such circumstances would understand what was involved in these decisions—the defilement aspect, at least, if not the lifelong stigma—and would acknowledge the actions of these women as honourable, perhaps admirable, certainly as comprehensible. There would be some sense of appreciation of actions that are consonant with martyrdom. Many would argue that such actions were the result of coerced choices, even Langer's 'choiceless choices'. But these women exercised their wills, their rational wills, in appalling contexts.

Other genocides and atrocities are also worth noting for the links to gender and suicide:

- Herero, Dama and Nama women in German South-West Africa [Namibia] following the genocide and rape of women by the German military between 1904 and 1906;
- Congolese women who suffered Belgian genocidal brutality between 1885 and 1908;
- Bosnian Muslim women forced into dedicated rape centres during the Wars of Yugoslav Succession between 1991 and 2001;
- The abduction and enslavement of Yazidi women and girls by ISIS in Iraq in 2014;
- Sexual violence and displacement of hundreds of thousands of Rohingyas in Myanmar from 2017;
- Brutal and violent treatment of arranged child brides in Syria and other countries.

We know less about the suicide of Armenian men than women, and not a great deal about Jewish men or women in the Nazi era, except that suicide among Jews in the early Nazi period was fairly common.[392] The esteemed suicide scholar David Lester found the suicide rate in concentration camps much higher than was once believed by the eminent survivor Elie Wiesel, a rate found to be of the order of 25 per 100,000.[393] That was remarkable because traditional Judaism regards suicide as unacceptable. Judaism, among major religions, generally has the fewest suicides. Yet suicides were common enough in crisis times and Jews experienced seemingly endless crises: they were deemed responsible for the death of Jesus, and as the transmitters of the Black Plague; they were expelled from European societies like Spain, Portugal and England; blamed for famines and the deaths of Christian children at Passover (the blood libel by which Jews were alleged to have made unleavened bread out of their blood); they endured pogroms in Russia, Ukraine and Poland; and a third died in the Holocaust.

There are two exceptions to the Jewish decree of suicide as sinful. One is *Kiddush Hashem*, the taking of one's life in defence of God, which is choosing martyrdom rather than forced apostasy (especially during the Crusades in the Middle Ages). The other, introduced by Rabbi Isaac Nissenbaum in the Warsaw Ghetto in the 1940s, is *Kiddush Ha-Hayim*, 'the sanctification of life', that one could and should defend one's soul against those who want to extinguish it by taking one's life away from the oppressor. In that sense, *Kiddush Ha-Hayim* is *defiant suicide* rather than *despairing suicide*.

The Roman Jewish historian Flavius Josephus was the first to describe what has come to be called 'the Masada complex'.[394] So the story goes that atop Herod's rocky citadel adjacent to the Dead Sea in Israel, the Jewish Zealots held out against the Roman army, but by 73 CE it was clear they could not sustain the siege. Rather than submit to slavery or possible 'de-Judaising,' 960 men, women and children took their lives. Regardless of the controversy about this 'complex'—that it is memorialised and celebrated as resistance by many, and condemned as a form of cowardice by others—it is a tale of terrible choices and of a political and wilful act of defiance in the face of the unthinkable, namely, the surrendering of one's Jewishness.

Whether German Jews in the 1930s consciously thought about Masada is not really known. But what is plain from the definitive analysis by historian Konrad Kwiet is that German Jewish suicide rates increased markedly in the Nazi era. There were two aspects of the escalation: suicide by those who had converted to

---

[392] Konrad Kwiet, 'The Ultimate Refuge: Suicide in the Jewish Community under the Nazis', *Leo Baeck Institute Year Book* 29, Iss. 1 (1984): 135–68.

[393] David Lester, 'The Suicide Rate in the Concentration Camps Was Extraordinarily High: A Comment on Bronisch and Lester', *Archives of Suicide Research* 8, no. 2 (2004): 199–201.

[394] Flavius Josephus, *The Jewish War* (London: Penguin Books Reissue Edition, 1984).

Christianity, even back two generations, and were then confronted by Nazi definitions of 'Jew' as anyone having at least one Jewish parent or one maternal or paternal grandparent. To be a devout Christian and a *Vaterland*-loving patriot, and to find one's citizenship removed by the Nuremberg Laws of 1935, being banished from public service of any kind and then having to wear a yellow armband, was more than enough for some who put an end to what they foresaw as an impossible Jewish life under the Nazi regime. Then there were those who, in a real sense, resisted the Nazis by taking their lives before the *Reich* took them. Some Jews bought and hoarded barbiturates and, judging that the time had come, found 'the ultimate refuge'. Remarkably, or perhaps not, wherever Nazis found Jews in a comatose or parlous state, they took them to hospitals to save them—in order to kill them in times and places of Nazi choosing. Here we see Lester's contention that victims seek freedom in death. We also see resistance in suicide during times of oppression.

The Austrian essayist, Jean Améry, who survived Auschwitz and Buchenwald, wrote agonising and acute analyses of the Holocaust, later a carefully considered book on suicide—and then ended his life.[395] People, he contended, kill themselves out of a sense of dignity, preferring annihilation to a continuing existence lived in ignominy, or in desperate pain (physical or mental), or in utter helplessness. Améry conceived of suicide not so much as an exit from life but entrance into another state, death—a cognition I came across in my years of fieldwork in Aboriginal societies.

Michel Foucault's concepts of biopower and biopolitics, and Barbagli's pairing are pertinent here.[396] The state exercises power over one's body in a range of ways—from birth control practices and compulsory sterilisation, to vaccination regimens, prohibitions on circumcision, marriageable ages, restrictions on multiple marriages, divorce, assisted dying and, as we have seen, suicide. Nazi administration of life and, of course, death is the ultimate example of total state control of the physical bodies under their domain. What would the biomedical world have to say about suicides among communities caught in the vortexes of genocidal catastrophe? The professionals may acknowledge the Hobson's choices and would likely agree that altruistic, defiant or despairing suicides did not occur as irrational acts, or as disordered behaviour arising from brain dysfunctions. Why then do the helping professions not accord to suicides among these populations, or indeed suicides of individuals in less calamitous circumstances, an attempt at understanding or accommodation of historical, social and cultural contexts?

---

[395] Born as Hanns Chaim Meyer (1912–78). See Jean Améry, *On Suicide: A Discussion on Voluntary Death* (Bloomington: Indiana University Press, 1999).

[396] Michel Foucault, *The History of Sexuality: The Will to Knowledge, Volume 1*, trans. Robert Hurley (London: Penguin Books, 2006).

There are two possible answers to the question. An obvious explanation is that biomedicine has little interest in the social history of medicine or in the anthropology of specific diseases, subjects no longer taught in medical schools. A few paragraphs may be offered on Ebola, HIV infection and similar esoteric killer infections. There was a time when every medical student in the West had to read Hans Zinsser's *Rats, Lice and History*, first published in 1935. The Harvard biologist's work has been replaced by writers on current epidemics and pandemics whose literature appears to be confined to those few who choose epidemiology as a profession. Then again, medical school curricula rarely offer space for social science elective courses, and where they do, few take up history, geography or anthropology.

Indigenous suicides

In some societies suicide is rare, in others, rampant. Several communities have an historic and cultural practice of suicide. However, a number of Indigenous communities have experienced an alarming escalation of suicide rates over recent decades, their common experience of genocide and colonialism undoubtedly a major factor. The affected groups are turning to community in preference to Western biomedical models of intervention.

We have an acute observation on the Western approach to suicide from the American psychologist James Hillman (1926–2011):

> Understanding is ... based on sympathy, on intimate knowledge, on participation. It depends upon a communication of souls and is appropriate to the human encounter, whereas explanation belongs to the viewpoint of the natural sciences. Understanding attempts to stay with the moment as it is, while explanation leads away from the present, backwards into a chain of causality, or sideways into comparisons.[397]

Today we can glimpse a different kind of suicide analysis in contemporary communities that have suffered one or more acts of genocide, especially Indigenous communities such as Aboriginal peoples and Torres Strait Islanders, Native Americans, Canadian First Nations and Inuit; Inuit Greenlanders; the Sami peoples of Norway, Sweden and Finland (once known as Lapps or Laplanders); Pacific Islanders and the New Zealand Maori peoples of Oceania. Several scholars of suicide in those regions are stepping outside the conventional box. Hillman asks who owns the soul. For him, 'self-killing ... means both a killing of community and involvement of community in the killing'.[398] Just as Dr Jack

---

[397] James Hillman, *Suicide of the Soul* (Woodstock: Springer Publications, 1997), 49.
[398] Ibid.

Kevorkian's assisted suicide campaign in the United States opened up that issue, so Hillman's plea was that suicide should be judged 'by some community court', comprising legal, medical, aesthetic, religious and philosophical interests, as well as by family and friends. In that way, self-death can 'come out of the closet'. The act of suicide will, of course, remain individualistic, 'but judgement of the suicide as part of, or interior to, a community may help to liberate Western civilisation's "persecutory panic" when suicide, or the threat of it, arises'. 'We must,' he concludes, get away from 'police action, lockups, criminalisation of helpers, dosages to dumbness'.[399]

We have done nothing of the sort, or very little of it, in North America or in Australasia. We insist on explanation, on causality—inevitably 'mental health issues', on seeking out 'at-risk' factors, on prescribing more medication rather than following Hillman's recourse to *understanding*. Some inroads have been made into the sovereignty of biopower and of the individualisation and isolation of suicide—by native communities in Australia, the United States, Canada and New Zealand. The communities—not the specialists' consulting rooms, the hospitals or Al Alvarez's 'isolation wards of science'—have become the locus and focus of suicide, especially that of youth. The 'community' has taken on the phenomenon and the problem it presents.[400] However defined or perceived by others, the community knows itself: who belongs, who does not, and where the social and geographic boundaries are drawn.[401]

Aboriginal Australia

The 2016 census enumerated the combined Aboriginal, Torres Strait Islander and South Sea Islander population as 649,200, or 2.8 per cent of the national population.[402] In northern Australia in the 1960s and 1970s there was no evidence, let alone any record of any suicide in remote, rural or in urban

---

[399] He means the benumbing of the emotions that often flows from antidepressant drugs.

[400] For example, a major segment of the second National Aboriginal and Torres Strait Islander Suicide Prevention Conference in Perth in 2018 was 'The Importance of Community Partnerships'.

[401] For example, while the word *Nyoongar* or *Nyungar* is the generic word of choice for, and by, Western Australian Aboriginal people, *Nyoongar* is also the name of a specific, tight geographic community in the south-west of Western Australia, from Geraldton on the west coast, to Esperance on the south coast, consisting essentially of fourteen language groups. Their Country numbers some 6,000 to 10,000 persons.

[402] New South Wales 216,176; Queensland 186,4582; Western Australia 75,978; Northern Territory 58,248; Victoria 47,788; South Australia 34,184; Tasmania 23,572; Australian Capital Territory 6,508.

communities—quite a contrast with suicide practice among Arctic Inuit and Indian communities.

'Ethnopsychiatry' became a research fad in Australia from 1960 to 1990, and several studies in the Northern Territory and Western Australia— by, among others, John Cawte in 1968, Malcolm Kidson and Ivor Jones in 1968 and Harry Eastwell in 1988—found no 'mental health issues' and 'nothing alarming about Aboriginal suicide'.[403] The specific suicide aspects of this research tended to be of the conventional variety, whereas the ethnopsychiatric approach to 'mental illness' was always less about studying native belief systems and much more about Western-perceived illness among the clans. This kind of ethnopsychiatry—always conducted in [academic] English among dialect-speaking people (and sometimes by observing 'subjects' at a distance through binoculars)—was, for the most part, a dismal art, unproductive and without any portending quality. Towards the end of the 1980s, Ernest Hunter began his pioneering work on Aboriginal history, health and suicide.[404]

My interest in suicide began in 1989 when I explored the role of sport in deflecting Aboriginal youth from criminal activity.[405] Conducted across 79 communities, this continent-wide fieldwork coincided with the appointment of a Royal Commission into Aboriginal Deaths in Custody, which was to investigate 99 such deaths between 1980 and 1989.[406] There was a mistaken belief that most of these deaths were 'assisted' and highly suspicious—but very few were. Noteworthy is that half of the custody deaths were of men who were members of the Stolen Generations; that is, children forcibly removed from their natural parents. Stories abounded of suicide and attempted suicide among young people, seemingly more common outside of custody than inside. So it proved to be.

---

[403] For evidence of that reality, see, *inter alia*, the following: J Cawte, D Baglin, G Bianchi, D McElwain, J Money, and B Nurcombe, 'Arafura, Aboriginal Town: The Medico-sociological Expedition to Arnhem Land in 1968' (n.p., 1968). Unpublished Manuscript; copy held by AIATSIS Library, Canberra (restricted use, call number MS 483). H. Eastwell, 'The Low Risk of Suicide among the Yolngu of the Northern Territory: The Traditional Aboriginal Pattern', *Medical Journal of Australia* 148, no. 7 (1988): 338–40. M Kidson, and I Jones, 'Psychiatric Disorders among Aborigines of the Australian Western Desert', (n.p., 1968). Unpublished Typescript, copy held by AIATSIS Library, Canberra (call number PMS 918).

[404] Ernest Hunter, *Aboriginal Health and History: Power and Prejudice in Remote Australia* (Cambridge: Cambridge University Press, 1993).

[405] Colin Tatz, *Aboriginals: Sport, Violence and Survival*, 1994 Criminology Research Council Research Report, http://crg.aic.gov.au/reports/18-98.pdf.

[406] *National Report, RCIADIC* (Royal Commission into Aboriginal Deaths in Custody) (Canberra: Australian Government Publishing Service, 1991).

Apart from a literal handful of cases, there was *no record* of Aboriginal suicides before 1960,[407] and suicide had no place in any Aboriginal belief systems, languages and material culture. Nor did Aboriginal suicide appear in prison, police or hospital records, the files of children's institutions, in anthropologists' writings or notes, or in any missionary or governmental documents. Yet in the past 50 years their rates of suicide have soared to among the highest in the world, especially in the younger age groups—not just 15 to 24 but the even younger 10 to 14 cohort. Lamentably, eight-year-olds are attempting suicide—'playing hangsies' as it is described in the Kimberley region of Western Australia. Even allowing for David Lester's comment at the head of this essay about Native American youth inured to death at an early age, how does an eight-year-old, deemed in law not to have the capacity to form *any* intent, understand, let alone intend, and then act out self-cessation?[408] Official statistics tell us that while the national suicide rate is now 10.4 per 100,000 of the population, for Aboriginal and Torres Strait Islander peoples it is 21.4. In three states the rate is closer to 30. For the years 1996 to 1998, I found rates of 40 in specific rural New South Wales Aboriginal communities.[409] In 2014, the Kimberley rate was 74.

My book *Aboriginal Suicide is Different* was first published in 2001. Reactions varied: most readers were surprised or astonished, and one or two critics demanded to know how and in what ways Aboriginal suicide was, or could even remotely be considered, 'different'. Academic psychologist Joseph Reser saw the 'differentness' as 'ostensible', 'rhetorical', with dangerous consequences for professional practice.[410] Wedded as they are to the axiom that an inexorable factor in suicide is previous suicide in families, Reser and others insist that there simply has to be a history of Aboriginal suicide—even in the absence of historical evidence.

In subsequent writings, and after research visits to New Zealand and Nunavut in Canada, the 'different' or varied quality was made clear: one sharp look at the social, political and historic contexts revealed the divide. While suicide

---

[407] Christine McIlvanie, 'The Responsibility of People' (BA honours thesis, University of New England, 1982). This thesis examined the death in custody of Eddie Murray in the cells at Wee Waa (NSW), and contained replies to the candidate from the NSW Prisons Service about records of Aboriginal deaths in custody for some eight decades.

[408] Sigmund Freud once proposed that youth understand physical death but believe their spirits live on. My experience of a few eight-year-old parasuicides is that despite 'playing' at hanging they appear to comprehend death as the outcome.

[409] Colin Tatz, *Aboriginal Suicide is Different: A Portrait of Life and Self-Destruction* (Canberra: Aboriginal Studies Press, 2005), 59–69.

[410] Joseph Reser, 'What Does it Mean to Say that Aboriginal Suicide is Different? Different Cultures, Accounts, and Distress in the Contexts of Indigenous Youth Suicide', *Australian Aboriginal Studies* 2, no. 23 (2004): 34–53.

is suicide, the origins, social factors and the legacies of history make for a very different kind of analysis, the kind most health professionals are not exposed to.

Aboriginal Australians trail a history like no other segment of the population, here or abroad. They experienced a genocidal era of episodic physical killings from 1804 to 1928, with some 250 massacre sites documented to date.[411] Some 20,000 to 30,000 people were killed, by intent, in sporadic but systemic acts of 'dispersal'. To prevent the killings, federal and state governments (between 1897 and 1912) introduced policies of protection-segregation—incarceration on isolated reservations. Between 1897 and the mid-1970s, governments sequestered between 70,000 and 90,000 people by erecting legal and geographic fences.[412]

A reign of systemic forcible child removal began in the late 1830s in colonial Victoria and lasted until the mid-1980s, with around 35,000 children taken. The aim—enshrined in government policy—was to eliminate Aboriginality by biological and social assimilation, by 'breeding out the colour' and by child re-acculturation, 'to erase them from the landscape'—to the point, said the authorities, that no one would know that Aboriginal people ever existed.[413] Throughout these phases, Indigenous individuals had no civil or civic rights as generally understood: they were officially declared wards of the state, with government officials and Christian missionaries their legal guardians, irrespective of their age or ability to manage their own affairs.[414]

Harsh as it was in terms of human rights and fundamental freedoms, the institutional era did maintain ordered communities. There were containable levels of physical violence, usually traditional methods of conflict resolution. But with the opening up of these near-prison-like regimes in the mid-1970s, disorder set in, with increasing deaths from non-natural causes. Officially called 'accidents and poisonings', this statistical category has, alarmingly, included high numbers of homicide and suicide.

In the name of 'protection', nomadic hunter-gatherers had become sedentary, stationary and segregated as welfare recipients, pauperised in all aspects of life. The draconian settlement and mission practices attempted to 'civilise' and

---

[411] Calla Wahlquist, 'Evidence of 250 Massacres of Indigenous Australians Mapped', *Guardian*, July 27 (2018), https://www.theguardian.com/australia-news/2018/jul/27/evidence-of-250-massacres-of-indigenous-australians-mapped. For further information see: https://c21ch.newcastle.edu.au/colonialmassacres.

[412] For a full account of these eras see: Colin Tatz, *Australia's Unthinkable Genocide* (Bloomington: Xlibris, 2017).

[413] See Anna Haebich, '"Clearing the Wheat Belt": Erasing the Indigenous Presence in the Southwest of Western Australia', in *Genocide and Settler Society: Frontier Violence and Stolen Indigenous Children in Australian History*, ed. A Dirk Moses (New York: Berghahn Books, 2005): 267–89.

[414] See Tatz, *Australia's Unthinkable*, and John McCorquodale, *Aborigines and the Law: A Digest* (Canberra: Aboriginal Studies Press, 1987).

Christianise them, to imbue them with notions of property ownership, aspiration and individualism. Then suddenly, in the early 1970s, these governing authorities moved out and effectively abandoned them under the policy slogans of 'self-determination', then 'self-management' and then 'autonomy'. The assaults on traditional culture thus occurred twice in less than 60 years. When the controlling authorities walked away, virtually overnight, there was loss of both the traditional *and* the imposed structure, resulting in the trauma that Durkheim would call 'anomie'; that is, instability and normlessness.

Johann Hari has written eloquently about 'lost connections' as the way to understand mental illness.[415] The Aboriginal loss of connections has been calamitous: loss of land, of life, of kin, children, language, traditional culture and ritual (often forbidden by statute), of freedom of movement, of lifestyle. They have experienced forcible relocation, loss of choice of living space. As recently as 2007, the conservative federal government introduced an 'intervention', ostensibly to quarantine Aboriginal communities from excessive alcohol, drugs, sexual predators and trespass from those deemed undesirable. This was essentially a reprise of the policies implemented in colonial Queensland in 1897: the strictest possible segregation and isolation but, in this instance, not to protect Aboriginal people from outside predators but from themselves.

In sum, in the period of 230 years since colonisation began, there have been massive impacts on Aboriginal lives: dispossession of land, massacres, isolation, strict segregation, forcible child removals, forced assimilation, fragmentation, denial of civic and civil rights, 'interventions' and, in more recent times, prison incarceration rates that are grossly disproportionate. For many, pretending that such events did not occur, or that they occurred in some less reprehensible way, is a preferable pathway. Such are the contexts of 'difference'. Public policies of equality that rely on 'levelling the playing fields', do not appreciate or accommodate difference: Aboriginal experiences get in the way of universality and expediency, two qualities precious to bureaucracies.

Both Louis Wekstein's *A Handbook of Suicidology* and Barbagli's book provide broad but definable categories of suicide. Both acknowledge something society wants to avoid, namely, the very idea of *rational suicide*, what Hillman would call 'persecutory panic'. There is no denying or relativising the reality that a percentage of the young who are bipolar or schizophrenic do commit suicide, but I emphasise that the majority of suicides I have studied did not have such professionally diagnosed and confirmed mental illness. Nor do coronial files and witness depositions reveal presentations of that kind. A fair percentage of the remote population does not have regular, or even irregular, contact with the professionals who can diagnose mental illness. As mentioned above, between 1960 and 1990 the major psychiatric studies by reputable researchers found no evidence of *any* mental illnesses among Aboriginal Australians. Certainly, the many doctors and nurses I met during my early 1960s work

---

[415] Hari, *Lost Connections*.

never reported or talked about mental illness cases. Individuals may have been unhappy, sad, even given to forms of melancholia, but they were neither clinically depressed nor inclined to undue violence, to self or to others. An inability to cope with neo-liberal expectations and aspirations in modern society, or to manage the symptoms of transgenerational transmission of trauma, is not an illness as such. Often in rational ways—at least according to many interviews of those who survived suicide attempts—they were not merely seeking an exit from life but, seemingly, an entrance to Amery's other state, death, a 'place' up there where life may possibly be better than the miserable lives they have down here. Just as rationally, there are many who reject broader society, and tell us so, more often than not by confrontational methods of death—like hanging in public places. In their own way, such public actions are political statements.[416] Hanging, generally, is hugely more prevalent than gun use, imbibing poison, jumping, train-surfing, drowning, self-immolating or climbing onto electricity power lines.

Two contextual factors loom large in the Aboriginal experience: their very short lives, forever confronted by young deaths, as well as the legacies of a recent past, and a never-certain present. A number of social indicators illustrate the gap between contemporary Aboriginal and non-Aboriginal life. One is life expectancy. Aboriginal males can expect to live to 67, some 11.5 years fewer than non-Aboriginal males. A recent book on Aboriginal sports achievers has an entry on the Rovers Football Club from Ceduna in South Australia, winners of a regional premiership in 1958.[417] Of the eighteen young men in that Australian Rules football team, only one lived to the age of 50.[418] The Rovers team is a truer indicator of Aboriginal life (and death) than the numerical portrait provided by the Australian Bureau of Statistics.

During decades of fieldwork it was obvious that in most communities there is at least one death, natural or unnatural, one funeral, one wake, every week. Children are inured to death at a very early age. Grief suffuses communities and the notion of grief counselling is not seen as culturally relevant. Horwitz

---

[416] Ernest Hunter, 'On Gordian Knots and Nooses: Aboriginal Suicide in the Kimberley,' *Australian and New Zealand Journal of Psychiatry* 22 (1988): 264–71.

[417] Colin Tatz and Paul Tatz, *Black Pearls: The Aboriginal and Islander Sports Hall of Fame* (Canberra: Aboriginal Studies Press, 2018).

[418] Australian football (sometimes called Australian Rules football, or Aussie Rules or 'footy'), is played by two teams on an oval-shaped field, with eighteen players on each team. The ball is kicked or handled in any direction between players, and the object is to kick the ball through the opponent's goalposts at the end of the field. The goalposts comprise four posts, each around 6.5 m apart; the two inner posts are taller than the two outer posts. Kicking the ball between the centre (or inner) goalposts scores six points, and through the adjoining side posts scores one point.

and Wakefield lament the 'loss of sadness' and the way psychiatry has turned sadness into a mental disorder.[419] There is no shortage of sadness in Aboriginal life. Sadness is not clinical depression; and sadness is reason enough to end the body that is overcome by it. Grief does not go away in specified timeframes. In a remote New South Wales town I was asked to meet four young Aboriginal men who had attempted suicide and were heavily dosed with the antidepressant Prozac. They took me to the cemetery where they pointed to the grave of a 16-year-old once promising footballer who had knocked down an old lady while trying to steal her purse and thought, wrongly, that he had killed her—whereupon he took a skipping rope from his gym bag and hanged himself, all too visibly, in the public park. The four had bought a 24-can carton of beer: as they each sank a can, so they poured a matching one into the grave for Peter. Why are you doing that? 'We want to join him', was the unanimous and unambiguous reply.

Native North America

The literature on suicide among Native Americans, Canadian First Nations and Inuit and Indigenous Alaskans has grown remarkably in the past three decades. In 1989, for example, David Lester's *Suicide from a Sociological Perspective* covered New Mexico Indian suicides in three pages; in 1997, he was moved to publish a full-length book on *Suicide in American Indians*. Suicide in Indigenous communities is increasing each year.

Andrew Woolford and Anthony Hall are leading the research into the genocidal legacy of Indian communities in North America, especially the impact on children who experienced the compulsory residential boarding schools (similar to the Stolen Generations in Australia).[420] Canadians have the benefit of major investigations: The Royal Commission on Aboriginal People (1991–96), and the Truth and Reconciliation of Canada Report of 2015. The latter gave an eloquent voice to the genocidal nature of colonial and post-colonial policies:

> Physical genocide is the mass killing of the members of a targeted group, and biological genocide is the destruction of the group's reproductive

---

[419] Allan Horwitz and Jerome Wakefield, *The Loss of Sadness: How Psychiatry Transformed Normal Sorrow Into Depressive Disorder* (New York: Oxford University Press, 2007).

[420] Andrew Woolford, *This Benevolent Experiment: Indigenous Boarding Schools, Genocide, and Redress in Canada and the United States* (Nebraska: University of Nebraska Press, 2015). See also Anthony J Hall, 'A National or International Crime? Canada's Indian Residential Schools and the Genocide Convention', *Genocide Studies International* 20, no. 1, (2018): 79–91.

capacity. Cultural genocide is the destruction of those structures and practices that allow the group to continue as a group. States that engage in cultural genocide set out to destroy the political and social institutions of the targeted group. Land is seized, and populations are forcibly transferred and their movement is restricted. Languages are banned. Spiritual leaders are persecuted, spiritual practices are forbidden, and objects of spiritual value are confiscated and destroyed. And, most significantly to the issue at hand, families are disrupted to prevent the transmission of cultural values and identity from one generation to the next. In its dealing with Aboriginal people, Canada did all these things.[421]

In 1994, the American and Alaska Mental Health Research Center published the proceedings of a major conference. 'Calling from the Rim' may well be the most important accounts of youth suicide amongst indigenous peoples.[422] Dozens of medical and psychiatric journal papers cite diverse rates of Indian suicide within tribal groups, while others point to sharp differences in prevalence between tribes. The diversity can be partly attributed to the different experiences between different tribes: some genocidal, some plain violent, a few with relatively peaceful relations. As discriminating as these studies appear to be, there remains the problem of the all-embracing title of 'tribe'. *Custer Died for Your Sins* by Vine Deloria Jr, a well-known Indian rights advocate and a former Executive Director of the National Congress of American Indians, remains the most searing, and unrebutted, indictment of American Indian policy, and of white academic attitudes, especially those of anthropologists.[423] He deplores the 'Little Big Horn' and 'wigwam' stereotyping of his people, and I suspect that, while he has not written specifically about suicide, his admonitions of anthropology would apply as strongly to suicidology. In essence, he condemns academe for creating 'unreal' Indians in their attempts to establish 'real' Indians. Thus, the 'bicultural people', the 'folk people', the 'drink-too-much people', the 'warriors without weapons people', the 'between-two-worlds people' are academic constructs imposed on a people who then came to believe, and live out, these external perceptions. Deloria reminds us that when academics talk of the Chippewas or the Sioux, they appear not to recognise that 'there are nineteen different Chippewa tribes, fifteen Sioux tribes, four Potawatomi tribes', and so on. There is an identical perspective among non-Aboriginal Australians:

---

[421] *Honouring the Truth, Reconciling for the Future* (Canada: The Truth and Reconciliation Commission of Canada, 2015), 1.
[422] 'Calling from the Rim: Suicide Behaviour Among American Indian and Alaska Native Adolescents', *American and Alaskan Mental Health Research Center, Journal of the National Center* 4 (1994).
[423] Vine Deloria Jr., *Custer Died for Your Sins: An Indian Manifesto* (Normanton: Oklahoma University Press, 1988).

Aboriginal people are Aboriginal, no matter how different their histories, cultures and experiences.

Anthropology may well have committed many 'sins' against Indian peoples. But the anthropological approach at least attempted to get to know 'their' people and 'their' tribes. Other social science and medical disciplines have adopted a distant, statistical approach, even where there are attempts at differentiation between reservation and non-reservation residents. There is no detail of lifestyle difference, only difference in geographic domain. There is no understanding of 'tribal memory' and the legacy of genocidal trauma. In short, there is no context—social, historical, political—provided in these studies, apart from stating the inevitably obvious that these communities are impoverished, with high rates of unemployment, and so on.

Every study is concerned about under-reporting and about inadequate protocols for identification. The 'Calling from the Rim' report states, 'suicide among aboriginal people cannot be studied through the use of such traditional data sources as vital statistics records, since ethnic background is not recorded on the death certificates in any jurisdiction.'[424] Every study reports more attempts by females, but makes an important point that clustering is more common among females and that more females succeed in their purpose when among the cluster. Without being explicit, there is a strong message that attempted suicide by female youth is in need of serious attention.

Lester provides the best statistical summary of youth suicide, albeit with data at least two decades old. Despite regional differences, there is a sameness about many of the figures and ostensible causes. Indigenous rates of suicide are at least *10 times higher* than the national rates. Attempted suicides are vastly more prevalent.

Lester admits the unreliability of standard psychology tests when used with Native Americans. His checklist of the 'standard' underlying factors is similar to the one in common use in Australia and New Zealand: depression, hopelessness, immaturity, aggressiveness, a history of suicidal behaviour, psychiatric problems, substance abuse, parent and family conflict, lack of family support, physical and sexual abuse and recent stress. He lists sociological factors as social disintegration, family breakdown and cultural conflict (noting the latter is rarely 'listed among the precipitating causes', although it is not clear whether he is being critical of that omission or whether he, himself, believes it not to be significant).

What we can learn from this brief excursion into North America is that there may well be room for a philosophy that is neither proactive nor intrusive, one that waits patiently until one is asked to intervene, explain, or better still, to understand. Of all human behaviours, suicide may just possibly be the one that *always* needs attention, that cannot be left alone, but which needs an attention of a very different kind from the present strategies.

---

[424] 'Calling from the Rim'.

Lost connections

To date, little has been written about the Indigenous genocide-suicide relationship. There is enough scholarship to say that in the more studied genocides of Armenians and Jews there is an understanding of 'tribal memory', an osmosis of the past that invades the present, or transgenerational transmission of trauma from genocide survivors to subsequent generations. That must surely be considered when examining the factors impinging on the predilection for suicide among Indigenous societies today.

We are beginning to comprehend the long-term legacy for Armenian, Jewish, Bosnian and Rwandan communities but the impact beyond the second and third generations is not yet recognised. Genocidal memory always lingers. It diffuses to the descendants; it hovers in the background and often permeates and suffuses the foreground. It surrounds and invades life, and is found in songs, stories, legends, attitudes to food, in art, language and idiom. And while youth may not know the details, they feel and absorb the emotions. One only has to ask an eight-year-old Armenian child, anywhere, what makes him or her Armenian, or different, and the essential answer will be heard. There is, indeed, an ineluctable phenomenon that Lester calls tribal memory, an *understanding* memory rather than an *explanatory* memory. Second generation Holocaust survivors say they can actually remember events their parents experienced, as though they were themselves present. They can hear the tragedies in their parents' silences and know there are ghosts all around them.

Indigenous peoples are among the world's best oral historians and the stories of their persecution transmit down the generations. In the space of some 180 years, six generations, Aboriginal Australians have endured genocidal massacres, culturally destructive incarceration on reserves, wholesale child removals and physical relocations, and then, in the name of autonomy with the election of the Labor government in 1972, the sudden removal of all infrastructure, however authoritarian, leaving an ill-prepared population to fend for themselves in isolation. Add former Prime Minister John Howard's 'intervention' in remote communities and the re-infantilising of whole populations in the name of saving them from themselves. In short, five (rather than just two) dramatic onslaughts on a people in a very short historical timeframe. Aboriginal suicide, unknown before 1960, erupted savagely after then, a time that coincided roughly with so-called equal rights, civil rights and 'autonomy'.

Among the many flaws in the *DSM* dictionary of disorders, the disregard of grief is one of the most grievous. Grief, or bereavement, is normal, not a medical condition, or a condition that can be limited to two weeks of compassionate leave. Grief is not a fortnight's worth of tears, or a yearlong sackcloth and ashes regimen found in some religions. Grief, as in a formal funeral and an alcohol-fuelled wake, may be the norm in Western Anglo societies but in many cultures mourning rituals are intrinsic to being (and dying). Much has been written about traditional Aboriginal mourning ceremonies and their significance. The present-day absence of those rites, and their lack of substitution, is a key factor in long-term grief, unresolved and unrequited grief. The grief of the Aboriginal quartet discussed earlier was manifesting a full two years after the footballer's suicide. What is unhelpful in all of these contexts is the particularly strident Australian penchant for an often inappropriate mantra—'move on'.

In the Aboriginal case—as with other persecuted minority victims—there is collective grief, a tone and a tension that is diffused across a community. It is not particularly difficult to comprehend what the German sociologist Ferdinand Tönnies termed *gemeinschaft*, commonly a tight-knit community of people with like tastes, values, attitudes and beliefs. Western society, urban society, with its more insular, privacy-seeking nuclear family structure (*gesellschaft*) tends in such situations to grieve alone, or in tighter circles.

We have before us a remarkable catalogue of collective grief in the 1997 report, *Bringing Them Home*.[425] After nearly two decades of Aboriginal agitation for an inquiry into the Stolen Generations of Aboriginal children, the federal Labor Government appointed Sir Ronald Wilson to inquire into 'the separation' of Aboriginal and Torres Strait Islander children from their families. The word 'separation' in the Commission's terms of reference was meant to infer that removal was temporary. It never was. The whole purport of the child removal policy was that 'transfer' would be permanent. Nevertheless, the Inquiry heard 523 witness testimonies and came to the conclusion that genocide was, indeed, committed by the act of forcible transfer of children from one group to another group (as defined in Article II(e) of the UN Genocide Convention).

The essential themes of *Bringing Them Home* were grief and loss. The stolen children's testimonies were, of course, gut-wrenching—endless tales of coercion, undue cruelty, physical and mental trauma while incarcerated in 'assimilation homes', constant sexual and physical abuse, humiliation, denigration, dehumanisation, all of which often led to attempts at self-harm. I have quoted a number of testimonies in *Australia's Unthinkable Genocide*; two short testimonies here illustrate the experiences. As Rosalie Fraser described:

> The date was 13 March 1961, the place was Beverley in Western Australia. On that day my brother and sister, Terry aged eight, Stuart aged six, Karen aged four-and-a-half, Beverley aged eight months, and myself, were all made Wards of the State through action taken by the Child Welfare Department of Western Australia. The boys and girls were sent to separate institutions and Rosalie was later 'collected' by her foster mother, Mrs Kelly. When we first went to the Kellys, we had no idea where our parents were, we never saw or heard from them and we were unaware of what efforts they might be making to get us back. The

---

[425] *Bringing Them Home: Report of the National Inquiry into the Separation of Aboriginal and Torres Strait Islander Children from Their Families* (Sydney: Human Rights and Equal Opportunity Commission, 1997).

Welfare communicated not with us but with the Kellys. The separation was total; our new life was the only one we knew.[426]

Marjorie Woodrow was born in a small New South Wales country town. It was alleged that she had stole (sic) a pair of stockings. Told that her mother was dead, she was sent to Cootamundra Girls' Training Home, one of the more notorious of many such institutions: 'We were all Aboriginal, we were never called by our names. It was always 'number 108, step forward!' We had numbers sewn on our uniforms. Everyone could see that we were from the Girls' Home. We were branded just like cattle'.[427]

There is a thread that runs through child removal practices: grandmothers, daughters and daughters' daughters; grandfathers, sons and grandsons endured such institutional lives. We know of several generations of families who have that experience. It was not often that an Aboriginal youth experiences a one-off incarceration: the norm was and still is systematic and systemic.

In the aftermath of the Holocaust, the eminent neurologist and psychiatrist Viktor Frankl published *Man's Search for Meaning* (1946). He wrote about those who survived the concentration camps but who had been beaten, starved, tortured. Survivors, he wrote, had purpose in life. Another camp survivor, Italian chemist Primo Levi, also attempted to discover the difference between those who survived and those who perished, in *The Drowned and the Saved*.[428] Reading Aboriginal testimonies, one can sometimes see who were *salvati*, people determined to 'outlive' those who incarcerated and mistreated them, and those who drowned—by alcohol, drugs, violence to others or to selves. Surviving, coping and resilience are nigh impossible to pinpoint as 'characteristics', as inherent or learned responses to grim circumstances. Decades of Holocaust and genocide research has not clearly determined why people behave the way they do in the immediacy of a crisis. Frankl and Levi based their beliefs on their own experiences of genocide.

Is there any correlation between these historical experiences and depleted reserves of serotonin? Can antidepressants address such contextual acts of violence and their transgenerational impact? I think not.

---

[426] Tatz, *Australia's Unthinkable*, 118.
[427] Ibid.
[428] Primo Levi, *The Drowned and the Saved* (New York: Abacus Books, 2013).

CHAPTER 7

Apprehending the Slow Violence of Nuclear Colonialism

Art and Maralinga

Jacob G. Warren

Standing in the south-eastern Western Desert, barely north of the Nullarbor Plain, at ground zero of a nuclear test, is an uncanny experience. From 1956 to 1963, seven 'conventional' nuclear weapons explosions and hundreds of other unconventional and dirtier experiments were carried out at the South Australian site that the British and Australian testing authorities named 'Maralinga' (an appropriated Garig/k word from the other side of the continent that meant 'thunder' or 'place of thunder').[429] We stood at the spot where the weapon

---

[429] Elizabeth Tynan, 'Thunder on the Plain', in *Black Mist Burnt Country: Testing the Bomb, Maralinga and Australian Art*, ed. Jan Dirk Mittman (Upwey: Burrinja, 2016), 21–35; Kingsley Palmer, 'Dealing with the Legacy of the Past: Aborigines and Atomic Testing in South Australia', *Aboriginal History* 14, no. 1 (1990): 206; HM Cooper, *Australian Aboriginal Words and Their Meanings*, second ed. (Adelaide: South Australian Museum, 1952), 16; Crawford Pasco, 'Port Essington', in *Australian Race: Its Origin, Languages, Customs, Place of Landing in Australia, and the Routes by Which It Spread Itself Over That Continent*, ed. Edward M Curr (Melbourne: John Ferres, Government Printer, 1886), 268–9.

How to cite this book chapter:
Warren, J. G. 2020. Apprehending the Slow Violence of Nuclear Colonialism: Art and Maralinga. In: Marczak, N. and Shields, K. (eds.) *Genocide Perspectives VI: The Process and the Personal Cost of Genocide*. Pp. 129–154. Sydney: UTS ePRESS. DOI: https://doi.org/10.5130/aaf.h. License: CC BY-NC-ND.

Breakaway was detonated from a 100-foot tower on 22 October 1956. There is still a large round clearing in the lightly wooded plain and lumps of Trinitite or 'bomb glaze', a green ceramic-glass created as the intense atomic heat melted the silica in the red sand, litter the surface (Figures 1 and 2).

Figure 1: Breakaway marker with tree line in background. Photo © the author.

Figure 2: The author holding Trinitite at Breakaway site. Photo © the author.

I stood there, taking notes in the furious wind, as part of a tour group composed mostly of caravaners, hoping to learn something not present in history books nor official documents.[430] Being there, I came to appreciate the 'sensory-disorientation produced by the phenomenon of radiation', what Joseph Masco has called the 'nuclear uncanny', as well as the many types of 'invisibility' that intersect in radioactively contaminated landscapes.[431] Radiation is itself not able to be visually sensed; the colossal burial pits that contain contaminated buildings, vehicles and soil also obscure this material from view; and finally, for many decades, Maralinga and its victims have been invisible to the national historical and cultural consciousness. In a way there was nothing to see; or, more precisely, what had happened and is still happening there could not be seen: half-lives are both too slow (tens of thousands to billions of years) and too fast (nanoseconds), and contamination too small (atomic) and too large (spread across thousands of square kilometres) to be apprehended first hand as they elude and disorient the senses. What I experienced was the strange and complex material reality of an invisibly scarred and toxic region only two hours north of the much-used Eyre Highway. The radiation, the multi-millennial half-lives of trans-uranic elements, and the ecological and physiognomic impacts of these materials were all nowhere to be seen under the banality of a midday sun. At the same time these violent realities were everywhere.

The overlapping invisibilities encountered at the site illustrate the many representational issues facing cases of what Rob Nixon has termed slow violence: violence so slow (like multi-millennial half-lives) that it is invisible as a form of violence at all.[432] Simply put, slow violence describes the manifestation of power relations (economic, political, racial, class) in the environment: in the case of the appropriated desert site known as Maralinga, these power relations are those of a nuclear colonialism. The slow violence of nuclear colonialism constitutes an example of what genocide scholar Kjell Anderson has termed 'cold genocide', a genocide that unfolds in slow-motion.[433] In this essay, the sand-covered painting *Maralinga* (1992) (Figure 3) by painter Jonathan Kumintjara Brown (Pitjantjatjara, 1960–97), and the five-metre tall installation of blown-glass bush yams *Thunder Raining Poison* (2015) (Figure 4) by artist Yhonnie Scarce (Kokatha, Nukunu, 1973–) are closely analysed in order to shape an account of the slow violence of nuclear colonialism in the context of Maralinga.

---

[430] Accompanying me on this trip was Hilary Thurlow, who took photos as furiously as I took notes.
[431] Joseph Masco, *The Nuclear Borderlands: The Manhattan Project in Post-Cold War New Mexico* (Princeton: Princeton University Press, 2006), 30.
[432] Rob Nixon, *Slow Violence and the Environmentalism of the Poor* (Cambridge, Mass.: Harvard University Press, 2011).
[433] Kjell Anderson, 'Colonialism and Cold Genocide: The Case of West Papua', *Genocide Studies and Prevention: An International Journal* 9, no. 2 (2015): 9.

Figure 3: Jonathan Kumintjara Brown, Maralinga, 1992, acrylic, sand and lizard skeleton on linen, 167 x 106 cm. Ebes Collection. Reproduced courtesy of Burrinja Cultural Centre. © artist estate.

These works of art grapple with the slow and uncanny violence of a colonially induced radiotoxicity and each, in its own way, explores the impacts of the Maralinga tests on the ecology, cultural meaning and inhabitants (human and non-human) of the desert in Australia's central south. Through these works the siting of a nuclear testing facility in the desert is argued to be an (re)iteration of colonial logics that read the continent as *terra nullius* more than two centuries ago: in fact, Brown's *Maralinga* was the first of a series entitled 'Maralinga Nullius' (1992–97). The South Australian desert, as will be shown,

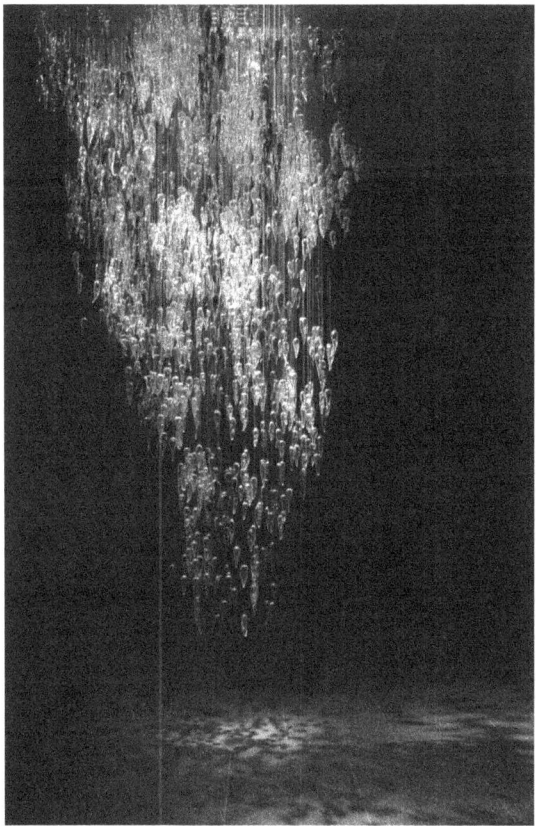

Figure 4: Yhonnie Scarce, Thunder Raining Poison, 2015, blown glass yams, dimensions variable. Installation view 'Tarnanthi', AGSA. Courtesy the artist and This is No Fantasy (Dianne Tanzer and Nicola Stein), Melbourne.

was fashioned in the ontology of the Anglo-Australian testing authorities as a barren wasteland, a *Maralinga nullius* and, as such, was deemed an appropriate void for the high-stakes experimentation of weaponised nuclear physics. The works by Brown and Scarce not only interrogate and problematise this colonial ontology and the multi-millennial violence of radioactive contamination that it delivered, but form examples of how works of art can make the invisible reality of nuclear harm visible and apprehensible. Unpacking the ways in which they do so will form the focus of this paper.

Slow violence, cold genocide and radioactive contamination

In his 2011 book *Slow Violence and the Environmentalism of the Poor*, Nixon writes in the folds of postcolonialism, environmental injustice and ecocriticism to introduce the concept of 'slow violence'.[434] The term seems oxymoronic as violence is commonly imagined as a burst, an instant, something fast and spectacular, such as machinegun firefight or an explosion. Radioactive contamination fails this imagination however, since it is 'cumulative, measured over the course of an entire life, not in individual doses. This means that radiation sickness or cancer is temporally separated from the moment of exposure'.[435] Nuclear harm lags, has gaps and is millennially ongoing. Nixon's observation of 'slowness' productively unearths precisely this different and often overlooked register of violence. Slow violence is, he writes:

> a violence that occurs gradually and out of sight, a violence of delayed destruction that is dispersed across time and space, an attritional violence that is typically not viewed as violence at all. … A violence that is neither spectacular nor instantaneous, but rather incremental and accretive, its calamitous repercussions playing out across a range of temporal scales.[436]

Forced child removal, mining induced erosion, heavy water and radioactive contamination are all examples of forms of violence that incrementally play out on the scale of years (decades, centuries, millennia), as well as the instant (the second, the minute, the present). This is not to say that explosions or gunshots do not have multi-generational impacts; instead, that within slow violence the moment of violence is considered as if the explosion lasted thousands of years, taking lives over a long period of time, rather than in an instant. This is violence reconsidered with a view to the massive timescales and global awareness produced by the Anthropocene and calamities like climate change. As such, Nixon's concept is one that addresses both human and environmental trauma, exploring damage done to 'peripheral' and 'disposable' ecologies as well as the politically, racially or economically (that is, neoliberally) irrelevant populations inhabiting them. All of this serves to decelerate understandings of the speed of violence so that, for example, genocides and ecocides that may not rhyme with traditional definitions can, first of all, become visible and named as such and, further, be addressed, analysed and remembered. Deceleration allows such events and situations that are so massively distributed in time and space to be considered as urgently as the 'immediate' manifestation of violence. The far-reaching and fundamentally interdisciplinary concept therefore allows for an adjustment to the spatiotemporal assumptions within the conceptualisation of forms of violence, such as genocide. Could the colonisation of Australia be considered an example of slow violence? Could colonisation that advances itself through policy, social and cultural assimilation, missionisation and so on, be

---

[434] Nixon, *Slow Violence*.
[435] Masco, *The Nuclear*, 32.
[436] Nixon, *Slow Violence*, 2.

understood as a slow genocide, supporting evidence of massacres and other more overt forms of violence?

Although missing the link to Nixon's theorisation of slow violence, Kjell Anderson's article 'Colonialism and Cold Genocide: The Case of West Papua' looks at precisely these questions from a genocide perspective. Anderson argues that the thinking of genocide is dominated by the model of the Holocaust, stating that 'many cases of genocide are atypical in the sense that they do not conform closely to these Holocaust-based understandings of genocide'.[437] This leads Anderson to decelerate orthodox understandings of genocide and demarcate between hot and cold genocides, wherein the latter occurs incrementally and is 'characterised by gradual destruction and limited killing' through 'systemic oppression or wilfully reckless policies ... rooted in dehumanising constructions of indigeneity'.[438] Such constructions of indigeneity and desert ecologies were, as will be shown, instrumental to the nuclear programme at Maralinga. To modify a passage on West Papua that rings true of the context of Maralinga, the policies and practices of the nuclear programme 'may not have been intentionally directed at the destruction of [Indigenous groups], yet they were undertaken with deliberate disregard for the welfare of the [group] and knowledge of the destructive consequences'.[439] The urge to reconstitute understandings of violence and genocide by Nixon and Anderson creates new perspectives that allow radioactive contamination, the subsequent inaccessibility of contaminated ancestral land and the intergenerational impacts to be reconsidered as violent and genocidal.

Reviewing *Slow Violence and the Environmentalism of the Poor*, Allison Carruth observes that slow violence expands on the tenets of structural violence by mixing in issues of large temporal and spatial protraction, and focussing on ways in which spatiotemporally 'invisible' traumas have been and can be represented.[440] With timescales so extended that they are beyond human perception or experience, Nixon argues that instances of slow violence, such as radioactive contamination with its multitude of half-lives in excess of a human lifetime, face and present representational, narrative and practical 'challenges of visibility'.[441] In the particular case of radioactive contamination, the difficulty in sensing radiation produces an uncanny experience, 'for the invisibility of radiation can make any space seem otherworldly, strange, and even dangerous'.[442] How do artists therefore render the representationally difficult and uncanny violence of radioactive contamination apprehensible?

---

[437] Anderson, 'Colonialism and Cold,' 9.
[438] Ibid. Emphasis on 'indigeneity' removed.
[439] Ibid., 13.
[440] Allison Carruth, review of *Slow Violence and the Environmentalism of the Poor*, by Rob Nixon, *MFS Modern Fiction Studies* 59, no. 4 (2013): 847.
[441] Nixon, *Slow Violence*, 5.
[442] Masco, *The Nuclear*, 33.

Unlike the news image, which thrives on mass killings and explosions, slow violence happens too slowly and over too large an area to become a spectacular image, bringing to mind my experience at Maralinga. Applying slow violence to a media studies account of art in the Anthropocene, Jussi Parikka summarises this representational upshot of Nixon's argument, wherein there is 'the necessity to apprehend this sort of slow reality … and to ask how to extend the cognitive and affective capacities of talking about what lies outside the first hand sensory, or even the time-span of human perception'.[443] How, following Nixon and Parikka, can artists, filmmakers and writers 'extend the cognitive and affective capacities' of representation, narrative and practice so that catastrophes that are hard to visualise (both in the sense of represent and imagine) begin to register in our consciousness? Through the work of Brown and Scarce I will begin to answer this question, focusing on how their art explores and renders visible the slow violence of radioactive contamination in the context of nuclear colonialism in South Australia. How, I ask, is the cosmically slow and 'invisible' presence of radioactive materials in the South Australian landscape made to appear in their work? In doing so, I necessarily address their formal and conceptual strategies for overcoming the 'challenges of visibility' presented by nuclear violence. The exploration of these questions necessarily flows through and requires an unpicking of the discourse and ontology of nuclear colonialism that both artists confront in their work.

Nuclear colonialism and the wasteland desert

The link to colonialism and environmental injustice along racial or class lines is a key factor in Nixon's assessment of the localities in which slow violence is played out: the use of socially or colonially peripheral land or labour in order to outsource, and therefore distance, toxicity and risk. In order to describe one such context of outsourced risk (the nuclear complex in and around the deserts of Nevada and its mapping over First Nations territories and reserves), Ward Churchill and Winona LaDuke introduce the notion of 'radioactive colonialism'.[444] Coalescing with the practice of internal colonialism, another practice based on the need to distance and 'minimise' risk, the authors used radioactive colonialism to describe the discourses and practices through which nuclear testing, storage and mining sites in Nevada (and, by extension, globally) were selected and came into existence. This radioactive or nuclear colonialism

---

[443] Jussi Parikka, *A Slow, Contemporary Violence: Damaged Environments of Technological Culture* (Berlin: Sternberg Press, 2016), 15–16.

[444] Ward Churchill and Winona LaDuke, 'Native North America: The Political Economy of Radioactive Colonialism,' in *The State of Native America: Genocide, Colonization, and Resistance*, ed. M. Annette Jaimes (Boston: South End Press, 1992), 241–66.

can be described as the system of imperial, governmental or corporate power that actively and disproportionately claims the lands and labour of subjugated groups of people in the name of nuclear development and production, subsequently concentrating radioactive toxicity in these regions and populations.[445] Summarised in connection with the idea of violence, Valerie Kuletz writes that:

> nuclear colonialism in the United States constitutes a peculiar sort of environmental violence deriving from its manifestation in vast desert areas, its association with the military, its execution in areas primarily occupied and used by indigenous groups and some marginalised non-indigenes, and its deployment of transuranic materials, which have complex and unique characteristics.[446]

Clearly, as Danielle Endres argues, nuclear colonialism is an instance of environmental injustice, the understanding 'that toxic waste and pollution are disproportionately linked to marginalised communities—people of colour and the poor'.[447] Slow violence is similarly tied to environmental injustice and the observation that waste sites and other toxic industry are often concentrated in economically, racially or politically subjugated communities and landscapes.[448]

---

[445] Churchill and LaDuke, 'Native North', 241–66; Valerie L Kuletz, *The Tainted Desert: Environmental Ruin in the American West* (New York: Routledge, 1998), 3–18; Danielle Endres, 'The Rhetoric of Nuclear Colonialism: Rhetorical Exclusion of American Indian Arguments in the Yucca Mountain Nuclear Waste Siting Decision', *Communication and Critical/Cultural Studies* 6, no. 1 (2009): 39–60; Elizabeth DeLoughrey, 'Radiation Ecologies and the Wars of Light', *MFS Modern Fiction Studies* 55, no. 3 (2009): 468–95; Robert Jacobs, 'Nuclear Conquistadors: Military Colonialism in Nuclear Test Site Selection During the Cold War', *Asian Journal of Peacebuilding* 1, no. 2 (2013): 157–77.

[446] Valerie Kuletz, 'Invisible Spaces, Violent Places: Cold War Nuclear and Militarized Landscapes', in *Violent Environments*, eds. Nancy Lee Peluso and Michael Watts (Ithaca: Cornell University Press, 2001), 243.

[447] Endres, 'The Rhetoric', 54; see also Robert D Bullard and Benjamin Chavis, Jr., eds., *Confronting Environmental Racism: Voices from the Grassroots* (Boston: South End Press, 1993); Richard Hofrichter, ed., *Toxic Struggles: The Theory and Practice of Environmental Justice* (Salt Lake City: University of Utah Press, 2002).

[448] The context of downwind Mormon communities in Utah should be acknowledged also, since the American government justified testing near these communities based on their pro-government and patriotic attitudes. This is a case where vehemently supportive, rather than subjugated communities, were exposed to risk because of a strong trust in the government. Since being affected by cancers and stillbirths however, this situation has

What Churchill and LaDuke point out, is that the Cold War nuclear arms race was a mid-twentieth century extension of old (or saw the creation of new) colonial projects. These were colonial projects of environmental injustice supported in turn by certain discourses and ontologies, certain imaginations of land and people, which allowed for the quick and careless production of the 'long dying' danger of radioactive contamination.[449]

In analysing the impacts of nuclear modernity in the United States upon First Nations, Kuletz has formatively linked nuclear colonialism with the West's 'wasteland discourse' of the desert.[450] For Kuletz, radioactive colonialism is supported by this lingering Anglo-European imagination of the desert as a barren wasteland—a convenient rhetoric for those seeking to distance risk and for those seeking to use and extract land that is already inhabited by others, who are rhetorically and literally made to disappear. The danger (known and potential) of atomic testing and radioactive materials required distant, 'empty' spaces outside and away from the dominant publics' view and imagination, spaces often found in desert landscapes.[451] Academic Robert Jacobs has argued that the inhabitants of these landscapes form a 'virtual nation' of victims rendered invisible by nuclear colonialism: 'their value to their colonial occupiers or national governments is that they could be dismissed as though their lives and health did not matter, without political consequence.'[452] Furthering an understanding of this dismissal of indigenous groups, Anderson, in linking colonialism and cold genocide, writes that 'colonialism seeks to exert total power over the environment of which indigenous peoples are [seen to be] a

---

been reversed. For an in-depth study of the Utah downwinders see Sarah Alisabeth Fox, *Downwind: A People's History of the Nuclear West* (Lincoln: University of Nebraska Press, 2014).

[449] Nixon, *Slow Violence*, 232.
[450] Kuletz, 'Invisible Spaces,' 13.
[451] A list of global test sites may be illuminating: the Los Alamos National Laboratory (LANL) and Jornada del Muerto desert site on Pueblo First Nations land in New Mexico; the Nevada Proving Grounds (or Nevada National Security Site) in the Shoshone First Nations deserts of Nevada; the Semipalatinsk nuclear testing site in the steppes of what is now Kazakhstan, Russia's former colony; the numerous Pacific Islands, used by the United States, France and Britain, in the blue desert of the Pacific Ocean; the Reggane region of the French colonised Algerian Sahara Desert; the corporately colonised uranium mines throughout sub-Saharan Africa; the Pokhran site in the Thar Desert of 'provincial' western India; the dried salt lake plain of Lop Nur in the north western deserts of China; the Montebello Islands off the arid coast of northern Western Australia; and the sites of Emu Field and Maralinga on Aṉangu land in the lower reaches of the Western desert of South Australia.
[452] Jacobs, 'Nuclear Conquistadors', 174.

part. ... Total possession is only possible if the indigenous inhabitants are a non-entity, either destroyed or invisible.'[453]

Within the wasteland discourse of nuclear colonialism, the desert is not only a physical site, but an uninhabited void empty of the possibility of life, let alone of anything actually living. In 1962, Ivan Southall captured such an imagination while musing on the landscape of the Woomera Long-Range Missile Base to which Maralinga was attached:

> It was the country in which they gave a man nine hours to live if he ran out of water and couldn't find shade. ... It was the country in which the sky was immense and glaring. ... It was silent country, and vast, and apparently empty, country in which only the gods could live in comfort. ... To the eyes of the stranger it was a cruel country, and worthless, baking in a blistering shimmer, with heat so intense that a man could scarcely breathe. ... It was dead country, or so it seemed. Its spirit had expired. Man had arrived too late. ... [It was] sterile land. ... It was a weird land, arid, alarming, blistered.[454]

Empty, cruel, worthless, dead, sterile, weird, masculine: Southall here emphatically combines the 'wasteland discourse' with what Roslynn D Haynes calls 'the wilderness image', an imagery that 'presents the desert as harsh, infertile and punitive'.[455] In *Wasteland: A History*, Vittoria di Palma contends that wasteland is a concept defined by absence and lack (of food, water and life) and writes that 'although wasteland may *be* many things, what it *does* is provide a space that figures as the antithesis, the absolute Other, of civilisation'.[456] Michael Marder, like di Palma, points out that in these dominant imaginings 'desert' is a doing word, it is 'an *invention*, a *creation* of emptiness in the plenitude of existence, an *introduction* of barrenness into the fecundity of being'.[457] In other words, the cultural imagination that arid landscapes are wild wastelands drives the active creation of actually uninhabitable spaces in this very image: mines, dumps, nuclear testing facilities, oil fields, toxic ecologies. 'Here it was', Southall writes again, indicatively of the instrumentalising logic of nuclear colonialism, 'one of the greatest stretches of uninhabited wasteland on earth, created by God

---

[453] Anderson, 'Colonialism and Cold', 13.
[454] Ivan Southall, *Woomera* (Sydney: Angus and Robertson, 1962), 1–2.
[455] Kuletz, 'Invisible Spaces', 13; Roslynn D Haynes, *Seeking the Centre: The Australian Desert in Literature, Art and Film* (Cambridge: Cambridge University Press, 1998), 26.
[456] Vittoria di Palma, *Wasteland: A History* (New Haven: Yale University Press, 2014), 3–4.
[457] Michael Marder, 'The Desert Is a State of Mind Cast over the Earth', *Cabinet: A Quarterly of Art and Culture* 63 (2017): 51. Emphasis added.

specifically for rockets, a magnitude of emptiness'.⁴⁵⁸ The introduction of slowly blossoming dangers and toxicities into these Othered, disposable landscapes demonstrates the performative nature of the wasteland discourse and the nuclear colonial ontology. It constitutes an example of 'perpetrator self-justification' wherein 'groups holding such ideological constructions may inculcate a self-fulfilling prophecy'.⁴⁵⁹ As Brown's *Maralinga* evidences, the concept of wasteland was a discursive mirage, an ontological concession that allowed the British and Australian testing authorities to plunge the landscape of Maralinga into the multi-millennial rhythms of slow violence while maintaining claims of safety.

Against the mirage of the desert as wasteland

Maralinga by Stolen Generations artist Jonathan Kumintjara Brown is just under two metres tall and over a metre wide, and was the first sand-covered work in what became the 'Maralinga Nullius' series (1992–97). In this work the majority of a dot-style painting is covered over by a light caramel body of sand adhered to the surface, and in the near centre of the work is affixed the skeleton of a lizard.⁴⁶⁰ Forcibly removed from his birth parents while only weeks old, Brown returned in 1984 to the diasporic mission of Yalata where he was born, a mission 200 km south of Maralinga that began as a refugee camp in 1952 after the Ooldea Mission 40 km away from the future test site was closed.⁴⁶¹ Having been introduced into the community over a number of months and years, Brown was taken out to visit his ancestral land, his grandfather's Country: the region that the British had named Maralinga. For the sand covering in *Maralinga*, Brown used the potentially contaminated and ancestrally charged sand of this land as a material for the first time, bringing the material reality of

---

[458] Southall, *Woomera*, 3.
[459] Anderson, 'Colonialism and Cold', 11; Ibid., 18.
[460] This gesture of obscuring the dotted painting is unlike the formal innovation in some Aboriginal communities of painting over sacred designs, a solution devised for the problem of putting down and communicating, but also protecting, secret knowledge. As such, it is a unique visual technique within the idiom of Western Desert painting.
[461] Helen Chryssides, 'Earthly Treasures: Paintings Has Brought Jonathan Kumintjara Brown Back to His People, His Culture and His Ancestral Land', *Bulletin*, May 7, 1996, 74–75; Maggie Brady and Kingsley Palmer, 'Dependency and Assertiveness: Three Waves of Christianity Among Pitjantjatjara People at Ooldea and Yalata', in *Aboriginal Australians and Christian Missions: Ethnographic and Historical Studies*, eds. Tony Swain and Deborah Bird Rose (Bedford Park: Australian Association for the Study of Religions, 1988), 236–49.

the ecological and spiritual 'poison' of slowly decaying radionuclides into his paintings. The skeleton of the lizard attached to the painting's surface was also possibly collected on Aṉangu (Pitjantjatjara) Country and perhaps even from around Maralinga itself.[462]

The coarsely textured surface of the painting conceals the majority of a dotted landscape that depicts culturally and spiritually significant sites of water, food and paths of ancestral beings on Brown's Country. The exposed concentric roundels that represent these sites and map the 'geospiritual' cartography of the region sit in a sea of sand in the middle of each perimeter, and in the corners and centre of the painting.[463] The partial and implied presence of lines that connect each of these roundels, as well as concentric patterns inside this grid, is suggested by an additional area of uncovered painting in the top right. Brown shows just enough of this painting beneath the sand to suggest that a vast majority of it has been obscured: to render visible the fact that something has been made invisible. By effacing the dotted painting as such, Brown produces a vision of environmental and cultural damage. He figures the abstract and non-spectacular violence of a radioactively contaminated space: something that is hard to experience even if standing at ground zero. The slow violence of radioactive contamination, it may be argued, is also presented in *Maralinga* in such a way that mirrors Brown's personal distancing from this land and culture by the assimilationist policy of forcible child removal. What Brown's covering technique achieves is the figuring of the shared experience of nuclear colonialism's diasporic virtual nation: the contamination of land, its inaccessibility, the invisibility of inhabitant populations, the increase in strange and unsure medical diagnoses and cultural denial (both the denial of culture and a bureaucratic culture of denial).

To reinforce the experience of a geospiritual catastrophe in the painting, Brown has attached the skeleton of a lizard to the lower right of the central roundel. The fragile skeleton, like the sand, operates as a material metaphor for the ecological violence of radioactive contamination, standing in for all animal life in this desert ecology that has been killed, maimed or genetically impacted. Lizards are a common sight in the region and in addition to providing a food source, the diversity of lizard species—from thorny devils and bicycle lizards to goannas and blue tongues—also feature as ancestral figures in major *tjukurpa*

---

[462] Possible lizards common to the area that fit this skeletal model are members of the *Ctenophorus* genus, specifically the Bicycle Lizard (*Ctenophorus Cristatus*); however, the remains are inconclusive and appear closer to the *Draco* genus of flying lizards (hence the very long rib bones) endemic to South East Asia. Brown may have come across this skeleton while working in Melbourne.

[463] The term geospiritual wonderfully captures the way in which ecology, geology, culture and spirituality intertwine in indigenous cosmologies. See Masco, *The Nuclear*, 108.

(stories, lore) for the south-eastern Pitjantjatjara. Examples include *Miniri*, the thorny devil (that Brown painted regularly as it relates to his grandfather's Country and to male initiation), and *Nintaka* and *Ninjuri*, a perentie lizard and black goanna respectively, whom are central to a major *tjukurpa* significant to the majority of Western desert groups, not only southern Aṉangu.[464] *Maralinga*'s skeleton, in chorus with the sand, renders the biological, ecological and cultural violence of nuclear contamination palpable, providing a haptic sense of the physical reality of the tests' impacts on this region that overcomes the challenges of visibility facing this context of colonial violence. A reading of slow violence enters here since, on the one hand, the object-painting figures the physical contamination and danger of the area's radioactive legacy and, on the other hand, *Maralinga* also figures the cultural poisoning of this land. In other words, this is violence wrought on both material and spiritual ecologies where the slow death of animal food sources hinders physical inhabitation of these spaces, and where these deaths likewise disturb the land's cultural and spiritual health, aligning with the push of missionaries at Ooldea and then Yalata to nix the '"satanic" influences of Aboriginal religion'.[465]

If the lizard bones reference the region's reptiles in general, then they may be understood as pointing to the important role the animals play in the diet of those humans and predatory animals living in such an ecology. The figured death of the lizard in *Maralinga* therefore underscores the slow violence of an interruption to food sources vital for Aboriginal people and other larger predators in the ecology, such as birds of prey or game marsupials. Thinking through this ecological violence also prompts a consideration of the multi-generational mutations and genetic damage that the reptiles and other animals of the contaminated landscape face. Most animals have faster generations than humans, speeding up the appearance of the mutagenic effects of radioactive exposure. Brown's lizard skeleton is therefore not just death now or in the past, but signals a slower, mutagenic violence that plays out on the scales of the cell and the gene. It suggests the denial of a food source at the time of the tests, at the time of Brown's painting and also into the future.

Spiritually as well as physically, *Maralinga* suggests that this land was also poisoned. As Maralinga tour guide Robin Matthews, the husband of an Aṉangu traditional owner, recounted to our tour group, Aṉangu avoid the site. Today's Aṉangu know that the spirits of missing people, having not been laid to rest in the correct manner, wander the former Prohibited Area, a sighting of one of these spectres bringing terrible misfortune. Materially and spiritually haunted, this land has also been poisoned by decades of forced ritual neglect. In other words, having been relocated 200 kilometres south and being barred access to their land and important sites, Aṉangu were largely blocked from carrying out

---

[464] Charles P Mountford, *Nomads of the Australian Desert* (Adelaide: Rigby Limited, 1976), 484–506, 269–309.

[465] Brady and Palmer, 'Dependency and Assertiveness', 238.

maintenance or performing site-specific rituals.⁴⁶⁶ In this way, the disconnection of the roundels (sites) in *Maralinga*, as well as the obscuring of the tapestry of their networked inter-relation, communicates the poisoning and interruption of this geospiritual ecology. Like assimilationist policies, the poisoning of certain areas and the denial of access worked to slowly obscure some connections to land. The presence of the roundels does, however, imply that regeneration and reconnection are possible (perhaps always-already happening). Yet the focus of *Maralinga* is to highlight these forms of violence and make the impacts of nuclear colonialism both palpable and visible. In addition, Brown also brings to the surface the underlying ontology of nuclear colonialism that mirrors the doctrine of *terra nullius* used by the British to claim Australia: that deserts are wastelands and, as such, are barren, empty and useless.

Maralinga nullius

Brown's *Maralinga* operates against the wasteland discourse that informs the Anglo-European ontology of desert landscapes. As philosopher Elizabeth A. Povinelli argues, 'the Desert', ontologically, 'is the space where life was, is not now, but could be if knowledges, techniques, and resources were properly managed'.⁴⁶⁷ But rather than try to make the barren landscape productive, it was instrumentalised precisely for its ontological emptiness of life and being. *Maralinga* counters the discursive and figural trope of the 'dead' heart of Australia—fuelled by the imagination of deserts as lifeless, uninhabited and useless—while interrogating the implications that such discourse has for understandings of the people who do inhabit them. Brown's compositional gestures insist that the desert was in fact alive and that it was spiritually and ecologically abundant. What Brown's effacing gesture performs then is the colonial opening of a void in 'the fecundity of being', made possible by the wasteland discourse and its ontological blindness to desert life.⁴⁶⁸ Emphatically underscoring how entrenched this logic was at the time is the fact that only one person, a native

---

⁴⁶⁶ Brady and Palmer, however, have respectively demonstrated that ritual and ceremony did not cease completely and that work-arounds for the spatial restraints were devised. These new practices were not developed for all ceremonies and rituals, some being site-specific. See Palmer, 'Dealing with', 197–207; Maggie Brady, 'The Politics of Space and Mobility: Controlling the Ooldea/Yalata Aborigines, 1952–1982', *Aboriginal History* 23 (1999): 1–14; Maggie Brady, 'Leaving the Spinifex: The Impact of Rations, Missions, and the Atomic Tests on the Southern Pitjantjatjara', *Records of the South Australian Museum* 20 (1987): 35–45.

⁴⁶⁷ Elizabeth A. Povinelli, *Geontologies: A Requiem to Late Liberalism* (Durham: Duke University Press, 2016), 16.

⁴⁶⁸ Marder, 'The Desert', 51.

Figure 5: Griffith Taylor's 1946 depiction of 'Empty Australia'. Drawn from Lesley Head, 'Zones and Strata, or How Aborigines Became Living Fossils', in *Second Nature: The History and Implications of Australia as Aboriginal Landscape* (Syracuse, NY: Syracuse University Press, 2000), 47.

patrol officer named Walter MacDougall, was employed to patrol the hundreds of thousands of square kilometres around the base to locate, notify and deter (or relocate) Aboriginal groups.[469] The task was impossible and the position a token one, illustrating an assumption that hardly any resources needed to be dedicated to it because the desert was empty (Figure 5).

When MacDougall reported to testing authorities about the dangers to Aboriginal people in the area and the impossibility of his task, he was reprimanded for 'apparently placing the affairs of a handful of natives above those of the British Commonwealth of Nations'.[470] As oral histories (most recently captured by Lynette Wallworth and Nyarri Nyarri Morgan's *Collisions* (2016)) and evidence given to the *Royal Commission into British Nuclear Tests in Australia* (1984–85) demonstrate, 'throughout the time Maralinga was operational, Aboriginal

---

[469] For many other examples that confirm this same point, see Frank Walker, *Maralinga: The Chilling Exposé of Our Secret Nuclear Shame and Betrayal of Our Troops and Country* (Sydney: Hachette, 2014), 148–63.

[470] William Alan Stewart Butement quoted in JR McClelland, Jill Fitch, and William Jonas, *The Report of the Royal Commission into British Nuclear Tests in Australia* (Canberra: Australian Government Publishing Service, 1985), 1: 308–309, section 8.4.38.

people still traversed the lands'.[471] Brown's *Maralinga* brings attention to the invisibility that Aboriginal people and their forms of life faced under this nuclear colonialism. The gesture of covering and the lizard skeleton highlights that the wasteland discourse operated to justify and secure the desert black hole within which nuclear experiments could be conducted with no consequence and, as Prime Minister Robert Menzies assured the public at the time, with 'no conceivable injury to life, limb or property'.[472]

In *Maralinga* the slow ecological and cultural violence of nuclear colonialism at Maralinga is rendered through a process of obscuring, a material and processual allegory of the invisibility of radioactive contamination and Aboriginal life within the desert site. The painting attests to the enduring presence of life at and around the nuclear outpost since even though the majority of the canvas is covered, not all is lost. Ecological, cultural and human life, the painting suggests, continues to persevere, although in a damaged, injured form. Rather than Mad Max-esque post-apocalyptic representations of his damaged desert Country, Brown figures the material (and spiritual) reality of a landscape upon and within which the signs of slow violence have begun and will continue to appear.

From ground zero to downwind

In Yhonnie Scarce's *Thunder Raining Poison* (2015) the slow and uncanny violence of radiation is explored through Maralinga's legacy of loosely mitigated and largely unmonitored fallout. The large-scale installation is a five metre tall 'cloud' composed of 2000 hand-blown glass bush yams that are suspended from the ceiling. It points to the scale and impacts of the fallout from the tests in South Australia (nine in total, including two at Emu Field in 1953), and explores the uncanny reality of living downwind, in the path of this fallout. I argue that Scarce employs 'fallout' as a vector of nuclear colonialism and the disregard testing authorities had for the safety of downwind, predominantly Aboriginal communities. The two thousand vitreous yams that make up *Thunder Raining Poison* are modelled off the long yam found in Scarce's Kokatha Country, land only a few hundred kilometres downwind of Maralinga that was exposed to fallout on numerous occasions. The glass yams, and the overall installation they shape, have been used by Scarce to surmount the representational hurdles that the slow and uncanny violence of radioactive colonialism presents.

Lit from above, *Thunder Raining Poison* glistens and shines radiantly, the contours and shapes of the glass tubers catching the light and throwing dramatic

---

[471] Tynan, 'Thunder on', 27.
[472] Robert Menzies in Question Time, Hansard, House of Representatives, October 21, 1953.

shadows on surrounding surfaces.⁴⁷³ In producing the multitude glass forms for the installation, Scarce worked with glass-blowing assistants from Adelaide's Jam Factory. Each one of the 2,000 hand-blown glass yams is therefore unique, but all share a roughly conical shape based on the top-heavy organic forms that the root vegetable takes as it burrows through sandy and rocky soil. In the work, the thicker end of each yam faces the ceiling that it is suspended from by nylon thread, while the thinner, pointed tip faces the ground, giving the overall installation a sense of both rising and falling movement. Does it resemble an atomic dust cloud rising up and expanding into the atmosphere above? Or, as the downward facing tips of the yams sculpturally suggest, is it the start of a contaminated rain falling to the ground below? The work allows, if not welcomes, both readings, since the rising and falling of radioactive debris (ash, dust, rain, bomb fragments and particulate matter) into and out of the atmosphere as clouds and rain, were both atmospheric realities through which radioactive particles spread across Australia, 'infecting' yam systems, land and water downwind.

The overall form of *Thunder Raining Poison*, despite being five metres tall and comprising 2,000 suspended objects (and 2,000 lengths of unconcealed supportive nylon), is nonetheless punctuated by gaps and space that contribute to a sense of expansive volume. The atmospheric quality created by the illusive emptiness of the work is supported by the many clear glass yams throughout its height that allow sight to pass through to the other side. While there are some dense clusters of yams, suggestive of cancer clusters that appeared in downwind communities in the months and years following the nuclear testing, *Thunder Raining Poison* is nonetheless almost transparent and is deceptively wisp like. The illusion of empty expanse created by the installation serves to highlight both the massive extent of fallout from the South Australian tests (Emu Field and Maralinga both being in the path of a prevailing westerly that carried fallout thousands of kilometres away), and the simultaneous everywhere-nowhere, that is, the 'nonlocalisable' and 'invisible' reality of radiation.⁴⁷⁴ It too is unseen and expansive.

Thunder Raining Poison's title came to Scarce while standing at ground zero of an explosion whose fallout was particularly widespread, the same ground zero described at the beginning of this essay. Breakaway was the fourth round of Operation Buffalo, a series of tests that alternately violated safe firing conditions or exceeded radiation levels deemed to be safe even at the time, when safe levels were far higher than what they are today. The test (like the first round, One Tree) was a tower blast and was therefore 'expected to have a higher level

---

⁴⁷³ The work was produced for the inaugural 'Tarnanthi' exhibition at the Art Gallery of South Australia in 2015, and has since appeared in 'Defying Empire: 3ʳᵈ National Indigenous Art Triennial' at the National Gallery of Victoria in 2017.

⁴⁷⁴ Masco, *The Nuclear*, 31.

of fallout' than the other two tests in the series.[475] This prediction was indeed the case as the dispersed cloud eventually stretched all the way from Darwin, in the country's north, to Newcastle, on the south-east coast, with radioactive rain being recorded at Oodnadatta (Kokatha Country), and Brisbane, in Queensland, days after the detonation.[476] The cloud's path also overlapped with those of previous tests, contravening a 'no overlap condition for firing' aimed at limiting the region's radioactive exposure.[477] The thunderous nuclear tests were raining poison, literally, across Australia (Figure 6).

Writing on how the British and Australian testing authorities approached fallout, Heather Goodall (who also played a role in the 1985 *Royal Commission into British Nuclear Tests in Australia*) has concluded that 'the early tests [Montebello Islands and Emu Field] were marked by a refusal to investigate, survey and monitor, whether in relation to human health or the spread of toxic fallout and residues, and later [at Maralinga] monitoring was more for publicity purposes than for any real safety effect'.[478] Goodall's (and the Royal Commission's) conclusion of negligence was not, however, the first time serious doubts about the safety of the test were raised. At the time of the tests an independent fallout monitoring programme conducted by The Commonwealth Scientific and Industrial Research Organisation (CSIRO) scientist Hedley Marston, who collected sheep thyroids from farmers all over Australia to test for radioactive isotopes of Iodine, and also collected air samples from Adelaide, reached similar conclusions. Both of Marston's studies produced results that dramatically undermined the information the testing authorities were sharing with the Australian government, let alone providing to the media.[479]

In repeating the yam form to build the nuclear weather of *Thunder Raining Poison*, Scarce maps the uncertain and winding passage of radioactive toxicity from ground zero (the yam), into the atmosphere (the cloud), back to the ground (through rain), into plants (the yam again), animals and water and, finally—we might deduce—into human bodies, blood streams and genetic code through ingestion. The multiple and ambiguous forms employed in *Thunder Raining Poison* (cloud, rain, yam) contribute to a gallery experience of the flow of irradiating materials between the fission weapons, the contaminated landscape, fallout atmospheres and the human body. In mapping these material

---

[475] McClelland, Fitch, and Jonas, *The Report*, 1: 294, section 8.3.21.
[476] Ibid., 1: 297, section 8.3.26, section 8.3.27.
[477] Ibid., 1: 297, section 8.3.25.
[478] Heather Goodall, 'Colonialism and Catastrophe: Contested Memories of Nuclear Testing and Measles Epidemics at Ernabella', in *Memory and History in Twentieth-Century Australia*, eds. Kate Darian-Smith and Paula Hamilton (Melbourne: Oxford University Press, 1994), 59.
[479] For a full account of the Hedley Marston saga and his reports, see Roger Cross, *Fallout: Hedley Marston and the British Bomb Tests in Australia* (Kent Town: Wakefield Press, 2001).

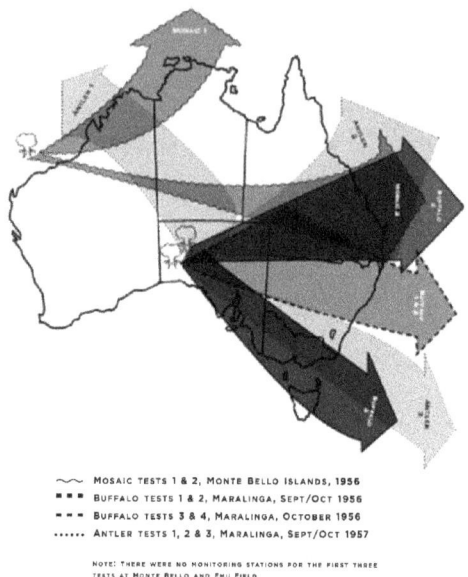

Figure 6: Direction of Fallout reproduced from Frank Walker, *Maralinga: The Chilling Exposé of Our Secret Nuclear Shame and Betrayal of Our Troops and Country* (Sydney, NSW: Hachette, 2014). © Frank Walker and Hachette.

flows, the suspended installation brings attention to the violent realities produced by the testing authorities' lack of any sense of consequence, highlighting the extent to which this colonised wasteland was exploited and remade as such. In doing so, it also charts the nuclear uncanny, since it renders tactile and visible the fact that 'radiation traverses space in ways that can make the air, earth, and water seem suspect, even dangerous, though no sensory evidence is at hand'.[480] This lack of sensory evidence recalls the challenges of visibility facing instances of slow violence: how can we know that eating a yam, for example, is dangerous or not if there is no sensory evidence, where instead, evidence may be cancer, still births, mutations or other non-instantaneous manifestations. The installation as a whole, and Scarce's yams in particular, are representations of these slippery dangers and as such become forms of material evidence that experientially mark the impacts and danger of the violent nuclear weather from Maralinga on the land and people of South Australia, and Australia more broadly. Like Brown's sand and lizard skeleton, the yam, the cloud and the rain are non-human witnesses of the slow and ambiguous spread of contaminating, mutating and potentially deadly radiation. By activating these forms and figuring fallout as a harbinger of colonial, even genocidal, violence, the installation

---

[480] Masco, *The Nuclear*, 32.

succeeds in representing radioactive contamination and making the nuclear colonisation of South Australia palpable and apprehensible. Scarce, further, achieves this powerful figuring in another way.

The bush yam

In *Thunder Raining Poison* (as in Scarce's practice more broadly), bush foods are used as vessels of meaning, referring to her Country and cultural heritage (the custodial knowledge of the bush yam belonging to her maternal grandfather) and at other times, standing in for Aboriginal bodies. They are important in a work such as *Thunder Raining Poison* because as a culturally significant plant and food source the yams not only suggest the slow and silent irradiation of the ecosystem and of human bodies that interacted with it, but also signal the colonial violence towards Aboriginal practices and forms of life. Each of the few thousand yams is unique, individualised, and as such generates a soft anthropomorphism wherein the yams became stand ins for individuals affected by the cell-altering dangers of radiation. Perhaps to the reading of the installation's form as a cloud or rain could be added the argument that these are the rising ghosts of the deceased victims (Aboriginal and non-Aboriginal) of Maralinga's radiotoxicity. As Marston's independent fallout data indicated, the nuclear tests were resulting in the large-scale introduction of irradiated debris into the atmosphere and environment (including crop growing and farming land). Especially on Kokatha Country, this unknown and uncertain irradiation of the ground would have compromised exposed food sources such as the yam and other bush foods like the bush banana or quandong. The vitreous surrogates of these quietly toxic yams in *Thunder Raining Poison* therefore serve as material and forensic evidence against the official mandates of the nuclear programme and its stubborn insistence that the tests were being conducted safely and with no prospect of harm. The slow, multigenerational and cumulative violence that produces nuclear harm is notoriously difficult to prove (as those ex-servicemen and downwinders who have attempted to gain compensation have discovered), so Scarce's cultural-ecological narrative, told through glass yams and the wisp-like mass they produce, serves as evidence against the culture of denial of 'any harm whatsoever' that still persists today. The installation of a cloud of these yams becomes an affective negation of the Safety Committee's self-defined task 'to ensure that the activity which does reach the ground outside the specified danger areas shall be at a level so low that it will not harm people exposed to it, or have any economic effect on plant and animal life'.[481]

Deepening our understanding of the use of the yam form in *Thunder Raining Poison* is an examination of the rhetoric and parameters of safety at the time of

---

[481] McClelland, Fitch, and Jonas, *The Report*, 1: 281, section 8.3.3.

the tests. One of the many criticisms levelled against the Atomic Weapons Tests Safety Committee (AWTSC), which was 'responsible for monitoring the British testing programme to ensure that the safety of the Australian environment and population were not jeopardised', was that they did not take into consideration exposure to internal radiation and simply focussed on external radiation, which is orders of magnitudes less dangerous, as a measure of fallout.[482] In their definitional blindness to Aboriginal agricultural practices the Safety Committee conveniently ignored the dangers of 'living close to the earth, hunting local animals, eating plants growing wild and walking barefoot'.[483] As Marston reported at the time:

> The grave danger of intensive internal irradiation resulting from the accumulation of long-lived isotope within certain tissues of the bodies of individuals subsisting on foodstuffs produced on the contaminated area *cannot be dispelled*. ... The situation is not one that may be pushed aside by denials of 'any danger whatsoever'.[484]

The continuing on in the face of this knowledge constituted an act of deliberately negligent and slow violence that would play out over decades and centuries to come, not only for those 'individuals subsisting on foodstuffs produced on the contaminated area' such as Aboriginal communities, but the broader population of Australia as well.

To visually emphasise the dangers that fallout posed to downwind communities, a portion of *Thunder Raining Poison*'s glass yams have been coloured in combinations of a sickly green and an opaque black that in more diluted areas appears purple. Metaphorically, each colour activates associations of sickness, contamination, burns, bruising and death. Materially, the colours reference Trinitite, the green (Maralinga) and black (Emu Field) atomic glass that is usually created at sandy nuclear test sites, as well as referencing the 'black mist', a fallout event that coated the small, predominantly Aboriginal community of Wallatina with a black, metallic smelling and oily mixture of radioactive debris.[485] In their colouration, the yams of *Thunder Raining Poison* become silent records of nuclear damage wrought by fallout events. Their shapes still resemble unaffected tubers, however the differing inflections of green, black

---

[482] PN Grabosky, *Wayward Governance: Illegality and Its Control in the Public Sector* (Canberra: Australian Institute of Criminology, 1989), 242.

[483] Tynan, 'Thunder on', 24.

[484] Hedley Marston cited in Roger Cross, *Fallout: Hedley Marston and the British Bomb Tests in Australia* (Kent Town: Wakefield Press, 2001), 103.

[485] The colour of Trinitite is determined by the mineral composition of the earth and sand at a given test site. Trinitite produced by the weapons at Emu Field is black because of a high iron content. It is, however, predominantly green.

and occasionally purple tones communicate that downwind yams bear the mark of irradiation. While being shaped and blown, the almost-molten glass is dipped and rolled in glass pigments, which melt into the form. Their colouring in this way creates a non-uniform finish, often appearing as if the sickly tones are flowing inside or as if they are in the process of swallowing the glass yam. With this method the glass yams visually capture the slow process of radiotoxic becoming. Nuclear contamination, mutation and danger are figured as processes of time and remain in process, happening now (still) at the genetic level of the colonially contaminated ecology.

'The colonisation of the future'

In their formal and metaphorical activation of this narrative of contamination, Scarce's glass yams visualise what Joseph Masco has called a 'mutant ecology'.[486] Mutation, as Masco defines it, describes changes, 'whether through improvement, injury or genetic noise' at 'biosocial, political, and ethnographic' levels.[487] The biosocial, political and ethnographic mutations brought about by the nuclear colonisation of Maralinga (and, in fact, any site involved in the nuclear process), saw 'the production of nuclear natures'.[488] Masco argues that nuclear natures and mutant ecologies are not only environmental, but since 'nuclear science has transformed human culture at the cellular level … producing new kinds of ecologies, bodies, and social orders', then they represent a locality, body or society that has, is, will or may undergo social, ecological and physical mutation because of the presence of nuclear material.[489] Atomic diaspora, mysterious unseasonal clouds, the cancers and stillbirths that plagued Aboriginal and non-Aboriginal families alike, and the defamiliarisation of Country: these were the new uncanny facts of life in the mutant ecology borne out of atomic testing in South Australia. What Scarce's yams tune into is the uncanny reality of South Australia's nuclear nature, a colonised landscape wherein the 'dangerous vulnerability of the human sensorium to an uncertain and uncertainly haunted universe' is revealed.[490] Scarce's vitreous bush food forms demonstrate a subtle and serious notion of nuclear violence and danger. Simply collecting foodstuffs, a once normal part of life in these arid ecologies, becomes a potentially dangerous and risky practice haunted by the invisible force of radiation. Scarce's contaminated yams capture the subtlety of experiences of radioactively contaminated spaces as food and water sources silently and without warning became irradiated, with daily practice going on,

---

[486] Masco, *The Nuclear*, 298.
[487] Ibid., 301, 326.
[488] Ibid., 293.
[489] Ibid., 301, 306.
[490] Ibid., 29.

unknowingly, as usual. The violence signalled by the yams of *Thunder Raining Poison* is slow, subtle and everyday. While the installation's ambiguous cloud form does partially vibrate on the register of the spectacular because of an association with the image of the mushroom cloud, other, far slower and more widespread considerations of violence are also (perhaps more strongly) signalled.

In Masco's unpacking of the concept of mutation, he describes its temporal dimension: it 'implies ... a complex coding of time (both past and future); it assumes change, but it does not from the outset judge either the temporal scale or the type of change that will take place. It also marks a transformation that is reproduced generationally, making mutation a specific kind of break with the past that reinvents the future'.[491] In *Thunder Raining Poison*, Scarce plots the coordinates of the new nuclear nature imposed upon those living within contaminated and slowly violent landscapes. The nuclear colonisation of Maralinga is therefore not simply an historical event, but an unfolding moment whose temporal scales reach into the billions of years. Masco has gracefully described this situation as a 'multimillenial colonisation of the future', the biological, cultural and ecological ramifications of which are still playing out and will continue to do so.[492] Radioactively contaminated ecologies, Masco urges, therefore require 'a different temporal analytic', and as I have made clear through the work of Brown and Scarce, these ecologies also prompt one to consider different registers of violence and to reconsider the manifestation of colonialism and genocide in Australia.[493] The nuclear colonisation of Maralinga and the subsequent contamination of land and people must therefore be recognised—as this essay has done—through the 'different temporal analytics' of slow violence and cold genocide. Until these other, decelerated impacts of colonisation in Australia are more widely recognised and acknowledged, the violence will continue, slowly and silently.

Conclusion

Jonathan Kumintjara Brown's *Maralinga* and Yhonnie Scarce's *Thunder Raining Poison* both explore and make visible the slow and subtle violence of a colonially delivered radioactive contamination, whether at ground zero or downwind. Both works emphasise ecological, cultural and biological damage, and in doing so invite further reflection on the spatiotemporal scales of nuclear violence in the arid lands of South Australia. They particularly figure the impacts that nuclear contamination and the irradiation of land have had on Aboriginal

---

[491] Masco, *The Nuclear*, 301.
[492] Ibid.
[493] Ibid.

people and their connection to these now toxic ecologies. Brown's sand, as a material, brings the ancestrally and radioactively charged reality of the landscape into the gallery, with the effacing gesture supporting a vision of a poisoned geospiritual region. The skeleton was likewise examined as expanding our consideration to the broader cultural-ecological impacts of the tests. In harmony, the vitreous yam objects of *Thunder Raining Poison* were thoroughly argued to present material evidence against claims of safety and 'no harm whatsoever' arising from the tests. Both works of art demonstrate conceptual and formal innovations that 'expand our affective and narrative capacities' for apprehending and representing the 'invisible' and slow traumas that nuclear testing delivers into bodies and landscapes.[494] The racist blindness towards Aboriginal people in this ontologically uninhabited region were also explored, demonstrating that in the mid-twentieth century Australia's 'empty' arid areas were colonised anew under the guise of nuclear weapons development. The land and lives of Aboriginal people and the lives of servicemen and contracted civilians who worked at Maralinga, as well Australians more broadly, were sacrificed to the slow rhythms of nuclear matter.[495] The slow violence of radioactive contamination presents, in Masco's words, a colonisation of the future, a colonisation whose genocidal violence Brown and Scarce have rendered visible through their work.

---

[494] Parikka, *A Slow*, 16.

[495] It must be noted that the Australian servicemen (no women were allowed at the site) who served at Maralinga have not had their time there recognised as military service by the Australian Government or Military. Many of these nuclear veterans died from unexplained cancers in their 20s, 30s and 40s as a result of the work they were ordered to do by controlling British regiments. For more on Australian nuclear servicemen and their treatment at Maralinga see Frank Walker, *Maralinga: The Chilling Exposé of Our Secret Nuclear Shame and Betrayal of Our Troops and Country* (Sydney: Hachette, 2014), 106–29; and Paul Brown, 'Maralinga: Theatre from a Place of War', in *Unstable Ground: Performance and the Politics of Place*, ed. Gay McAuley (Brussels: P.I.E. Peter Lang, 2006), 205–26.

CHAPTER 8

The 2017 Myall Creek Massacre Commemoration Speech

Mark Tedeschi AM QC

The Myall Creek massacre on 10 June 1838, that resulted in the horrific murder of 28 men, women and children of the Weraerai tribe of the Kamilaroi nation, has come to represent the multitude of massacres of Indigenous people that occurred all over Australia during a period of more than 120 years. This is because we know more today about the murders at Myall Creek than any of the hundreds of other massacres. We know so much today about this one largely because of the investigation and two trials of the perpetrators conducted in 1838.

The man who successfully prosecuted the two trials of those responsible for the massacre was the then Attorney-General of New South Wales, John Hubert Plunkett. It was, in my view, the greatest challenge of his long career and one of his greatest achievements. Unusually for the times, two trials arose from the massacre, and both provoked enormous controversy and hostility throughout the colony towards the prosecutor. The powerful forces of the landowning settlers were pitted against Plunkett and caused him endless difficulties. Plunkett's approach to these prosecutions was innovative and bold in equal measure. He faced massive difficulties in overcoming bigotry and vested interests. Despite the fact that there had been an eyewitness to the massacre—the Indigenous stationhand Yintayintin (known as Davy)—the law at that time prevented

How to cite this book chapter:
Tedeschi, M, AM QC. 2020. The 2017 Myall Creek Massacre Commemoration Speech. In: Marczak, N. and Shields, K. (eds.) *Genocide Perspectives VI: The Process and the Personal Cost of Genocide*. Pp. 155–158. Sydney: UTS ePRESS. DOI: https://doi.org/10.5130/aaf.i. License: CC BY-NC-ND.

any Aboriginal person from giving evidence in court. Plunkett spent the next 20 years trying to remedy this deficiency—without success. New South Wales was, in fact, one of the last jurisdictions in Australia to allow Aboriginal people to give evidence in court.

It is instructive to look closely at the long-term effects of the 1838 Myall Creek murder trials. They marked one of the few times in the history of Aboriginal displacement that Europeans were punished for the murder of Aboriginal Australians. Those trials stand as an early statement of principle that Australian courts had at least the capacity to operate without fear or favour and to treat all people, including those on the margins of white society, equally. That is not to say that the law always operated in this way, or even that it frequently did during the colonial period; but on the occasion of the Myall Creek murder trials it certainly did. Plunkett's advocacy and tactics at the second trial succeeded in persuading a jury of 12 white, free men to convict seven white defendants for the brutal slaying of an Aboriginal child, who represented the 28 members of that infant's kinship group that had been murdered. That Plunkett was able to do this in the face of almost universal hostility to the prosecution was nothing short of miraculous. It would never happen again during the colonial period, or even after the federation of the Australian States in 1901.

Tribute should also be paid to others who did the right thing in 1838: George Anderson, the convict hut keeper on Myall Creek Station, who attempted to convince the perpetrators not to commit the atrocity, and who later bravely gave evidence against them. Yintayintin (Davy) was the Aboriginal station worker on Myall Creek Station who at great risk to himself followed the perpetrators at a distance while hidden in the bush and personally witnessed the murders, so that he could report back to George Anderson. William Hobbs was the station manager on Myall Creek Station who was so repulsed by what had happened in his absence that he reported the atrocity in writing to the Governor, and in retaliation was then sacked by his employer, landowner Henry Dangar. Police Magistrate Captain Edward Denny Day conducted an exemplary investigation of the incident and managed to arrest and charge 11 of the 12 perpetrators, and then to bring them to Sydney for trial. The trial judge at the second trial, Justice William Westbrooke Burton, reinforced to the jury the sanctity of all life and set the tone for a fair hearing. And the 12 white jurors in the second trial who were brave enough to convict the seven defendants in the face of extreme public hostility; and especially juror William Knight, who spoke up to correct the initial, incorrect verdict of acquittal, so that convictions were eventually recorded.

There is no doubt that the trials failed to stop the attempts to annihilate Aboriginal people. The hanging of seven of the Myall Creek murderers merely served to drive future perpetrators underground, so that more surreptitious means, such as poisonings, were used instead of brutal, bloody slayings by sword or bullet, or herding over cliffs or into swamps. However, one cannot assess the significance of the Myall Creek murder trials merely by that measure, just as one cannot assess the success of the Nuremberg trials in Europe after the Second World War by the number of genocides that have since taken place in various parts of the world.

In my view, the two trials in 1838 were more akin to modern-day war crimes trials than to domestic murder trials, even though the concept of war crimes lay more than 100 years in the future. There was undoubtedly an ongoing, internal, frontier war at the time, albeit quite one sided, between the white settlers and the Indigenous inhabitants, whom the former were attempting to displace and disperse. The war against the Indigenous population involved a systemic policy, often approved or acquiesced in by the white authorities, of unlawfully exterminating those Aboriginal people who stood in the way of the expansion of English settlement, or who posed a threat to the white pastoralists and their farming activities. In my view, the perpetrators of the mass murders at Myall Creek Station on 10 June 1838 were motivated by genocidal intentions and their actions were an example of what today we call 'ethnic cleansing'. The fact that almost the whole tribe was decimated—including old men, women and children—demonstrated clearly the genocidal intent of the perpetrators. The subsequent sexual abuse of one female Indigenous victim, who was spared her life on the day of the massacre, but only for what must have been a few excruciating days, illustrated the objectification of the victims. Recent history has shown that sexual violence often goes hand-in-hand with genocide, and that is why systemic sexual offences against enemy populations in war zones are now categorised as war crimes.

In addition, the actions of the perpetrators can be viewed as an example of what has become known as 'collective punishment'—a form of retaliation whereby a suspected offender's family, friends, acquaintances, neighbours or an entire ethnic group is targeted for punishment, and where the punished group may have no direct association with the act that is being punished. The victims in this case had been living peacefully on Myall Creek Station for several months and had done nothing to justify their victimisation. Collective punishment has been categorised as a war crime since the 1949 Fourth Geneva Convention and genocide has been categorised as an international crime by the Genocide Convention as adopted by the United Nations General Assembly in 1948, which came into force in 1951.

By modern-day standards, the actions of the Myall Creek murderers were war crimes and part of a deliberate, state-sanctioned genocide of the Aboriginal people that today would be punishable by the rules of international criminal law. The fact that vast numbers of genocidal murders in colonial Australia went unpunished would today provide evidence of state sanction, justifying international intervention in the prosecution of the perpetrators and their national leaders. While such laws did not exist in 1838, the approach taken by John Hubert Plunkett towards the case was consistent with these legalities, and demonstrated an enlightened and visionary attitude that was unparalleled in his time, or for more than 100 years afterwards. John Plunkett did not just prosecute 11 men for murder. He prosecuted his entire society for its connivance in the attempted annihilation of the Aboriginal people and their culture, and that is why it aroused such prevalent hostility. His contemporaries vehemently resented him during the trial and for years afterwards. It was a testament to his perseverance and tactical skills that he convinced 12 jurors to convict seven of the perpetrators, because they were not only condemning those men to their deaths, but also stingingly rebuking their own society. So, while the 1838 trials and convictions did not prevent future massacres, they stand as a beacon of humanity and interracial justice that illuminated the way for Australia to develop as a civilised nation.

Australian schools, both primary and secondary, have always devoted much time to teaching students about the great, white explorers—people like John Oxley, Charles Sturt and Major Thomas Mitchell. Very few schools, however, teach what almost invariably happened within a few years of these explorers' discoveries: the expansion of white pastoralists into areas that had for millennia been occupied by Indigenous clans. What followed was the expropriation of their land, the destruction of their culture and society, and the massacres of tens of thousands of Indigenous peoples in hundreds of locations all over Australia.

In my opinion, the story of what happened to the Aboriginal inhabitants in colonial times should be taught in our schools as readily as we teach the exploits of the great, white explorers. The two accounts are inextricably intertwined. One almost inevitably followed the other. A real acceptance by mainstream Australia of the horrors perpetrated against our Indigenous communities in the colonial period will bring with it an understanding of the long-term trauma transferred through the generations. We readily recognise that the trauma of other genocides and crimes against humanity—such as those during the Nazi period in Europe, in the former Yugoslavia during the 1990s, and in countries like Rwanda and Cambodia—can be deeply felt for many generations after the killings have ended. If we acknowledge that Aboriginal communities were subjected to massacres in a multitude of locations all over Australia for more than a century, there may be more sympathy for the current generations striving for equanimity, understanding and acceptance.

Until we recognise that what occurred was a war of extirpation or annihilation, until we acknowledge that what was perpetrated amounted to genocide and that today it would be categorised as a war crime, and until we teach this to all children throughout Australia, we will not reach our full maturity as a nation.

CHAPTER 9

Long Shadows—The Great War, Australia and the Middle East

From the Armenian to the Yazidi Genocide

Caroline Schneider and Hans-Lukas Kieser

This essay is based on the exhibition 'Long Shadows—The Great War, Australia and the Middle East', displayed at the University Gallery of the University of Newcastle (Australia) from 5 September to 11 November 2018.[496] The essay synthesises the exhibition's main content and focus, and adds reflection. 'Long Shadows' made a connection between Australia's military operation on the Gallipoli peninsula and what would come to be known as the Armenian Genocide, and presented detailed information on the persecution of the

---

[496] A website has been established to make the exhibition online accessible. See 'Long Shadows – The Great War, Australia and the Middle East', The University of Newcastle Art and Museum Collection, accessed February 7, 2019, https://gallery.newcastle.edu.au/pages/longshadows. We acknowledge the work of our colleagues Dr Kate Ariotti, Gillean Shaw and the whole team of the University Gallery. In the following, content will be drawn from the physical exhibition as well as its online attribution. For an exhibition review see Burcu Cevik-Compiegne, 'Long Shadows: The Great War, Australia and the Middle East', *History Australia* 16, no. 1 (2019): 210–11.

How to cite this book chapter:
Schneider, C. and Kieser, H-K. 2020. Long Shadows—The Great War, Australia and the Middle East: From the Armenian to the Yazidi Genocide. In: Marczak, N. and Shields, K. (eds.) *Genocide Perspectives VI: The Process and the Personal Cost of Genocide*. Pp. 159–175. Sydney: UTS ePRESS. DOI: https://doi.org/10.5130/aaf.j. License: CC BY-NC-ND.

Armenian population. 'Long Shadows' implicitly suggested that a fair public memory of the night of 24 to 25 April 1915, must address both the Australians' (Anzac) and the Armenians' (Armenian Genocide) trauma. France—whose soldiers fought alongside Britain and Australia in 1915—has recently decided to do so: it named 24 April a national day of genocide commemoration.[497]

The exhibition in Newcastle drew long historical lines from the 1910s to the 2010s and provided an unusually broad context to the Armenian Genocide. It highlighted a genocide that targeted Armenians primarily, but also other Ottoman Christians and minorities, and the impact on all for generations to come. Also, it shed light on lesser-known traumatic experiences of Anzac soldiers at Gallipoli or during captivity. Furthermore, 'Long Shadows' joined dots not only between Gallipoli and genocide in Ottoman Turkey in 1915, but also between this genocide during the Great War and the recent genocide of Yazidis, and between patterns of violence in the Middle East then and now. Finally, it connected stories of persecuted people and the efforts of Australian humanitarian organisations then and now. Although not all problems in today's post-Ottoman region can be directly traced back to the decade of 1911–22, many major issues have important historical connections there, such as radical Islamism, the Kurdish question and several instances of mass violence that have remained unrecognised. Ethno-religious stigmatisation, extreme violence and human trafficking were common during the decade of the Ottoman war; many of its patterns have since re-emerged in recent years in Syria and Northern Iraq (although the number of civilian victims was much higher a century ago). In short, the Great War casts long shadows of violence, trauma and unresolved conflicts over current times.

While the Great War was physically undertaken in one geographic region, its consequences and memory have affected and still affect international diplomacy and countless individuals belonging to migrant communities all over the world. In this essay, the focus will be on the shared war experience of two regions: Australia and the Middle East. As in the exhibition, the essay will weave from Australia to Gallipoli, to Asia Minor, Syria and Northern Iraq, from 1915 through to 2018.

I

Every year on 25 April (since 1916), Australians and New Zealanders come together to commemorate their servicemen and women. While this day offers

---

[497] 'Macron fait du 24 avril la journée nationale de commémoration du génocide arménien', *Le Figaro*, accessed February 6, 2019, http://www.lefigaro .fr/actualite-france/2019/02/05/01016-20190205ARTFIG00309-macron -fait-du-24-avril-la-journee-nationale-de-commemoration-du-genocide -armenien.php.

honour and respect to Australians and New Zealanders who served their country in any conflict or peacekeeping mission, it has its origins in the Gallipoli campaign of 1915. At the time, World War One was already underway, but somewhat in a deadlock. To contain the Central Powers (Germany and its main allies Austria-Hungary and the Ottoman Empire), to lessen the pressure on certain fronts (for example, the Caucasus), and foremost to connect with Russia through the Bosphore, British strategists decided on a new front against the Ottoman capital. The Gallipoli peninsula seemed to be the ideal location. A successful attack would eventually ease the way for Allied forces to capture Ottoman's capital Constantinople (today's Istanbul), which would knock the Ottomans out of the war and allow for Allied control of the Dardanelles, a waterway linking the Black and Mediterranean seas. After a British/French naval attack failed on 18 March 1915, a joint offensive of British, French and Anzac soldiers launched a few weeks later. This campaign would come to play a fundamental role in Australia's national memory and identity.

In the early morning hours of 25 April 1915, the first Anzac troops landed on the Gallipoli peninsula. From the very beginning, the troops faced enormous challenges. The terrain, with its steep cliffs, deep gullies and thick scrub, proved difficult to conquer and the Ottomans were determined in their resistance. Less than a month after the landing on the peninsula, and following a strong counter-offensive by the Ottomans, the fighting stalled. The Australians and New Zealanders managed to occupy a little ground around the beach and on the ridges above, but life on the peninsula was hard. In extreme heat, the soldiers had to carry their own supplies from the beach to higher ground, the trenches were overcrowded, sanitation was limited, lice and fly plagues were present and sniping and bombing were incessant. The Anzac soldiers became more and more exhausted. In fact, more men suffered from sickness than were wounded. Anzac soldiers had to be evacuated *en masse* for medical reasons. To counteract this harsh reality, in early August 1915 an 'all or nothing' offensive was launched. This led to high losses and only little ground gained. With no real prospect for improvement and the need for more troops in Europe, the decision was made to withdraw the Anzac soldiers from the Gallipoli peninsula. Without a single casualty, all Anzacs were safely evacuated by 20 December 1915. Ironically, the safe removal of the troops was the most successful aspect of the campaign. All forces involved—Allies and Ottomans—endured great losses. Australia suffered 26,000 casualties, including over 8,700 dead. Furthermore, 67 Australians were taken prisoners of war by the Ottomans.[498] Joined by light horsemen and members of the Australian Flying Corps captured in Mesopotamia, the Sinai Desert and Palestine, these POWs were used for forced labour and many died in captivity. However, some also became

---

[498] For further information on Australian Prisoners of First World War see Kate Ariotti, *Captive Anzacs. Australian POW's of the Ottomans during the First World War* (Cambridge: Cambridge University Press, 2018).

witness to atrocities committed by the Ottomans against the Armenians and other ethnic minorities (Christian Assyrians and Pontus Greeks) in the Empire.

Writing about the Armenian Genocide while in captivity was risky, but there are several eyewitness accounts from captive Anzacs. John Wheat, a captured member of the Australian submarine AE2, would write the following in his diary: 'At Afyonkarahissar ... officers had houses to live in. The owner of these houses had been taken away "somewhere" ... driven into the desert, and were numbered among the victims of the Armenian atrocities'.[499] What John Wheat refers to as 'the Armenian atrocities' is today known as the Armenian Genocide. The genocide started in the evening of 24 April 1915, in Constantinople, just a few hours before the Anzac landing on Gallipoli and in close proximity to the peninsula. Signs of an extermination policy could be observed earlier, but on that evening approximately 300 Armenian intellectuals, clergy and community leaders were taken into custody. The systematically implemented genocide started by first depriving the Ottoman Armenian community of its leaders.

II

The Ottoman Armenian population had achieved advanced self-organisation, welfare and educational institutions by the late nineteenth century, and was increasingly vocal in its claims for equality. The Armenian community was under the rule of Sultan Abdülhamid II (1876–1909) when it became the target of social envy and violence, including large-scale massacres carried out in 1894–96. At the time, the Ottoman Empire faced domestic crises and began to crumble. Dissatisfaction with the ruling sultan led to the rise of a broad underground opposition movement of the so-called Young Turks. The group's strongest organisation was the Committee of Union and Progress (CUP), which was formed by young army officers and comprised students and state functionaries. In the hope for a better, more democratic future, the main Armenian party, the Armenian Revolutionary Federation (ARF), entered into an alliance with CUP in 1907. In July 1908, supported by ARF, the Young Turks initiated a constitutional revolution to overthrow the despotic regime of Sultan Abdülhamid II. Constitutional rule was restored, the Ottoman parliament reopened and elections took place in the same year. The revolution ultimately led to an 'Ottoman Spring', a short phase in which a more democratic collective Ottoman identity was emphasised. This period, however, did not last long, and Armenian hopes for equal rights and the end of violence against minorities in the Empire were soon destroyed. The aims of the ARF and the CUP diverged with the Young Turks' desire to restore imperial power and create a homogeneous Turkish

---

[499] John Wheat, Diary, August 18, 1915, 3DRL/2965, AWM, in Vicken Babkenian and Peter Stanley, *Armenia, Australia and The Great War* (Sydney: NewSouth Publishing, 2016).

identity. In 1909, the Armenians once again became victims of massacre, this time in Adana.

Adding fuel to anti-Christian sentiments and a warmongering attitude within the CUP were the Balkan Wars (1912–13). With the rise of ethnic nationalism and the simultaneous increase in dissatisfaction among diverse population groups, non-Muslim as well as Muslim, the situation within the Empire became increasingly tense. The Balkan Wars emerged both from unresolved problems in Ottoman Macedonia and the irredentism of young post-Ottoman Balkan states. The Ottomans were defeated and lost almost all their territory west of Istanbul. The Balkan Wars resulted in several peace treaties, mainly the Treaty of Constantinople in September 1913. This was the first treaty in a long series of similar agreements in the twentieth century that foresaw population exchanges with the aim of an 'ethno-religious un-mixing' (in contrast with future treaties, however, this one was not compulsory).

The two Balkan Wars had severe consequences: approximately 500,000 soldiers plus an unknown number of civilians lost their lives, the Ottomans lost massive amounts of territory, and about 300,000 Muslims became refugees. During the turmoil of the First Balkan War, the CUP—which had temporarily lost power in July 1912—launched a successful *coup d'état* on 23 January 1913. It then established a dictatorial single party regime in the Ottoman Empire. Interior Minister Mehmed Talaat Bey, later the mastermind of the Armenian Genocide, evolved to become the strongest, most influential figure in the Empire.[500] His aim was not only to restore by means of coercion and violence the sovereignty and territory of the Ottoman Empire, but also to build a centralised Turkish-Muslim state based in Asia Minor. The Balkan Wars were a catalyst for this policy, and thus for World War One in the Middle East and for the Armenian Genocide.

III

The main events of the Armenian Genocide lasted from April 1915 to September 1916 and killed more than a million Ottoman Christians. When Mehmed Talaat gave the order to arrest hundreds of members of the Armenian elite on that night of April 24 1915, and to question, torture and eventually murder most of them as well as those arrested in provincial towns, the first phase of the Armenian Genocide began. Provincial and military authorities, as well as party commissaries were sent to the provinces to spread propaganda about supposedly treacherous Armenian neighbours, accusing them of stabbing the Empire in the back by changing sides and helping the enemy. Some

---

[500] For further information on Talaat Pasha, his rise to power and his role in the Armenian Genocide see Hans-Lukas Kieser, *Talaat Pasha. Father of Modern Turkey, Architect of Genocide* (Princeton: Princeton University Press, 2018).

Armenians had indeed turned to the Russians, yet the Armenian community in general had been one of the most loyal to the constitutional state. Nevertheless, the Armenians became a useful scapegoat for CUP's broader problems. Attacks on Armenians and other Christians and minorities involved massacres, deportations, death marches and concentration camps. The genocide was carried out in gender-specific ways: men were often killed on the spot, while many women and children were abducted and enslaved, either trafficked or forcibly married and converted. Thousands were forced to march through the desert to squalid concentration camps in Northern Syria. They were either transported in railway cattle wagons or on foot. Many were massacred in their home provinces or died *en route* to the camps. The ones who were able to escape fled to the Caucasus, Northern Iran, the Sinjar mountains of the Yazidis in Northern Iraq and into the Alevi-Kurdish province of Dersim in Eastern Anatolia.

Based on CUP policies and correspondence, including a letter sent in May 1915 from Mehmed Talaat to another CUP member, Grand Vizier Said Halim, it is clear that Talaat's ultimate goal was the almost total elimination of the Armenian population in the Ottoman Empire. He argued that the Armenian 'trouble occupies an important place among the vital problems of the Sublime [Ottoman] state' and that now 'means were prepared and considered to remove this trouble in a radical, fundamental and comprehensive way'.[501] Furthermore, Cavid Bey (Talaat's party friend and unofficial finance minister) wrote in his diary in September 1915: 'Ottoman history has never known before such monstrous murder and enormous brutality. ... I am of the opinion that Talaat was involved in this [extermination] with full conviction'.[502] Talaat ordered the relocation of more than a million Armenians, of whom more than half a million arrived in Syria. Here, the survivors of the deportation faced the next phase of the genocide. The conditions in the camps led to hundreds of thousands of deaths from starvation, disease and exposure. In a final massacre between August and September 1916, tens of thousands were killed.[503] On the intitiative of Syria governor Cemal Pasha, many more Armenians were forcibly converted to Islam and resettled further in the South, including in Palestine. Although

---

[501] Talaat, from the interior Ministry's Directorate for Resettlement of Tribes and Migrants, to the grand vizier, Ottoman State Archives: BOA BEO, 4357-326758.

[502] Mehmed Cavid Bey, *Meşrutiyet Rûznamesi* (Ankara: TTK, 2015), 3:136–37.

[503] See notably Taner Akçam, *The Young Turks' Crime against Humanity: The Armenian Genocide and Ethnic Cleansing in the Ottoman Empire* (Princeton: Princeton University Press, 2012); Taner Akçam, *Killing Orders: Talat Pasha's Telegrams and the Armenian Genocide* (Cham [Switzerland]: Palgrave Macmillan, 2018); Kieser, *Talaat Pasha*; Khatchig Mouradian, *The Resistance Network: The Armenian Genocide and Humanitarianism in Ottoman Syria, 1915-1918* (East Lansing: Michigan State University Press, forthcoming in 2021).

their individual lives were saved, the policy of forced assimilation effectively contributed to the destruction of the Ottoman Armenian Christian community.

The plight of the Armenians was well known in wartime Australia. In addition to the POWs who witnessed atrocities against the Armenians, wounded and sick Australian servicemen, who were sent to Egypt for treatment and recovery, also became aware of the Armenians' desperate situation.[504] In September 1915 a large refugee camp was established in Port Said in Egypt. Around 4,000 Armenians found refuge there, employed by the Allies to make, for example, army shirts and fishing nets.

Humanitarian relief efforts were crucial for the survival of Armenian refugees. Underground networks, in which Western missionaries were also involved, had already helped rescue Armenians via Dersim in 1915. These and other networks were partly built on existing humanitarian groups that had been established in Europe, the United States of America and Australia after the 1894–96 massacres. Together with workers from neutral countries still resident in the Ottoman Empire, they formed the active nucleus of the Near East Relief that started in late 1915. Australia had its first fundraising campaign for the Armenians in mid-late 1915. It was a success. Several organisations were involved in arranging collections, which grew over the years with heart-breaking reports from overseas. The fundraising efforts also helped to open an orphanage in Antelias in Lebanon, which took in about 1,700 genocide survivors. Australian aid to the Armenians lasted well into the 1940s, despite the official denial of the Armenian Genocide by the Turks and the push for healthy diplomatic relations with Turkey after the Treaty of Lausanne in 1923. The aid provided to the Armenians is considered to be Australia's first major international relief effort and set the path for Australia's future worldwide humanitarian efforts. Despite this, the aid had limited impact on the overall suffering of the Armenians. In hindsight, a successful Gallipoli campaign could have prevented or at least mitigated the Armenian Genocide.

The suffering of the Armenians did not end with the war; expropriation and cultural suppression continued. Many Armenians deal with transgenerational trauma even today. The first commemorations of the Armenian Genocide took place in the Ottoman capital on 24 April 1919, but ceased abruptly in 1923 when the occupation of Istanbul by the Allies ended. It was not commemorated again until 1965, its fiftieth anniversary, when protests in Yerevan and among the Armenian Diaspora revitalised this day of remembrance. Until 1991 Armenians did not have a state of their own, which made it difficult to create a platform to advocate for justice.[505] The struggle for recognition and

---

[504] For further information on encounters between Australians and Armenians see: Babkenian and Stanley, *Armenia, Australia*.

[505] Harutyun Marutyan, 'April 24: Formation, Development and Current State of the Armenian Genocide Victims Remembrance Day', in: *Remembering the Great War in the Middle East: From Turkey and Armenia to Australia*

commemoration of the Armenian Genocide continues to date in the face of Turkish Government denial.

One critical aspect that created a long-lasting problematic political matrix was the Treaty of Lausanne. Initially, another peace treaty was concluded between the Allied forces and the Ottoman Empire, the 1920 Treaty of Sèvres. The Turkish nationalists (also named 'Kemalists' after their leader Mustafa Kemal, later Atatürk), who had founded a counter-government in Ankara, refused the stipulations in the treaty that foresaw the prosecution of war criminals and included financial and military restrictions. Also, the Sèvres Treaty planned to attribute parts of Asia Minor to Greeks, Armenians and Kurds. Ankara's victory in the Greco-Turkish war led to the renegotiation of the treaty. The new Treaty of Lausanne—a compromise between the nationalist leaders in Ankara and imperialist Britain and France—came into force in 1923.

From the very beginning, this treaty was highly criticised by international lawyers, scholars and humanitarians. It not only withdrew provisions for minorities, but also offered impunity for crimes against humanity—a term that was first used on 24 May 1915, in relation to the Ottoman authorities' atrocities against the Armenians. Ultimately, this meant that members of the Ottoman Empire who were responsible and active actors in the genocide were not prosecuted. Moreover, the treaty endorsed compulsory mass population exchanges. The treaty ended the conflict, but not without long-term consequences for ethnic minorities living in the region, and for a political culture that allowed for impunity. Finally, the treaty defined the borders of Turkey and, as a result, in October 1923 the Republic of Turkey was internationally recognised. The Lausanne Treaty not only shaped the modern Middle East, but established a seminal international paradigm of conflict resolution that consisted in 'un-mixing peoples' for the sake of unitary, authoritarian, ethnic nation states.[506]

In the following years the Turkish government was confronted with Kurdish insurrections. Initially the Kurdish had fought on the side of the Kemalists

---

and New Zealand, ed. Hans-Lukas Kieser and Thomas Schmutz (London: I.B. Tauris, forthcoming in 2021).

[506] For further information on the Treaties of Sèvres and Lausanne see Eric D Weitz, 'From the Vienna to the Paris System: International Politics and the Entangled Histories of Human Rights, Forced Deportations, and Civilizing Missions', *American Historical Review* 113, no. 5 (2008): 1313–43; Roland Banken, *Die Verträge von Sèvres 1920 und Lausanne 1923. Eine völkerrechtliche Untersuchung zur Beendigung des Ersten Weltkrieges und zur Auflösung der sogenannten „Orientalischen Frage' durch die Friedensverträge zwischen den alliierten Mächten und der Türkei* (Berlin: LIT-Verl, 2014); Renée Hirschon, ed., *Crossing the Aegean: An Appraisal of the 1923 Compulsory Population Exchange Between Greece and Turkey* (New York: Berghahn, 2008); Umut Özsu, *Formalizing Displacement. International Law and Population Transfers* (New York: Oxford University Press, 2015).

during the wars for Asia Minor against non-Muslim competitors (1919–22), as they had alongside CUP in World War One. However, they soon realised that the Turkish government intended to implement a radical Turkish-nationalist agenda. There was no room for other languages or cultural autonomy, and all religious expression was subjected to strict state control. In the interwar period several rebellions took place, which led to massacres such as the one in Dersim in 1937–38. Overall, these resulted in the death and displacement of hundreds of thousands of Kurds. Since the mid-twentieth century, violence and conflict in the Middle East have led to much higher death tolls than in continental Europe. For several decades, the Israel-Palestine conflict has taken centre stage, while other domestic and interstate wars have occurred such as the Lebanese civil war, the Iran-Iraq war, the anti-Kurdish Anfal campaign, Kurdish guerrilla wars in Turkey, the Persian Gulf War, the US invasion of Iraq in 2003, the civil war in Syria and the war in Yemen. These conflicts claimed millions of lives and resulted in the displacement of many more people. New elements of warfare were combined with patterns of violence, genocide and human trafficking present in World War One. Most recently, the shadows of the past have been cast over Syria and Northern Iraq by the so-called Islamic State (IS) and its treatment of minorities—Christians, Shi'a Muslims and especially the Yazidis.

IV

Almost 100 years after the Armenian Genocide began, the Yazidis were confronted with genocide in their homeland around Mount Sinjar, where they had offered asylum to fleeing Armenians a century earlier. The Yazidis are an ethno-religious minority with their own distinct religion. As heterodox non-Muslims, they have been regularly persecuted, and there are testimonies of Yazidi survivors of attacks by Ottoman rulers during the Armenian Genocide. They were viewed by IS and other non-Yazidis as heathen infidels and, therefore, 'fair prey for conquest'.[507]

The so-called Islamic State's roots can be traced back to the US-led invasion of Iraq in 2003 and much earlier.[508] After loosening its ties with the Islamist

---

[507] IS produced several documents for propaganda purposes and for the distribution of instructions and guidelines for its supporters. For instance, it released an official propaganda magazine to promote the recruitment of new soldiers, its attempt to legitimate an IS Caliphate ('Khilafah'), the promotion of slavery and to encourage worldwide atrocities and individual terror attacks.

[508] For further information on IS, its ideology and rise, see, for example Robert Manne, *The Mind of the Islamic State* (Carlton: Redback Quarterly, 2016); Patrick Cockburn, *The Rise of Islamic State. ISIS and the New Sunni Revolution* (London: Verso, 2015).

terror organisation Al-Qaida, IS proclaimed itself a caliphate in June 2014 in Mosul and promised the worldwide establishment of an Islamic order. The implementation of the genocide launched in August 2014 against the Yazidis has many parallels with the Ottoman attacks against Armenians: displacement, dispossession and massacre, enslavement and sexual violence against women and girls, and the brainwashing of children.

On 3 August 2014, IS launched its attack by invading the area from various locations: Mosul and Tal Afar in Iraq, and Al Shaddadi and Tel Hamis region in Syria. The Yazidis had little chance to escape. They were given no evacuation orders beforehand, nor could they display any significant resistance themselves. Many Peshmerga soldiers, who were supposed to defend and protect the Yazidi population, reportedly left their posts when IS approached—without warning the Yazidis.[509] Tens of thousands of Yazidis fled to Mount Sinjar Plateau where they remained for several days surrounded by IS fighters, with no belongings, water, food or heat protection, and with no escape route. Within a matter of days after the initial IS attack, thousands of Yazidis were killed— murdered by IS fighters or perishing on their escape. Many more were taken captive by IS members and the whole community of the region was displaced. The atrocities committed by IS fighters against the Yazidis have been recognised as genocide by the United Nations and other authorities, including the Australian Parliament.[510] It is a genocide that is still ongoing as the United Nations' expert body in this matter argues: 'Thousands of Yazidi men and boys remain missing and the terrorist group continues to subject some 3,000 women and girls in Syria to horrific violence including daily rapes and beatings'.[511]

IS sought to destroy the Yazidis via multiple strategies. Their actions were planned, and the genocide systematically conducted by strict 'rules'. The systematic nature can be seen in the categorisation of Yazidis into groups, which

---

[509] '"They came to destroy": ISIS Crimes Against the Yazidis', UN Independent International Commission of Inquiry on the Syrian Arab Republic, June 15, 2016, accessed March 20, 2019, 6–7, http://www.ohchr.org/Documents/HRBodies/HRCouncil/CoISyria/A_HRC_32_CRP.2_en.pdf.

[510] Ibid., 1; 'House Debates, 26 February 2018, Motions Yazidi People', Open Australia, accessed March 20, 2019, https://www.openaustralia.org.au/debates/?id=2018-02-26.195; Susan Hutchinson, 'The Pain of Hearing: Australia's Parliament Recognises Yazidi Genocide', The Lowy Institute, accessed March 20, 2019, https://www.lowyinstitute.org/the-interpreter/pain-hearing-australia-parliament-recognises-yazidi-genocide.

[511] 'ISIL's "Genocide" Against Yazidis is Ongoing, UN Rights Panel Says, Calling for International Action', *United Nations News*, accessed February 7, 2019, https://news.un.org/en/story/2017/08/562772-isils-genocide-against-yazidis-ongoing-un-rights-panel-says-calling; the exact number of captives is hard to establish as many might have been killed while in captivity by IS, allied airstrikes, etcetera.

occurred consistently across different locations, clearly indicating the planned nature of the attacks. These are the fates of the captives.[512]

Men and women were immediately separated. Men and boys who had reached puberty were often immediately massacred, shot into mass graves. Others were forced to convert to Islam and killed if they refused. In some cases, family members were forced to watch the executions or were taken later to see dead bodies lying on roadsides.[513] The bodies of the Yazidi men and boys were often left *in situ*. Most killings were groups that consisted of two to 20 captives, but there are several documented and yet to be documented sites of bigger mass killings. The Yazidi men and boys who converted to Islam were transferred to different sites in Syria and Northern Iraq, where they were put to forced labour such as construction projects, digging trenches, and cleaning streets. They were also forced to pray, to grow their beards and hair, and to follow other religious 'rules'. Attempted escape resulted in immediate execution. It has to be highlighted that even converted Yazidis were by no means equal to IS fighters, nor were they protected. Male Yazidis, even boys around the age of 12, were often beaten and verbally abused, called '*kuffar*' (infidel), and forced to commit heinous acts of violence against each other.

Yazidi women and girls aged nine and above suffered severe sexual abuse, frequent rape, enslavement, physical violence, human trafficking, starvation and verbal and mental abuse. Once separated from the men, the women and girls were themselves categorised into groups of married or unmarried, with children or without, with young, unmarried girls being the most 'valuable'. After weeks or sometimes months of living in poor conditions, where basic human needs were barely met, the women and girls were sold, mainly to IS fighters. Some were sold in slave markets, which would later become accessible online. Once sold, the fighter held the woman captive in his home, where she was raped, sometimes several times a day, and forced to do housework for the fighter's family. Most of the Yazidi women and girls were sold and trafficked several times. The younger children could stay with their mothers, and

---

[512] For more detailed information on the treatment of the captive Yazidis and the Yazidi Genocide in general see inter alia: '"They came to destroy": ISIS Crimes Against the Yazidis', UN Independent International Commission of Inquiry on the Syrian Arab Republic, June 15, 2016, accessed February 7, 2019, http://www.ohchr.org/Documents/HRBodies/HRCouncil/CoISyria/A_HRC_32_CRP.2_en.pdf; 'An Uncertain Future for Yazidis: A Report Marking Three Years of an Ongoing Genocide,' Yazda, accessed February 7, 2019, https://docs.wixstatic.com/ugd/92f016_230c3d32aa44498db557326046ad5ca7.pdf.

[513] For further information on genocidal acts that specifically target the family unit see Elisa von Joeden-Forgey, 'The Devil in the Details: "Life Force Atrocities" and the Assault on the Family in Times of Conflict', *Genocide Studies and Prevention: An International Journal* 5, no. 1 (2010): 1–19.

were also treated poorly, including having to watch their mothers being raped. Any attempt to escape had severe consequences. The women and girls were the property of the buyer, which meant he could do to them whatever he wanted. Already pregnant women were sometimes subjected to forced abortion. Some Yazidis who were forcibly married to IS fighters were confronted with forced pregnancy, others with the use of forced contraception to facilitate ongoing trafficking. Some were gifted from one IS fighter to another. Ownership rights reflected in purchase contracts were yet another indication of the rigid system, hierarchy and official governance of the treatment of captive Yazidis.

Furthermore, captive female Yazidis and children were not allowed to practise their own culture and religion. Boys under the age of puberty were considered to have a pliable identity, able to be converted to Islam and trained in IS ideology. Thousands of boys were brought into 'schools' and taught how to pray, fight and kill. The boys were registered, had to convert to Islam and were given Islamic names. From that moment on, the boys were treated as IS recruits. The boys had to attend daily indoctrination of IS ideology, Quran lessons and military training sessions. Furthermore, they were forced to watch propaganda videos of armed battles, beheadings and suicide missions. If the boys performed poorly in training sessions or could not remember Quranic verses, they were beaten. IS did everything to erase the boys' past. Instead, a new identity was forcibly imposed on the boys, the identity of an IS fighter. They were taught to hate their own community. One boy said: 'They told us we had to become good Muslims and fight for Islam. They showed us videos of beheadings, killing and battles. My instructor said "you have to kill kuffars even if they are your fathers and brothers"'.[514] After weeks or months in the training camps, the boys were distributed according to IS's needs: some became fighters on the battlefield; others had to perform duties including suicide attacks.

For the Yazidis who fled towards Mount Sinjar, limited international efforts were initially made, including humanitarian airdrops by the US government, which were announced by then President Obama while acknowledging the risk of an imminent genocide. Australia was one nation that launched an airdrop with much needed supplies.[515] For Australia, this was one of the most complex humanitarian operations in more than a decade. However, the overall international intervention was extremely limited. Further action could have

---

[514] '"They came to destroy": ISIS Crimes Against the Yazidis', UN Independent International Commission of Inquiry on the Syrian Arab Republic, June 15, 2016, accessed February 7, 2019, 18, http://www.ohchr.org/Documents/HRBodies/HRCouncil/CoISyria/A_HRC_32_CRP.2_en.pdf.

[515] 'Recent History of Air Force Humanitarian Assistance', Royal Australian Air Force, accessed March 20, 2019, https://www.airforce.gov.au/operations/humanitarian-support/recent-history-air-force-humanitarian-assistance.

prevented many more deaths and saved thousands of women and children from abduction. Australia is continuing its assistance for the Yazidis to date.[516]

V

IS's actions against the Yazidis, which include the crime of genocide, crimes against humanity, war crimes and human rights abuses, have had dire short-term as well as long-term consequences for the Yazidi community. Already faced with individual, collective and transgenerational trauma, the Yazidis have lost their homeland. There are approximately 350,000 Yazidis living in camps for internally displaced people in Northern Iraq. A small number of Yazidis have found refuge in Europe as well as in the United States of America, Canada and Australia, but several thousand are still missing or captive. So far it has almost been impossible for Yazidis to return to their homeland. Approximately 80 to 85 per cent of cities in the region have been destroyed. IS has officially been defeated, but ongoing geopolitical conflict between the Kurdish and Iraqi authorities complicate any rebuilding of the area.[517] Poor safety and infrastructure, including uncleared landmines, make resettling difficult. The lives of the Yazidis drastically changed on 3 August 2014 and they continue to suffer enormous daily challenges.[518]

The suffering of the Armenian Genocide survivors did not end with the atrocities—some scholars even recognise the ongoing denial as the last stage of the genocide.[519] The genocidal strategies of Ottoman forces such as massacres of local Armenian men, forcible transfer and brainwashing of children, enslavement, forced marriages and sexual violence against women and girls, trafficking, forced conversions and cultural, biological and social destruction, had severe long-term consequences for the Armenian community. The gendered nature of the Armenian Genocide proved to be a central tactic of the

---

[516] For example Nathan Morris, 'Yazidi Refugees Fleeing Northern Iraq Arrive in Toowoomba to Write a New History in Australia', ABC, accessed February 7, 2019, https://www.abc.net.au/news/2018-06-21/yazidis-write-a-new-history-in-toowomba/9889238.

[517] For further information on the on-going conflict between different groups in the region see 'An Uncertain Future for Yazidis: A Report Marking Three Years of an Ongoing Genocide', Yazda, accessed March 20, 2019, 32–42, https://docs.wixstatic.com/ugd/92f016_230c3d32aa44498db557326046ad5ca7.pdf.

[518] For more information on the Yazidis' trauma, see for example several works from Jan Ilhan Kizilhan.

[519] For example Fatma Müge Göçek, *Denial of Violence. Ottoman Past, Turkish Present, and Collective Violence against the Armenians, 1789–2009* (Oxford: Oxford University Press, 2015), 11.

genocide itself, and continued to have an impact in the aftermath.[520] Rescued or escaped Armenian women and children who were sexually abused had to deal with long-lasting stigma; re-integration was often difficult. Turkification and Islamisation processes of orphaned children, and assimilation in general, could often not be reversed and had severe consequences for individuals and the whole community.[521] The aim was not only to destroy the Armenian population, but also its heritage: identity, history and culture. As a central policy, the Armenian Genocide displayed mainly a race-based social Darwinist character that is comparable to exterminatory patterns of the Holocaust. Yet, in many provinces, religion-based Islamist ideology prevailed.

Similar Islamist strategies are now being reinforced by IS in their treatment of the Yazidis. Knowing what the Armenians had to face after the genocide—stigma, problems around re-integration, trauma and re-traumatisation, hidden or permanent loss of Armenian identity—reflects the situation of the Yazidis today. Many Yazidi boys who return from captivity have forgotten their identity and language, Kurmanji. They suffer from post-traumatic stress disorder. The women and girls have to live with the stigma from sexual violence, despite statements from Yazidi leadership that welcomed them back into community (although not their children born of rape). They are severely traumatised. Some male Yazidis have a hard time dealing with their perceived failure to protect women and children. Many Yazidis have lost their lives and the fate of many others remains unknown. Combined with all the existential challenges, this is an unbearable situation. All of this should awake the international community and call for more concrete action.

However, despite everything known about the Yazidi Genocide, the first prosecution of an IS member for crimes against Yazidis only began in April 2019, in Germany.[522] The lack of accountability for perpetrators is seemingly repeating the history of the Armenian Genocide. This fact highlights the need for a joint international effort to bring IS fighters to justice. Future coexistence in the region is impossible without justice. The survivors of the Yazidi Genocide bear

---

[520] For detailed information on the gendered nature of the Armenian and Yazidi Genocide, especially on the enslavement of women and its long-term consequences see Nikki Marczak, 'A Century Apart: The Genocidal Enslavement of Armenian and Yazidi Women', in *A Gendered Lens for Genocide Prevention. Rethinking Political Violence*, eds. M.M. Connellan and C. Fröhlich (London: Palgrave Macmillan, 2017), 133–62.

[521] For more information on the treatment of Armenian children in orphanages see for example Selim Deringil, '"Your Religion is Worn and Outdated" Orphans, Orphanages and Halide Edib During the Armenian Genocide: The Case of Antoura'. Études arméniennes contemporaines 12 (2019): 33–65.

[522] 'German IS Member on Trial for War Crimes in Munich,' *Deutsche Welle*, April 9, 2019, https://www.dw.com/en/german-is-member-on-trial-for-war-crimes-in-munich/a-48259664, accessed April 22, 2019.

witness to the atrocities of IS and are willing to fight for justice. Nadia Murad, Human Rights activist, United Nations Goodwill Ambassador and Nobel Peace Prize winner, stated: 'It never gets easier to tell your story. Each time you speak it, you relive it … Still, I have become used to giving speeches, and large audiences no longer intimidate me. My story, told honestly and matter-of-factly, is the best weapon I have against terrorism, and I plan on using it until those terrorists are put on trial'.[523] Murad highlights the importance of raising awareness through the honest telling of peoples' experiences, despite the challenges. Descendants of Armenian Genocide survivors still recount their stories today, and memoirs of descendants of Islamised Armenians are finally being published.[524] This aspect of the genocide—the secret Armenian grandmothers in Turkish or Kurdish families—was for generations a taboo topic in Turkey. Turkey's continued denial of the Armenian Genocide, and decades of passive or active support from Western partners for this position, are a major stumbling block against any credible accountability for mass violence in the post-Ottoman Middle East.

A principled international stand and, in the current case of the Yazidis, significant action, would help in preventing repeated patterns of violence that burden the political cultures in the region. Sadly, patterns of demographic and economic engineering, enslavement and dispossession, common during the last Ottoman decade, have once again taken centre stage in the Middle East of the 2010s.

Conclusion

The Armenian Genocide casts to this day a particularly long and dark shadow, both in the region it occurred, and indeed globally. It is the unnamed black spot in the Lausanne Treaty and represents a continued, even reinforced culture

---

[523] Nadia Murad, *The Last Girl. My Story of Captivity, and my Fight against the Islamic State* (New York: Tim Duggan Books, 2017), 306; for further accounts also see Farida Khalaf, *The Girl Who Escaped ISIS. Farida's Story* (London: Vintage, 2016); Shirin with Alexandra Cavelius and Jan Kizilhan, *Ich bleibe eine Tochter des Lichts. Meine Flucht aus den Fängen der IS-Terroristen* (München: Knaur, 2017); Jinan mit Thierry Oberlé, *Ich war Sklavin des IS. Wie ich von Dschihadisten entführt wurde und den Albtraum meiner Gefangenschaft überlebte* (München: mvg Verlag, 2016).

[524] See for example Fethiye Çetin, *My Grandmother: An Armenian-Turkish Memoir*, trans. Maureen Freely (London: Verso Books, 2012); Ayşe Gül Altınay and Fethiye Çetin, *The Grandchildren. The Hidden Legacy of 'Lost' Armenians and Turkey*, trans. Maureen Freely (Somerset: Taylor and Francis, 2014); Kemal Yalçın. *Hayatta Kalanlar* (Istanbul: Birzamanlar Yayıncılık, 2006); İrfan Palalı, *Tehcir Çocukları: Nenem Ermeniysmiş* (Istanbul: Su Yayınevi, 2005).

of impunity for the most serious collective crimes of genocide during the twentieth century. As a consequence, the foundation for human rights in the juridical systems of the post-Ottoman states was weak from the start. The Lausanne Treaty had implicitly accepted the CUP's demographic engineering, even completing it through the agreement on the so-called Greek-Turkish population exchange. Also, it endorsed the single-party rule of the Kemalists, the successors of the CUP single-party regime, and its unitary, ultra-nationalist rule over Asia Minor.

The CUP's legacy has marked Turkey and the Ba'ath regimes of Syria and Iraq. Most post-Ottoman countries followed, one way or another, in the footsteps of the warring Young Turk regime; its rule was a paradigm for post-Ottoman power struggles: for military coups; leader centrism; deep states (within states); partisanship instead of meritocracy; and use of religion and propaganda against scapegoats. All this was and is incompatible with constitutional rule and comprehensive social contracts. As a consequence, lasting social peace has remained elusive.

Visitors to the Australian War Memorial who possess some knowledge of World War One in Ottoman Turkey, are struck by the omission from this large exhibition of the slightest allusion to the extermination of the Armenians, which constituted a major chapter of the Ottoman Great War and evolved simultaneously with the Anzac landing on Gallipoli. In fact, for the CUP rulers, one was logically connected to the other in a total war that they directed against domestic groups declared enemies as well as official foreign enemies. Any comprehensive exhibition on World War Two without inclusion of the Holocaust would be seen as entirely unacceptable. After 1945, Europe could only be rebuilt based on the explicit rejection of the former criminality of the German single-party rulers and their allies in Europe. Analogous reasons are valid for World War One and the post-Ottoman world.

Both the Armenian Genocide and the Anzac experience had in common the deep trauma that they left among Armenians and Australians. In Australia, both traumas, however, are remembered entirely separately, although it was for different reasons that they were not addressed in Australian public history or collective memory for generations. On the one hand, the reason was diplomatic convenience and partly historical ignorance; on the other, it was based on the need for national heroism to make sense out of great loss. In Australia, the Gallipoli campaign is held up as an event signalising the 'birth' of the nation and used by politicians to invoke a sense of patriotic pride and military virtue. But for many soldiers and their families it was, and remained, a profound trauma that they were largely left alone to deal with—as were Armenian survivors.

In contrast to this genre of memorial framing, the exhibition 'Long Shadows' exposes links between the Armenian Genocide and the Gallipoli campaign, as well as between past and current patterns in the Middle Eastern region—especially between the Armenian and Yazidi Genocides. With images, maps, texts, artefacts and songs, the visitors of the exhibition are taken from 1915 Australia to Gallipoli, and with witness accounts of Anzac POWs they are introduced to the Armenian Genocide. After a section on the Armenian Genocide, 'Long Shadows' introduces the public to knowledge of Australian aid sent to Armenians. Reflecting on the fatal consequences of the Lausanne Treaty and violent events in the Middle Eastern region since, it then leads visitors to the Yazidi Genocide, again highlighting Australian aid to the targeted group. The last wall of the exhibition shows a selective timeline on violent conflicts in the modern Middle East. Past events join contemporary events and have long-term consequences for people around the globe. No longer looked at separately, they must be connected in authentic ways without national or diplomatic strings and constraints.

In 1985, an official memorial exchange between Turkey and Australia took place: the site of the Anzac landings was renamed 'Anzac Cove' by the Turks and a memorial to Atatürk was built close to the Australian War Memorial in Canberra. Furthermore, every year on Anzac Day thousands of Australians make a pilgrimage to Turkey to commemorate their ancestors.[525] Turkey has threatened the cancellation of these events should Australia formally recognise the Armenian Genocide. Understanding the linkages in this history, it becomes easier to explain the Australian humanitarian efforts on behalf of the Armenians and Australia's simultaneous inability to face the reality of the Armenian Genocide. It touches on deep ambivalences and hypocrisies in politics and diplomacy. Because of Turkey's political weight, several Western states still do not recognise the atrocities against the Armenians as genocide, preferring a diluted vocabulary like 'tragedy' or 'catastrophe'. Australia is one of those states. It is certainly time to cast off the shadows.

---

[525] See also Nikki Marczak, 'Armenian Genocide Forgotten in ANZAC Commemorations', The Lowy Institute, accessed March 20, 2019, www.lowyinstitute.org/the-interpreter/armenian-genocide-forgotten-anzac-commemorations.

CHAPTER 10

'It's Happening Again'

Genocide, Denial, Exile and Trauma

Armen Gakavian

This essay explores the ways in which survivors of the Armenian Genocide and their descendants have responded to the ongoing trauma of the genocide in the last three decades. In 1986, Donald E Miller and Lorna Touryan Miller published a chapter identifying six responses to the genocide, drawing on their oral history work: repression, rationalisation, resignation, reconciliation, rage and revenge.[526] In this essay I offer two extensions to this typology. First, I suggest a seventh response that has emerged in recent years: engagement with the Turkish government, civil society and individuals. Second, building on the

---

[526] Donald E Miller and Lorna Touryan Miller, 'An Oral History Perspective on Responses to the Armenian Genocide', in *The Armenian Genocide in Perspective*, ed. Richard G Hovannisian (New Jersey: Transaction Publishers, 1986), 187–204. Miller and Miller later published their findings in a book, *Survivors: An Oral History of the Armenian Genocide* (Berkeley: University of California Press, 1993).

findings of Miller and Miller[527] and of Ani Kalayjian and Marian Weisberg,[528] I explore how the continuing sense of exile, the unresolved trauma of the genocide and denial by Turkish governments have fuelled the fear that the genocide 'is happening again'. This fear has shaped the response by Armenians to events in the last three decades: in Armenia (the 1988 earthquake, the 1991–94 war with Azerbaijan and the 2016 Four-Day War); in Azerbaijan (pogroms against Armenians in 1987–90); and in the Middle East (the Syrian civil war and the brief occupation of Kessab by the Syrian opposition in 2014).

Exile and trauma

Classic diasporas are characterised by 'a collective trauma, a banishment, where one dreamed of home but lived in exile'.[529] Exile and dispersion have been, in one form or another, part of the Armenian experience since the sixth century AD. Those who have remained in the homeland have lived with the constant *threat* of exile, domination or annihilation, with these experiences becoming 'normalised'.

The genocide of the Armenians, launched by the Ottoman Turkish government during World War One and completed by its successor Kemalist state, created conditions of exile and trauma on an unprecedented scale. Up to 1.5 million Armenians were killed, and hundreds of thousands were forcibly converted to Islam or deported into the Syrian Desert.[530] The millennia-old Armenian homeland was emptied of its indigenous inhabitants in what former Armenian Foreign Minister Raffi Hovannisian has referred to as the 'Great National Dispossession',[531] with survivors eventually scattered across the world

---

[527] Donald E Miller, 'The Role of Historical Memory in Interpreting Events in the Republic of Armenia', in *Remembrance and Denial: The Case of the Armenian Genocide*, ed. Richard G Hovannisian (Detroit: Wayne State University Press, 1998).

[528] Ani Kalayjian and Marian Weisberg, 'Generational Impact of Mass Trauma: The Post-Ottoman Turkish Genocide of the Armenians', in *Jihad and Sacred Vengeance*, eds. JS Piven, C Boyd, and HW Lawton (New York: Writers Club Press, 2002), 254–79.

[529] Robin Cohen, *Global Diasporas: An Introduction* (London: UCL Press, 1997), ix.

[530] Greeks and Assyrians were also subjected to genocide, with an estimated 1,000,000 killed.

[531] See, for example, Raffi Hovanissian, 'Forward To The Past: Russia, Turkey, And Armenia's Faith', *RadioFreeEurope, RadioLiberty*, October 21, 2008, https://www.rferl.org/a/commentary_Russia_Turkey_Armenia/1331509.html, accessed April 10, 2019.

or making their way to the newly declared independent Republic of Armenia that lasted from 1918 to 1920.[532]

Kalayjian and Weisberg's 2002 study documented the transmission of the trauma of the genocide to the second and third generations.[533] Eight participants aged 22 to 78, consisting of both survivors and their offspring, all reported feelings of grief, sadness, anger, pain and confusion over the genocide and its continued denial by the Turkish government, experiencing this denial as 'an attack on their personhood, feeling like a non-person'.[534] Both survivors and their offspring reported a distrust of outsiders and 'deep and intense feelings of helplessness', mostly in response to persistent Turkish denial.[535] They found that 'anger that was not expressed internally was expressed horizontally: toward one another, to other Armenians, toward the facilitators in the workshop'.[536] Offspring of survivors felt 'like orphans: no roots, no relatives, no uncles and great aunts'. Importantly, they felt 'burdened by having to carry emotional memories of previous generations', for which 'some second-generation respondents reported resentment'.[537]

In both the diaspora and Armenia, events throughout the twentieth and early twenty-first centuries reinforced the sense of exile and made the healing of the post-genocide trauma more difficult. Among the diasporan communities, this trauma was compounded by the growing realisation that exile was now permanent. The creation of the Armenian Soviet Socialist Republic in 1922 confirmed Armenia's re-absorption into the Russia sphere, and any chance of regaining independence and returning from exile now seemed lost. The second wave of emigration during and after World War Two from the long-established Middle Eastern and European communities to North and South America and Australia, pushed the epicentre of the diaspora further away from the homeland, making it more difficult to contemplate return if Armenia were to regain independence. For those living in Soviet Armenia and in other parts of the Soviet Union, a series of events reinforced the sense of trauma: the Stalinist purges of the 1930s and the exile of thousands to Siberia were followed by heavy losses during World War Two, and more recently the earthquake in 1988, the pogroms in Azerbaijan, the war over Nagorno-Karabakh (*Artsakh* in Armenian) in the 1990s, the Four-Day War in 2016 and the ongoing economic, political and

---

[532] The independent Republic of Armenia was established, along with the Republics of Georgia and Azerbaijan, following the Bolshevik Revolution and collapse of the Russian Empire in 1917. It was reabsorbed into what was by then communist Russia in 1920, and became one of the 15 republics of the Soviet Union in 1922.

[533] Kalayjian and Weisberg, 'Generational Impact'.

[534] Ibid., 11.

[535] Ibid., 16.

[536] Ibid., 17.

[537] Ibid., 15.

social challenges in post-Soviet Armenia leading to mass emigration from the homeland.

These conditions created what poet Vahe Oshagan refers to as a sense of 'constant vigilance'—'sleeping with one eye open'.[538] The unresolved post-genocide trauma, along with the ongoing denial of the genocide by Turkey, is key to understanding the response of many Armenians to those events, particularly in the last three decades.

Responses to the genocide and to Turkish denial

In 1986, Donald and Lorna Miller carried out in-depth interviews with 92 Armenian Genocide survivors in California. They identified six responses to the experience of genocide: repression, rationalisation, resignation, reconciliation, rage and revenge.[539] Miller and Miller argued that an individual's experience of these six responses is often sequential, though there is overlap between stages and different people experience each stage differently. Their research showed how individual responses are shaped, among other things, by the extent and type of trauma, by pre- and post-genocide positive or negative interactions with Turkish people, and by the level of involvement in the Armenian community and its religious, political and cultural organisations.[540]

I suggest that Miller and Miller's typology also describes the *collective* Armenian response to both the genocide itself and to its denial by successive Turkish governments. Furthermore, I suggest that, in the decades since Miller and Miller developed their typology, there has emerged a seventh response: engagement with Turkish government, civil society and individuals. This seventh response is qualitatively different to the previous six responses, in that it has an outward, positive focus. I also explore how the ongoing trauma of the genocide and its denial have fuelled the fear that the genocide 'is happening again', shaping the response by many Armenians to events in the homeland and the Middle East in the last three decades.

Repression, rationalisation, resignation and reconciliation (1918–1965)

Repression, rationalisation, resignation and reconciliation are inward-looking, essentially reactive responses to trauma. Repression involves 'putting a lid on' painful memories as a way of coping with past events that are 'too horrible to

---

[538] Notes from lectures by Vahe Oshagan at Macquarie University, Sydney, in 1992–93.
[539] Miller, 'An Oral,' 187–202.
[540] Ibid., 189–190.

contemplate'.⁵⁴¹ The sheer trauma of the genocide, along with 'survivor guilt',⁵⁴² left the Armenian exiles numb, with barely enough motivation to focus on personal survival and the preservation of their cultural heritage in the face of 'white massacre' (*jermag chart* or assimilation without bloodshed).⁵⁴³ Aside from the targeted assassination of members of the former Committee for Union and Progress (Young Turk) government in the 1920s, the desire for justice and recognition of the genocide by Turkey and the world did not translate into consistent, organised political activism until 1965.

Rationalisation can take the form of political, pragmatic or religious explanations for a traumatic experience. Miller and Miller found that, while many survivors were reluctant to allow repressed memories to resurface, they tried to give meaning to the genocide. Some viewed the genocide as a means of 'salvation'; that is, as an opportunity for personal and collective religious or political awakening, while others suggested that exile from the homeland provided better opportunities for long-term national flourishing.⁵⁴⁴ The Armenian Apostolic, Catholic and Protestant churches have drawn on sacred concepts of martyrdom, death-burial-resurrection, moral victory and redemption through suffering to make sense of the genocide and its aftermath.⁵⁴⁵ However, beyond these basic rationalisations, there has been little philosophical or theological reflection on the meaning and impact of the genocide, making it difficult for diasporan thinkers and leaders to achieve true 'reconciliation' with self and the Turkish nation due to the inability to derive meaning from the genocide.⁵⁴⁶

As memories become submerged beneath the realities of everyday life, and simplistic rationalisations seem increasingly inadequate, resignation expresses a sense of helplessness in the face of a past that cannot be changed and of a recognition that is increasingly elusive. The sense of resignation was fuelled by the international community's abandonment of Armenia in the immediate post-war period, whose recognition of Kemalist Turkey and its borders in 1923, along with the sovietisation of the Armenian Republic, removed any hope for

---

⁵⁴¹ Miller, 'An Oral', 192.
⁵⁴² Lorne Shirinian, 'Survivor Memoirs of the Armenian Genocide as Cultural History', in *Remembrance and Denial*, ed. Richard G Hovannisian (Detroit: Wayne State University Press), 171–72.
⁵⁴³ Rouben Manuel Torossian, 'The Contemporary Armenian Nationalist Movement' (PhD diss., United States International University, 1980), 48.
⁵⁴⁴ Miller, 'An Oral', 193–94.
⁵⁴⁵ For discussion of religious explanations for the Genocide, see for example Leonardo Alishan, 'Crucifixion Without "The Cross": The Impact of the Genocide on Armenian Literature', *Armenian Review* 38, no. 1 (1985): 27–50; and Vigen Guroian, 'When Remembering Brings Redemption: Faith and the Armenian Genocide', *Liturgia Special Issue* 3 (1993): 77–88.
⁵⁴⁶ Alishan, 'Crucifixion Without', 149.

return or recognition. Meanwhile, the Turkification of Armenian place names in historical Armenian lands was completed by the 1930s.

French-Armenian writer Shahan Shahnour expressed this sense of resignation in his novel, *Nahanch Arants Yerki* (*Retreat without Song*), published in 1929, in which six Parisian survivors of the genocide angrily reflect on their powerlessness in the face of the pressures of assimilation:

> Parents, sons, uncles, and sons-in-law, retreat;
> customs, conceptions, morals, and love, retreat.
> The language retreats, the language retreats, the language retreats.
> And we are still retreating in words and in deed,
> willingly and unwillingly, knowingly and unknowingly:
> forgive them, forgive them, Ararat!547

Reconciliation is an acceptance of things as they are, but unlike resignation it involves a conscious decision. Reconciliation on an individual level might involve confronting one's own anger, or concluding that disasters are 'part of life' and that one needs to 'move on', or beginning to recount stories of Turks who saved them. However, until the perpetrator acknowledges their crime, full reconciliation is impossible. Miller and Miller found that 'Turkey's current denial campaign simply fuels feelings of resentment and hostility' among survivors. Denial is the 'salt' that is rubbed into the open wound.548 Collectively, this means that it is difficult for the nation to 'be at peace' within itself.

Rage and revenge (1965–2001)

Fifty years of Turkish denial and continuing exile have made full reconciliation impossible, and have given birth to rage and, in some cases, revenge. While rage is generally an 'internalised' emotion, revenge is the acting out of these 'hostile feelings' or giving approval to others who do so.549

Among some Armenians, rage was and continues to be expressed in the form of hatred towards the Turkish population and for anything Turkish: boycotting Turkish goods; avoiding travel to Turkey; expressing anger at annual commemorative events; or preventing their children from befriending Turks. However, 1965 marked the beginning of the politicisation of that rage; that is, its outward expression in non-violent form. Aside from ongoing Turkish denial, the emergence of activist rage was triggered by several factors: the

---

[547] From Shahan Shahnour, *Retreat Without Song*, cited in Hagop Oshagan, *Hai Kraganoutiun* [*Armenian Literature*] (Jerusalem: St. James Patriarchate Press, 1942), 634–35.
[548] Miller, 'An Oral', 195–98.
[549] Ibid., 198–200.

environment of activism in the Western world of the 1960s; the symbolism of the 50-year anniversary; the tensions of the Cold War; and the emergence of a second generation of diasporans who carried the historical memory ('trauma by proxy')[550] but who did not carry the burden of repressed memories.

On 24 April 1965, the government of the Armenian Soviet Socialist Republic held an official commemoration of the genocide. While delegates inside the theatre delivered solemn and cautious speeches, over 100,000 people gathered outside calling for the return of Turkish occupied Armenian lands.[551] On the same day, services commemorating the genocide were held in diasporan communities throughout the world. As a result of this awakening, Armenian National Committees were established throughout the world to pursue the 'Armenian Cause', by lobbying world governments for official recognition of the genocide.

This recognition was slow to come. Rage turned into revenge for some Armenians who saw violence as a means of expressing their frustration with ongoing Turkish denial and of expediting international recognition.[552] In 1973, a lone gunman, genocide survivor Gourgen Yanikian, assassinated the Turkish Consul and Vice-Consul in Los Angeles. Over the next decade, a number of Armenian terrorist organisations were formed that targeted Turkish consular staff, businesses and citizens around the world.[553] Cohen suggests that 'it is easy to see that the 60-year silence about the genocide and the obstinate denials of the Turkish government were at some point going to provoke open rage rather than resignation and repressed anger'.[554] While violence is never an inevitable (or justifiable) expression of trauma, terrorism was an act of desperation by those who lived with either the direct or inherited unresolved trauma of the genocide.

Armenian response to the terror attacks was mixed. Most Armenians in the United States were opposed to terrorism,[555] and the acts of terror were publicly

---

[550] Amanda Wise, *Exile and Return Among the East Timorese* (Philadelphia: University of Pennsylvania Press, 2006), 11.

[551] Richard Hrair Dekmejian, 'Soviet-Turkish Relations and Politics in the Armenian SSR', *Soviet Studies* 19, no. 4 (1968): 513–15.

[552] Khachig Tololyan, 'Cultural Narrative and the Motivation of the Terrorist', *Journal of Strategic Studies, Special Issue: Inside Terrorist Organizations* 10, no. 4 (1987): 226.

[553] See Torossian, 'Contemporary Armenian,' 231–37, for a complete list of Armenian terrorist organisations and a breakdown of terrorist activities until 1980.

[554] Cohen, *Global Diasporas*, 54.

[555] Anny Bakalian states that 65 per cent of the American-Armenians she interviewed did not agree with terrorism as a means of furthering the Armenian cause. The percentage was highest among American-born Armenians. Anny Bakalian, *Armenian-Americans: From Being to Feeling Armenian* (New Brunswick: Transaction Publishers, 1993), 53–54.

condemned by most Armenian organisations. However, a number of Armenian writers and commentators expressed sympathy with the frustration that had given impetus to the killings, and some media outlets even praised the 'bravery' of the terrorists.[556] By appealing to 'shared symbols'[557] associated with the Armenian revolutionary movements in the Ottoman Empire in the nineteenth century[558]—martyrdom, justice and revenge—terrorists were able to appeal to the popular imagination. In any case, the spate of terrorist attacks succeeded in placing the issue of the genocide and its ongoing denial on the global agenda.

In response to Armenian lobbying and terrorism, the Turkish government launched a propaganda counter-offensive. Beginning with the publication of booklets distributed to governments, embassies and libraries across the world, the denial campaign grew into a multi-million dollar industry, with a large proportion of the funds spent paying public relations firms in Washington DC in an attempt to prevent the US President, Congress and Senate from publicly affirming the genocide. Turkish Studies Chairs were established in the United States, funded by the Turkish government and often run by known denialists of the Armenian Genocide. In Australia, in 1988, Turkish consular representatives attempted to prevent the Centre for Comparative Genocide Studies at Macquarie University, Sydney—the forerunner of the Australian Institute for Holocaust and Genocide Studies—from teaching the Armenian Genocide. The ongoing denial of the genocide has had a profound psychological impact on the Armenian survivors and on subsequent generations:[559] 'The distortion of the truth impacts directly upon his own identity, and therefore the identity

---

[556] For examples of overt or tacit support in the Armenia press, see Torossian, 'Contemporary Armenian'.

[557] Jenny Phillips, *Symbol, Myth and Rhetoric: The Politics of Culture in an Armenian-American Population* (New York: AMS Press, 1989), 142.

[558] A number of Armenian nationalist revolutionary groups and parties formed in the Ottoman Empire in the late nineteenth century. Of these, two continue to operate today: the Social Democrat Hunchak Party, founded in 1887 by a group of students in Geneva; and the Armenian Revolutionary Federation founded in 1890 in Tbilisi, Russia (now in Georgia). These parties initially pursued the recognition of Armenian minority rights within the Ottoman Empire, but later sought independence for Armenians. They engaged in both terrorist and self-defensive acts in pursuit of their goals.

[559] Vigen Guroian, 'Collective Responsibility and Official Excuse Making: The Case of the Turkish Genocide of the Armenians', in *The Armenian Genocide in Perspective*, ed. Richard G. Hovannisian (New Jersey: Transaction Publishers, 1986), 135–36; and Leo Hamalian, 'The Armenian Genocide and the Literary Imagination', in *The Armenian Genocide in Perspective*, ed. Richard G Hovannisian (New Jersey: Transaction Publishers, 1986), 153–203, *passim*.

of his children, because their identity formation is so closely tied to his own perceptions and feelings about himself, his past, and his worth.'[560]

Engagement (2001–present)

As an alternative to rage and revenge, I suggest that some Armenians have more recently adopted a seventh response to the genocide and its denial: engagement with Turkish government, civil groups and individuals. This has involved reflection on the current reality and a re-adjustment of goals and methods, and is qualitatively different to the previous six responses in that it has an outward, positive focus.

On the Armenian side, engagement has been prompted by the conditions of their host countries, in particular Europe, the United States of America, Canada and Australia, where Armenian intellectuals and community members alike have the opportunity to interact with their Turkish peers in a less restrictive environment. In addition, since a large number of countries have now formally recognised the Armenian Genocide, there has been a call by some Armenians to move from a strategy of seeking recognition to seeking reparations.[561]

On the Turkish side, a growing number of journalists, scholars and other leaders have publicly acknowledged the Armenian Genocide, or have recognised that Armenians died as a result of government-sponsored massacres rather than employing the previous euphemisms of 'mutual massacres' or 'civil war'. This is despite Turkish laws prohibiting such acknowledgement.[562] Early Turkish voices included prominent authors Elif Şafak and Orhan Pamuk, and historian Taner Akçam who has gained access to Ottoman records and written a number of important books outlining Turkish responsibility for the genocide. More recently, journalist Hasan Cemal, the grandson of Cemal Paşa who was one of the Young Turk triumvirate responsible for the Armenian Genocide, has acknowledged the reality of the genocide.

---

[560] Levon Boyajian and Haigaz Grigorian, 'Psychosocial Sequelae of the Armenian Genocide', in *The Armenian Genocide in Perspective*, ed. Richard G. Hovannisian (New Jersey: Transaction Publishers, 1986), 183.

[561] For example Harut Sassounian, 'Genocide Recognition and a Quest for Justice', *Loyola of Los Angeles International and Comparative Law Review* 32, no. 115 (2010): 115–22.

[562] The first part of Turkish Penal Code 301 reads: 'A person who publicly denigrates the Turkish Nation, the State of the Turkish Republic or the Grand National Assembly of Turkey and the judicial institutions of the State shall be punishable by imprisonment from 6 months to 2 years'. The code has been used to charge authors, writers and activists who use the term 'Armenian Genocide'.

The Turkish-Armenian Reconciliation Commission (TARC, 2001–04) was the first major attempt at organised dialogue between Armenians and Turks. TARC highlighted the challenges of such engagement: conflicting agendas; the involvement of known denialists on the Turkish side; and the involvement of third party governments. Nevertheless, TARC created a precedent for civil society engagement. The assassination of Turkish-Armenian journalist Hrant Dink in January 2007 gave further impetus to grassroots initiatives in Armenian-Turkish relations. Gatherings to commemorate Dink's death were held throughout the world, initiated by members of the Armenian, Turkish and Kurdish communities. Also, the 'I Apologise' campaign, launched in December 2008 in Turkey by a group of academics, journalists and others, was endorsed by over 30,000 signatories. The apology stated: 'My conscience does not accept the insensitivity showed [sic] to and the denial of the Great Catastrophe that the Ottoman Armenians were subjected to in 1915. I reject this injustice and for my share, I empathise with the feelings and pain of my Armenian brothers. I apologise to them.'[563] Turkish Prime Minister Tayyip Erdoğan refused to endorse the apology campaign, arguing that Turkey had done nothing for which to apologise.[564] Instead, in a statement made on 23 April 2013, he called the 'mass killings' by Ottoman forces 'inhumane' and offered his 'condolences' to the grandchildren of those killed. However, he embedded his comments in the language of 'shared pain', arguing that all Ottoman citizens suffered and that it was 'inadmissible' for these events to be used as a way of stirring up hostility against Turkey today.[565] Erdoğan's comments came against the backdrop of the failed Armenian-Turkish Protocols initiated by Turkey in 2009, aimed at restoring diplomatic relations with Armenia and opening up discussion about the genocide. The impetus for this initiative came from Erdoğan's initial push for entry into the European Union, and subsequently from his desire to raise Turkey's profile in regional affairs. In the end, the Protocols were buried, in part due to Turkey's insistence that Armenian forces withdraw from Nagorno-Karabakh as a pre-condition.[566]

---

[563] *Özür diliyorum* (I Apologise), http://www.ozurdiliyoruz.com/. The site has since been shut down and the signatories punished under Article 301 of the Turkish Penal Code—see '"Özur diliyorum" yine takip altında', *Radikal*, March 3, 2009, www.radikal.com.tr/turkiye/ozur-diliyorum-yine-takip-altinda-924313/, accessed October 10, 2018.

[564] İlgili Gündem Haberleri, 'Turkish PM Says Apology Campaign to Armenians Unacceptable', *Hurriyet Daily News*, December 17, 2008, http://www.hurriyet.com.tr/english/domestic/10587736.asp, accessed October 10, 2018.

[565] Constanze Letsch, 'Turkish PM Offers Condolences Over 1915 Armenian Massacre', *Guardian*, April 24, 2014, http://www.theguardian.com/world/2014/apr/23/turkey-erdogan-condolences-armenian-massacre, accessed October 10, 2018.

[566] For the text of the Protocols and a discussion of the reasons for their suspension, see David L Phillips, Michael Lemmon, and Thomas de Waal,

The response from Armenians to these initiatives is mixed. Some have viewed them as a 'crack' in the wall of denial, seeing the narrative of 'shared pain' as an improvement on the argument that 'it never happened, but they deserved it anyway'. However, critics pointed out that the language and content of the 'I Apologise' campaign were problematic and that Armenians were not consulted in formulating the wording.[567] They saw Erdoğan's comments as an attempt to 'soften' the Armenians in the lead-up to the 100th anniversary of the genocide in 2015. Overall, critics saw Turkish efforts as a way of strengthening Turkey (rather than bringing about justice for the Armenians), or of simply neutralising Armenian efforts at obtaining recognition and reparation while reinforcing the unequal power relations between Armenians and Turks.

The narrative of 'it's happening again' has been a strong factor in shaping the response of some Armenians to these apologies. For many, it is difficult to trust any Turkish overtures. This distrust is shaped by previous experience. When the Young Turks came to power in 1908, Armenians were promised reforms that would give them equal rights within the Ottoman Empire. By 1915, the Armenian dream of freedom and fraternity under the Young Turks had transformed into a genocidal nightmare.

Unresolved trauma, re-traumatisation and 'history repeating'

So far, I have explored how the seven responses to the genocide and its denial have been experienced sequentially. Yet the unresolved nature of the trauma means that it is possible for Armenians to continue to experience a number of different responses at any given time. For example, a genocide survivor might relive rage or resignation, or even the very same emotions they experienced during the genocide itself, in the face of fresh trauma.

On 8 December 1988, a magnitude 6.8 earthquake struck northern Armenia. The earthquake flattened several villages and a major town, Spitak, and caused severe damage to Armenia's second largest city, Gyumri. The death toll was estimated at between 25,000 and 50,000, with 130,000 injured and up to half a million rendered homeless. In her work among earthquake survivors, Anie Kalayjian found that some elderly survivors who had lived through the genocide

---

Diplomatic History: The Turkish-Armenian Protocols (Harvard: Institute for the Study of Human Rights, 2012), https://carnegieendowment.org/2012/04/17/diplomatic-history-turkey-armenia-protocols-event-3630, accessed October 10, 2018. For background to the Nagorno-Karabakh issue, see the next section.

[567] Ayda Erbal, 'Mea Culpas, Negotiations, Apologias: Revisiting the "Apology" of Turkish Intellectuals', in *Reconciliation, Civil Society, and the Politics of Memory: Transnational Initiatives in the 20th and 21st Century*, ed. Birgit Schwelling (Blelefeld: Transcript Verlag, 2012), 53–54.

were now experiencing nightmares of the horrors of 1915.⁵⁶⁸ The fresh trauma (the earthquake) gave opportunity for the repressed trauma of the genocide to surface, with the earthquake being seen through the lens of the 'memory of trauma'.⁵⁶⁹

Survivors and eyewitnesses of the pogroms against Armenians in Azerbaijan between 1988 and 1990 also interpreted their experience through the lens of previous trauma. Armenians had lived in what is now Azerbaijan for hundreds of years. There had been massacres and inter-ethnic conflict in the early part of the twentieth century (the Armenian-Tatar massacres in 1905–07 and three massacres of Armenians between 1918 and 1920), followed by seven decades of relative stability under Soviet rule. However, in February 1988, Azerbaijani mobs killed dozens of Armenians and looted their homes in the city of Sumgait just north of the Azerbaijani capital, Baku, with police standing by. This was followed by similar pogroms in Kirovabad, north of Nagorno-Karabakh, in November 1988, and in the capital, Baku, in January 1990.

The death toll from the pogroms ranged from the official figure of 120 to unofficial estimates of several hundred. Eerily, Harutyun Marutyan noted that 'the method of killing was the same as that used by the Turks during the genocide'. Victims in both cases 'were beaten, tortured, raped, and thrown out of windows, slain with metal rods and knives, chopped with axes, beheaded and burnt in fires … '.⁵⁷⁰ This similarity was confirmed by interviews conducted by Donald E. Miller with the observers of the Sumgait massacres.⁵⁷¹

Armenians around the world immediately linked the pogroms to the genocide. Evan Pheiffer added that 'Armenians seem incapable of separating the 1988 pogroms from the 1915 Ottoman atrocities—mention of one immediately triggers talk of the other'.⁵⁷² Mari Hovhannisyan noted that 'the posters carried by the Armenians on April 24, 1988 were verifications of the fact that Armenians saw the Sumgait massacres as the continuation of the genocide. … The events in Sumgait are the sequence of 1915 Genocide. Reluctance to acknowledge the 1915 Genocide led to the Genocide of 1988'.⁵⁷³ As a result

---

[568] Anie Kalayjian, Rania Lee Kanazi, Christopher L. Aberson, and Lena Feygin, 'A Cross-Cultural Study of the Psychosocial and Spiritual Impact of Natural Disaster', *International Journal of Group Tensions* 31, no. 2 (2002): 178.

[569] Erica Resende and Dovile Budryte, *Memory and Trauma in International Relations: Theories, Cases and Debates* (London: Routledge, 2013), 65.

[570] Harutyun Marutyan, 'Iconography of Armenian Identity: The Memory of Genocide and the Karabagh Movement', *Gitutyun* (Yerevan: Publishing House of The National Academy of Sciences, Republic of Armenia, 2009).

[571] Miller, 'The Role', *passim*.

[572] Evan Pheiffer, 'A Place to Live For', *Jacobin*, June 1, 2016, https://www.jacobinmag.com/2016/06/nagorno-karabakh-armenia-azerbaijan-four-day-war/, accessed April 10, 2019.

[573] Mari Hovannisyan, *The Collective Memory of the Armenian Genocide* (Budapest: Central European University, 2010), 21–22.

of the pogroms, 350,000 Armenians fled Azerbaijan to neighbouring Armenia or Russia. As Miller and Miller point out, 'The pogroms, while horrific, did not justify in themselves the mass exodus that occurred unless viewed as the precursor to an actual genocide'.[574] The reason for this 'overreaction' lies in the memory of the Armenian Genocide a century earlier: the Azerbaijani 'other' was reminiscent of the Turkish 'other' of that genocide. (Azerbaijanis are a Turkic people and speak a language similar to Turkish). The Armenians of Azerbaijan were re-traumatised, fearing that 'it is happening again'. Their fears may have been well-founded: one wonders what the fate of these Armenians would have been if they had remained in Azerbaijan during the ensuing war over Nagorno-Karabakh.[575]

The pogroms in Azerbaijan raised fears that Armenians in Nagorno-Karabakh could meet a similar fate. In 1921, in an effort to appease Kemalist Turkey and the more numerous Muslim inhabitants in the region, the newly formed Soviet Union had placed the Armenian-populated enclaves of Nagorno-Karabakh and Nakhichevan under Azerbaijani control.[576] Large-scale demonstrations calling for greater autonomy for Nagorno-Karabakh, and eventually for re-unification with Armenia, began in Armenia and Nagorno-Karabakh in 1987, and gained impetus after the pogroms. Tensions escalated between Armenia and Azerbaijan,[577] leading to a successful referendum for Nagorno-Karabakh's independence in 1991, followed by military conflict that erupted into full-scale war in 1992 and ended with a ceasefire in 1994. By that time, the former Nagorno-Karabakh Autonomous Oblast of Soviet times and its surrounding territories were under Armenian military and political control—a total area of approximately 12,000 square kilometres. Since then, regular peace talks between Armenia and Azerbaijan have failed to make progress, and clashes have become a regular occurrence on the frontline.

The Armenians were victorious in the war; however, the ceasefire is precarious and there remains a threat of renewed hostilities. Azerbaijan's military budget is greater than Armenia's total state budget, and the rhetoric of Azerbaijan's leadership has become increasingly bellicose.[578] The Four-day War in 2016

---

[574] Miller, 'The Role', 187.
[575] Ibid., 188.
[576] Subsequently, while Nagorno-Karabakh had retained its Armenian majority, Nakhichevan's Armenian minority reduced from 40 per cent in 1917 to 15 per cent in 1926 and 1.5 per cent in 1979, mainly through emigration to Armenia and Russia.
[577] For discussion of this escalation, see Armen Gakavian, 'Armenia: From Irredentism to Independence: The Dynamics of the Nagorno-Karabagh Crisis' (Honours thesis, University of Sydney, 1991).
[578] For example Joshua Kucera, 'Following Armenian Uprising, Azerbaijan's Saber Rattling Grows Louder', *Eurasianet*, July 3, 2018, https://eurasianet.org/following-armenian-uprising-azerbaijans-saber-rattling-grows-louder, accessed April 10, 2019.

confirmed Armenia's fear that war could erupt at any time. On 2 April 2016, fighting broke out between Armenian and Azerbaijani forces on the Nagorno-Karabakh frontline. As a result, dozens of soldiers and civilians were killed on both sides, and Azerbaijan obtained approximately eight to 20 square kilometres of land from Nagorno-Karabakh, marking the first time that the line of contact had shifted since 1994.[579] There were reports of war crimes by Azerbaijani troops, including 'torture, execution, and mutilation', and 'beheadings, ears and hands cut off, and throats cut',[580] again reminiscent of methods used in the genocide. The most famous case was that of three elderly members of the Khalapyan family who were discovered by Armenian photojournalist Hakob Poghosyan in the village of Talish. The family appeared to have been tortured, mutilated and killed.[581] A photo of the deceased family was widely circulated in the Armenian media,[582] again feeding the sense of 'it's happening again'.

Armenians in the Middle East have similarly experienced this sense of history repeating. Genocide survivors and their descendants were 'gripped with fear' at the possibility of mass violence against Christian minorities during the 1956 nationalist revolution in Egypt.[583] More recently, the advance of Islamic fundamentalism in Iraq, Egypt and Syria following the 'Arab Spring' has created a

---

[579] For an analysis of the causes, course and outcome of the Four-Day War, see Masis Ingilizian, 'Azerbaijan's Incremental Increase On The Nagorno Karabagh Frontline', *Bellingcat*, April 12, 2016, https://www.bellingcat.com/news/rest-of-world/2016/04/12/detailing-azerbaijans-incremental-increase-in-nagorno-karabaghs-frontline/, accessed April 10, 2019. Estimates of the number of casualties vary. While both sides blamed the other for the hostilities, the evidence points to Azerbaijan as the instigator. Mikayel Zolyan argues that: 'Arguably, apart from testing the defences on the line of contact, the operation pursued external and internal political goals: modifying the status quo in the peace process and testing the international community's reaction to military action in the region, as well as consolidating Azerbaijani society around its ruling government'. See Mikayel Zolyan, 'The Karabakh Conflict After the "Four-Day War": A Dynamic Status Quo', *Turkish Policy Quarterly*, March 14, 2017.

[580] Artsakh Ombudsman's 'Second Interim Report on Atrocities Committed by Azerbaijan During the 2016 April War', *Karabakhfacts.com*, December 9, 2016, https://karabakhfacts.com/tag/4-day-war/, accessed April 10, 2019.

[581] See Maria Titizian, 'War Crimes in Spring: The Four Day War One Year On', *EVN Report*, April 1, 2017, https://www.evnreport.com/spotlight-karabakh/war-crimes-in-spring, accessed April 10, 2019.

[582] See, *inter alia*, 'Azerbaijani Soldiers Execute Elderly Armenian Couple in Artsakh; Then Cut Off Their Ears', *HETQ*, April 4, 2016, https://hetq.am/en/article/66976, accessed April 10, 2019.

[583] Based on my conversations with Egyptian-Armenian *émigrés*.

new wave of refugees and nurtured a new narrative of exile, massacre and even genocide in describing these events.

The #SaveKessab campaign of the first half of 2014 epitomised this fear. On 21 March 2014, the predominantly Armenian village of Kessab in northeastern Syria was captured by opposition forces. Most Armenian residents had been evacuated to safety in nearby towns before the capture, with only a handful of residents left behind. While the Kessab 'genocide' narrative circulated by some of the Armenian mainstream and social media did not hold up to analysis, the fact that the #SaveKessab campaign resonated so quickly and so widely, and the panic spread so easily, is telling. The sense of 'it's happening again' was fuelled by several factors: Kessab had twice before experienced deportations (in 1909 and 1915); Kessab was one of the only two remaining Armenian villages along the Mediterranean coast (the other being Vakıflı, across the border in Turkey); Turkey's involvement in allowing Islamic militant groups to cross the border into Syria aroused suspicions of Turkey's intentions regarding the Armenians; and the killing, rape, forced conversion and deportation of Christian, Yazidi and Shia minorities in Syria and Iraq by ISIS were a haunting repetition of some of the methods used during the Armenian Genocide.[584]

Conclusion

The unresolved post-genocide trauma, continuing sense of exile, denial by successive Turkish governments and geopolitically driven reluctance of some countries to acknowledge the Armenian Genocide have had a profound psychological impact on the survivors of the genocide and subsequent generations. The six responses identified by Miller and Miller—repression, rationalisation, resignation, reconciliation, rage and revenge—and the more recent response of engagement provide a helpful framework for documenting this impact and explaining the fear that 'it's happening again'. This fear is key to understanding the response to events in the past three decades in Armenia (such as the earthquake and the war with Azerbaijan), Azerbaijan (pogroms) and the Middle East (the Syrian civil war and the brief occupation of Kessab). Until there is a resolution of the trauma there can be no collective healing or closure, and each subsequent traumatic experience will reinforce the fear that 'it's happening again'.

---

[584] For an excellent discussion of the post-genocide dynamics around events in Kessab, see Elyse Semerdjian, '#SaveKessab, #Save Aleppo, and Kim Kardashian: Syria's Rashomon Effect', *Jadaliyya*, April 24, 2014, http://www.jadaliyya.com/Details/30576#SaveKessab,-#Save-Aleppo,-and-Kim-Kardashian-Syria%E2%80%99s-Rashomon-Effect, accessed October 10, 2018.

Biographies

Alex J Bellamy
Alex J Bellamy is Professor of Peace and Conflict Studies and Director of the Asia Pacific Centre for the Responsibility to Protect at The University of Queensland, Australia. He is also a Fellow of the Academy of Social Sciences in Australia. With Stephen McLoughlin, Alex is author of *Rethinking Humanitarian Intervention* (Palgrave, 2018). His most recent book is *World Peace (And How We Can Achieve It)* (Oxford, 2019). He is currently completing *The Betrayal of Syria: War, Atrocities and the Failure of International Diplomacy* (Columbia).

Susan Benedict
Susan Benedict is Professor Emerita at the Medical University of South Carolina, United States of America, and is the world's leading scholar of the role of nurses in the Nazi era. Among numerous other publications she is co-editor of the book *Nurses and Midwives in Nazi Germany: The 'Euthanasia' Programs* (with Linda Shields, Routledge, 2014).

Armen Gakavian
Armen Gakavian's PhD examined Armenian Diasporan identity and a longing for home. He was the founding convenor of the Armenian Genocide Research Unit of the Centre for Comparative Genocide Studies, the predecessor of the Australian Institute for Holocaust and Genocide Studies. He was a researcher at Macquarie University, The Salvation Army and other NGOs, with a focus on social inclusion, social services, multiculturalism and social change. He is

currently Associate Director and Editor at Ethos, a Christian think tank. Armen and his wife Karina Kreminski recently established Neighbourhood Matters to train reflective practitioners for service in the urban neighbourhood.

Katharine Gelber
Katharine Gelber is Head of the School of Political Science and International Studies, and Professor of Politics and Public Policy at The University of Queensland. She researches freedom of speech and the regulation of public discourse and has been awarded several ARC competitive research grants including a Future Fellowship (2012–15). She is the author of three monographs, *Free Speech After 9/11* (OUP, 2016); *Speech Matters* (UQP, 2011), *Speaking Back* (John Benjamins, 2002), and three edited books including *Free Speech in the Digital Age* (OUP, 2019). Katharine is a Fellow of the Academy of Social Sciences Australia and a former President of the Australian Political Studies Association, and has served on its Executive Committee (2010–18).

Hans-Lukas Kieser
Hans-Lukas Kieser is an historian and Associate Professor at the University of Newcastle (Australia). He is also Honorary Adjunct Professor at the University of Zurich. His teaching focus is on modern global and Middle Eastern history. His research focus is on late Ottoman and early post-Ottoman history, especially of violence and peace-making. He is a member of the Advisory Council of the Federal Foundation Displacement, Expulsion and Reconciliation in Berlin, and in 2017 received the President of the Republic of Armenia Prize. Recent publications include *Talaat Pasha: Father of Modern Turkey, Architect of Genocide* (Princeton University Press, 2018), and as co-editor, *End of the Ottomans: The Genocide of 1915 and the Politics of Turkish Nationalism* (I.B. Tauris-Bloomsbury, 2019).

Nikki Marczak
Nikki Marczak is the Atrocity Prevention Coordinator at the Asia Pacific Centre for the Responsibility to Protect at The University of Queensland, leading the Centre's work on atrocity prevention with regional partners. Nikki is a genocide scholar and survivor advocate whose work has been published by academic journals, policy think tanks and media outlets. She has worked with the Armenian, Yazidi and Jewish communities on issues for survivors and descendants of genocide, recognition and justice, and has researched women's experiences during genocide. Nikki is a member of the Australian Institute for Holocaust and Genocide Studies and co-editor of *Genocide Perspectives V: A Global Crime, Australian Voices* (UTS ePRESS, 2017).

Stephen McLoughlin
Stephen McLoughlin is an Assistant Professor at the Centre for Trust, Peace and Social Relations, at Coventry University. His research interests

include mass atrocity prevention, the role of the United Nations in conceptualising and carrying out prevention, the causes of genocide and mass atrocities and the Responsibility to Protect (R2P). He is the author of *The Structural Prevention of Mass Atrocities* (Routledge, 2014) and *Rethinking Humanitarian Intervention* (co-authored with Alex Bellamy) (Palgrave, 2018).

Melanie O'Brien
Melanie O'Brien is Senior Lecturer in International Law at the University of Western Australia, an award-winning teacher of international humanitarian law, public international law and legal research. Melanie is the 2nd Vice-President of the International Association of Genocide Scholars (IAGS) and co-convened the 2017 IAGS conference. She is on the WA International Humanitarian Law Committee of the Australian Red Cross and the Editorial Board of *International Journal of Human Rights*. Melanie is an admitted legal practitioner who has previously worked at several Australian universities; the National Human Rights Institution of Samoa; and the Legal Advisory Section of the Office of the Prosecutor at the International Criminal Court.

Caroline Schneider
Caroline Schneider is a PhD candidate within the Research Centre for the History of Violence at the University of Newcastle (Australia). Within the context of a modern global history she is interested in exploring the connection between past violent events and current political and social on goings. Her thesis is about the genocidal practice of forcible child transfers and its long-lasting multifaceted consequences. Her current research focuses predominately on the Middle Eastern region. She was part of a team that developed the exhibition 'Long Shadows—The Great War, Australia and the Middle East'.

Kirril Shields
Kirril Shields teaches in the field of cultural studies, genocide studies and the Holocaust. He teaches at The University of Queensland, Australian Catholic University and the University of Southern Queensland. He is a member of the Australian Institute for Holocaust and Genocide Studies. He is also a Research Fellow at the Asia Pacific Centre for the Responsibility to Protect, and current Atrocity Prevention Grants Program Manager. Kirril was co-editor of *Genocide Perspectives V: A Global Crime, Australian Voices* (UTS ePRESS, 2017).

Linda Shields
Linda Shields, DMed, PhD, FACN, Centaur Fellow, holds the position of Honorary Professor in the Faculty of Medicine at The University of Queensland and Adjunct Professor, School of Nursing, Midwifery and Paramedicine, University of the Sunshine Coast. She recently retired from a research career in universities in Australia and Europe. She is co-editor of the book *Nurses and*

Midwives in Nazi Germany: The 'Euthanasia' Programs (with Susan Benedict, Routledge, 2014).

Colin Tatz
Colin Tatz was Visiting Professor of Politics and International Relations at the Australian National University, Canberra. He wrote and taught about comparative race politics, Holocaust and genocide studies, Aboriginal affairs, migration, youth suicide, and sports history. Colin edited seven books, co-authored six, and was sole author of 12. His most recent books were *The Magnitude of Genocide* (co-authored with Winton Higgins, Praeger Security International, 2016), *Australia's Unthinkable Genocide* (Xlibris, 2017) and *The Sealed Box of Suicide: The Contexts of Self-Death* (co-authored with Simon Tatz, Springer, 2019).

Mark Tedeschi
Mark Tedeschi AM QC is a barrister practising at Wardell Chambers in Sydney. He was formerly the Senior Crown Prosecutor for New South Wales. He has prosecuted some of the most significant criminal trials in New South Wales. Mark has also prosecuted two high profile trials of government officials in Fiji. He was the Counsel assisting the Coroner during the Inquest into the deaths of five Australian journalists at Balibo in East Timor during the Indonesian invasion in 1975. Mark has authored a number of books and journal articles, including *Murder at Myall Creek* (Simon & Schuster, 2017) that was shortlisted for the Ned Kelly Awards. He is currently a Councillor of the State Library of NSW and a Trustee of Sydney Grammar School, and has been a successful exhibiting photographer for many years, with photographs included in the collections of the Art Gallery of New South Wales, the National Library in Canberra, the State Library of New South Wales and numerous private collections.

Amanda Tink
Amanda Tink is a PhD candidate at Western Sydney University's Writing and Society Research Centre. Her research interests include the influence of impairment and disability on the writing of Australian disabled authors, and the Nazi genocide of disabled people, both of which inform her PhD on the Australian poet Les Murray. Her PhD is supported through an Australian Government Research and Training Program Scholarship. Her essays have been published in *Southerly*, *Overland*, and *Sydney Review of Books*, and she is co-editor (with Dr Jessica White) of the forthcoming special issue of *Australian Literary Studies* 'Writing Disability in Australia'.

Jacob G Warren
Jacob G Warren holds a Master of Philosophy in Art History from The University of Queensland (2019) where he has taught as a casual academic tutor since 2018. His research centres on politics and colonialism in modern and contemporary art. His writing has appeared in *The Australian and New Zealand Journal of Art*, *Art and Australia Online* and has an accepted article in *Third Text*.

Index

Page numbers in *italics* indicate an illustration or its caption.

A

Abdul Hamid II, Ottoman
    sultan   38, 162
Aboriginal Australians
    colonialism as cold genocide
        134, 138
    Myall Creek massacre   155
    nuclear colonialism and   131, 140,
        149, 151
    Stolen Generations   117, 126, 140
    suicide and collective grief
        116, 125
activism   182
Africa   11, 20, 25, 29, 31, 112
African National Congress (ANC)   26
Aktion Reinhard   102
Aktion T4   74, 91, 97–98, 104
Alawites   16
Albanians   23
Altschul family   58–59, *58*

Améry, Jean   36, 114
ANC (African National Congress)   26
Anderson, George   156
Anderson, Kjell   131, 135
Annan, Kofi   8, 27, 29
antisemitism   56, 62, 90
    see also Holocaust
Anzac   160, 174
Apartheid   25
Arab Spring   7, 17, 190
Armenian genocide   163, 178
    Anzac eyewitnesses   162
    background to   162
    denial of   165–166, 171, 173, 175,
        179, 182–183
    eliticide   162, 163
    freedom of religion violations   37
    gendered nature of   40, 111,
        164, 171
    long-term consequences   165, 171,
        173, 177

Armenian genocide (*Continued*)
  post-genocide exile and
    trauma   165, 177, 187
  suicide in   110
  survivors' responses to   180
  Treaty of Lausanne   166, 173
Armenians
  and Azerbaijan   188
  and the earthquake (1988)   187
  in the Middle East east   190
  see also Armenian genocide
art *see* literature; visual art
al-Assad, Bashar   7, 17, 28
al-Assad, Hafez   15
atomic weapons testing   129, 136, 143
Atomic Weapons Tests Safety
    Committee (AWTSC)   150
Aung San Suu Kyi   8
Auschwitz   42, 59–60
Australia
  Gallipoli campaign and the
    Armenian genocide   161,
    165, 174, 184
  humanitarian aid provision
    165, 170
  see also Aboriginal Australians
Australian Institute for Holocaust
    and Genocide Studies   184
Australian War Memorial   174
AWTSC (Atomic Weapons Tests
    Safety Committee)   150
Azerbaijan   188

B

Ba'ath Party   15
Balkan Wars   163
Ban Ki-moon   12–13
Barbagli, Marzio   110, 114, 120
Belzec   41
Bernberg, Germany   98
biopower   114, 116
Boeckh, Rudolf   96
Bosnia   13, 112
Botswana   11
Boughny, Houphoet   11
Brandenburg, Germany   97
Brandt, Karl   92, 95
Bringing Them Home report   126
Brown, Jonathan Kumintjara   131,
    132, 140, 145, 152
Buddhism and Buddhists   44, 49
Burton, William Westbrooke   156
bush foods   149, 151

C

Cambodia   44, 49
Canada   122
Card, Claudia   50
Catel, Werner   94
Ceduna, South Australia   121
Cemal Pasha   164
Cham Muslims   44, 46–47
children
  born of rape   172
  child brides   112
  forcible conversion of   40, 43, 111,
    164, 170, 172
  forcible removal or transfer   117,
    119, 126, 140, 164
  killed prior to mother's
    suicide   111
  Nazi 'euthanasia' of disabled   92,
    103, 105
  Nazi 'euthanasia' propaganda
    for   89
  suicide of   118
  Yazidi   169
Christianity and Christians   43,
    46–47, 112, 119, 181, 190
  see also Armenian genocide
Church
  response to Armenian
    genocide   181
  objections to Nazi 'euthanasia'   89,
    92, 102
  and suicide   112

Churchill, Ward   136, 138
cold genocide   131, 135, 138
collective punishment   157
colonialism   134, 138
   see also nuclear colonialism
Committee of Union and Progress
      (CUP)   162, 164, 174
Commonwealth Scientific and
      Industrial Research
      Organisation (CSIRO)   147
communists   20, 43
compensation   73
concentration camps   41, 59, 164
Congo   112
Constantinople Treaty   163
Convention on the Prevention and
      Punishment of the Crime of
      Genocide (Genocide
      Convention)   51, 126, 157
conversion, forcible   40, 43, 111,
      164, 169–170, 172
Côte d'Ivoire   11
crimes against humanity   166
Croatia   13
CSIRO (Commonwealth Scientific
      and Industrial Research
      Organisation)   147
cultural genocide   51, 123
CUP (Committee of Union and
      Progress)   162, 164, 174

D

Day, Edward Denny   156
de Klerk, F. W.   25
death camps   102
Deloria, Vine, Jr   123
denial
   of Aboriginal genocide   120
   of Armenian genocide   165–166,
      171, 173, 175, 179, 182–183
   of nuclear harm   141, 149
deportations   164
des Pres, Terrence   110

descendants of survivors
   activism of   183
   alienation from culture and
      tradition   50
   second generation storytelling   54,
      68, 173
   transgenerational trauma   68, 125,
      158, 165, 179, 183
desert   129, 136
di Palma, Vittoria   139
diasporas   178
Dieng, Adama   14
Dink, Hrant   186
disability   69, 88
   alternative strengths   78–79
   and capacity for
      development   82
   drawing lines of difference   83
   future worth of disabled
      people   83
   and language use   69, 71–72, 75
   Nazi 'euthanasia' of disabled
      people   70, 73, 77, 79, 81–83,
      85, 88
   social model of   72
dispossession   171, 178
doctors, in Nazi 'euthanasia'
      programme   91–93, 95, 99,
      100–104
'Dog Fox Field' (Murray)   71
Durkheim, Émile   108, 120

E

earthquake (Armenia 1988)   187
East Asia   18
ecology   133
Edison, Thomas   67
education   158
Egypt   165, 190
Endres, Danielle   137
engagement, as survivor
      response   185
environment   133

Erdoğan, Tayyip   186–187
ethnopsychiatry   117
eugenics   72, 79, 83, 85, 88
Evans, Suzanne   70, 73
exile   171, 178, 181
eyewitness testimony   39, 45, 60, 111, 161, 173
Eysler, Edmund   66

F

family *see* children; descendants of survivors
Feierstein, Daniel   49
films, Nazi propaganda   89
'final solution'   97, 102, 110
First Nations *see* indigenous peoples
First World War *see* World War One
footballers, Aboriginal   122, 126
forced labour   45, 161, 169
forcible conversion   40, 43, 111, 164, 169, 170, 172
forcible marriage   40, 45, 111, 164, 170
forcible removal of children   117, 119, 126, 140, 164
forcible sterilisation   72, 73, 80, 83, 90
Foucault, Michel   114
France   43, 160–161
Frankl, Viktor   127
Fredy Neptune (Murray)   72, 74

G

Galen, Clemens August Graf von   92, 102
Gallipoli   159, 161, 174
gas chambers   97
Gelber family   53, *56*, *58*, *62–63*, *63*
Gelber/Altschul Collection   53, 56
gender
   Armenian genocide   40, 111, 164, 171
   suicide and   111, 124
   Yazidi genocide   168–169, 172
   see also women
Geneva Communiqué   28
Geneva Conventions   157
genocide
   cold and hot   131, 135, 138
   definition   34, 48, 108, 122
   as international crime   157
   prevention   12, 18, 23, 29, 52
Genocide Convention   51, 126, 157
German South-West Africa   112
Germany *see* Holocaust; Nazis
Gligorov, Kiro   23–24, 27
Goodall, Heather   147
Grafeneck, Germany   74, 98–99, 105
Great War *see* World War One
grief   121, 125

H

Hadamar psychiatric hospital   98–99, 105
Hari, Johann   120
Hartheim, Austria   98
Heinze, Hans   94
Herero and Nama genocide   112
Hillman, James   115
Hirsch, Marianne   55
Hitler, Adolf   70, 81, 89, 91–92, 95
Hobbs, William   156
Hoffman, Eva   54, 68
Holocaust
   Aktion Reinhard   102
   as dominant model of genocide   135
   freedom of religion violations   40
   second generation storytelling   54, 68
   social contract violated in   36
   suicide during   110, 113
   survivor characteristics   127

see also Gelber/Altschul Collection; Nazis, 'euthanasia' of disabled people
Hong Kong   19
Howard, John   125
human rights   33, 36, 47, 174
Human Rights Watch   17
human trafficking   111, 160, 164, 169
humanitarian aid   165, 170

I

ICISS (International Commission on Intervention and State Sovereignty)   12
ICTY (International Criminal Tribunal for the former Yugoslavia)   50
IFP (Inkatha Freedom Party)   26–27
impairment   72
  see also disability
indigenous peoples
  colonialism as cold genocide   134, 138
  Myall Creek massacre   155
  nuclear colonialism and   131, 136, 140, 149, 152
  suicide among   115
Indonesia   19, 20, 27
Inkatha Freedom Party (IFP)   26–27
intergenerational trauma   68, 125, 158, 165, 179, 183
International Commission on Intervention and State Sovereignty (ICISS)   12
International Covenant on Civil and Political Rights   35
international criminal courts   51–52
International Criminal Tribunal for the former Yugoslavia (ICTY)   50
intervention (Aboriginal)   120, 125
Iraq   112, 190

Islam and Muslims   44, 46, 112, 163
Islamic State (IS, ISIS)   112, 167, 171–172, 191

J

Jacobs, Robert   138
Jacobs, Steven Leonard   48
Jadid, Salah   16
Japan   18
Jews and Judaism   40, 53, 90, 113
  see also Holocaust
JNA (Yugoslav National Army)   23

K

Kalayjian, Ani   179, 187
Kamilaroi people   155
Kaufbeuren, Germany   103
Kayibanda, Grégoire   11
Kemalists   166
Kenya   29, 31
Kenyan Private Sector Alliance (KEPSA)   31
Kessab, Syria   191
Kévorkian, Raymond   111
Khmer Rouge   43
Kibaki, Mwai   29
Kiir, Salva   8
Kindertransport   53, 56
Kneissler, Pauline   99
Knittel, Susanne C.   74
Kosovo   13
Kristallnacht   42, 56
Kuletz, Valerie   137
Kuper, Leo   48
Kurds   40, 166
Kwiet, Konrad   113

L

LaDuke, Winona   136, 138
Langer, Lawrence   110
Lausanne Treaty   166, 173
laws, Nuremberg   90, 114

leadership, political 7
  drivers and inhibitors 19
  mass atrocities and 10
  prolongers and terminators 27
  risk makers and risk breakers 15
Lemkin, Raphael 48, 50
Lester, David 107, 113, 122, 124–125
Levi, Primo 127
literature 72, 74
'Long Shadows' exhibition 159, 174

M

Macedonia 13, 23, 27
Machar, Riek 8
Malaysia 19
Mandela, Nelson 25
Maralinga, South Australia 129, 135, 139
Marder, Michael 139
marriage
  forcible 40, 45, 111, 164, 170
  laws limiting 90
Marston, Hedley 147, 149–150
martyrdom 112, 113, 181
Marutyan, Harutyun 188
Masada 113
Masco, Joseph 131, 151–152
Mehmed Talaat 163–164
memorials 74, 175
memory 55, 68, 180, 183, 188
Mencken, HL 110
mental health
  freedom of religion and 51
  loss of connections and 120
  Nazi 'euthanasia' of the mentally ill and disabled 89–90, 92, 95, 100, 102
  suicide and 108, 117, 120
Menzies, Robert 145
Meseritz-Obrawalde hospital 105
Middle East 18, 166, 190
midwives, in Nazi 'euthanasia' programme 93

Miller, Donald and Lorna Touryan 111, 177, 180–182, 188, 189
Milošević, Slobodan 8, 27
missionaries 119
Mount Sinjar 168, 170
Mukhabarat (security agencies), Syria 17
Murad, Nadia 173
Murray, Les 70, 74
Muslims 44, 46, 112, 163
Myall Creek massacre 155
Myanmar 8, 112

N

Nagorno-Karabakh 189
Namibia 112
Nasution, Abdul Haris 22
nationalism 19, 24, 110–111, 166–167, 174
Native Americans 122
NATO (North Atlantic Treaty Organization) 28
Nazis
  'euthanasia' of disabled people 70, 73, 77, 79, 81–82, 83, 85, 88
  'euthanasia' promoted by 88
  'final solution' 97, 102, 110
  freedom of religion violations 40
  medical experiments 94
  in Vienna 56, 59
Near East Relief 165
New South Wales 118, 122, 127, 155
New Zealand *see* Anzac
Newcastle, Australia 159
Nightingale, Florence 87
Nissenbaum, Isaac 113
Nixon, Rob 131, 133, 135–136
Northern Territory 117
nuclear colonialism 129
  artistic representation of 131, 135, 140, 151–152
  definition 136

desert as wasteland   136
  as slow violence   131, 134
nuclear tests   129, 136, 143
Nuremberg Laws   90, 114
nurses, in Nazi 'euthanasia'
    programme   87, 92–94,
    96–97, 99, 102–103

O

Obama, Barack   170
Odinga, Raila   29
orphans   40
Ottoman Empire   37, 161, 167, 171,
    174, 186

P

Parikka, Jussi   136
Pavese, Cesare   107, 110
Philippines   19
PKI (Communist Party of
    Indonesia)   20
Plunkett, John Hubert   155, 157
pogroms   188
Poland   61, 100
Poore, Carol   73
post-memory   55, 68
Powell, Christopher   49
prevention of genocide   12, 18,
    23, 29
prisoners of war   161
propaganda   22, 89, 92, 163, 170, 184
prosecutions see trials
psychiatric hospital, Hadamar   98,
    99, 105
psychiatry   117

Q

Qatar   29

R

R2P (Responsibility to Protect)   12
radioactive colonialism see nuclear
    colonialism

radioactive contamination   131,
    134–135, 137, 140–141, 145
rage, as survivor response   182
rape see forcible marriage;
    sexual violence
rationalisation, as survivor
    response   181
reconciliation, as survivor
    response   182
religion   33
  Aboriginal   142
  in Armenian genocide   37
  in Cambodian genocide   43, 49
  freedom of   35, 47
  genocide and   47
  genocide prevention and   52
  in the Holocaust   40
religious leaders
  killing of   38–39, 46
  role in resistance and prevention
    14, 89, 92, 102
religious responses to
    trauma   181
reparation   49, 73
repression, as survivor
    response   180
Reser, Joseph   118
resignation, as survivor
    response   181
resistance   49, 92, 102, 112–113
Responsibility to Protect
    (R2P)   12
revenge, as survivor response
    182–183
Rohingyas   112
Russia   28–29
Rwanda   11

S

Saudi Arabia   29
Scarce, Yhonnie   131, *133*, 145
school education   158
Second World War see World
    War Two

Serbia and Serbs   8, 23, 27
sexual violence   40, 111, 157,
    168–169, 172
Shahnour, Shahan   182
Shahtahmasebi, Said   109
Shoah *see* Holocaust
Sicher, Efraim   54
Singapore   19
Sinjar, Mount   168, 170
slavery   164, 169
slow violence   131, 134, 137,
    140–142, 145, 149, 152
Solingen, Etel   18
Sonnenstein, Germany   98–99
South Africa   25
South Korea   19
South Sudan   8
Southall, Ivan   139
Springer, Gisela   67, *67*
sterilisation, forcible   72–73, 80,
    83, 90
Stolen Generations   117, 126, 140
Straus, Scott   9, 11, 19
Suharto   20
suicide   107
  Australian Aboriginal people
    116, 125
  biomedical approach to   108, 114
  genocide and   107, 125
  in Indigenous communities   115
  lost connections and   125
  native Americans   107, 122
  as rational choice   110
  understanding rather than
    explaining   110, 115, 124
Sumgait massacres   188
survivors
  characteristics of   127
  children as   43
  post-genocide exile and trauma
    165, 177, 187
  silence and silencing of   55, 73, 74
  social death   50
  testimony of   39, 45, 60, 111, 173
  see also descendants of survivors
Sydney Jewish Museum   54
Syria   7, 15, 27, 164, 190

T

T4 programme   74, 91, 97, 98, 104
Taiwan   19
Talaat Pasha   163, 164
Tanzania   11
Tatz, Colin   1
Temoney, Kate   48
terra nullius   132, 143
terrorism   183
testimony, witness   39, 45, 60, 111,
    161, 173
Thailand   19
theological responses to
    trauma   181
Theresienstadt/Terezin   59, 60
Thunder Raining Poison
    (Scarce)   131, *133*, 145
Torres Strait Islanders   116, 118, 126
torture, right to freedom from   36
trafficking   111, 160, 164, 169
transgenerational trauma   68, 108,
    125, 158, 165, 179, 183
trauma
  communal   178
  continuing   187
  survivors' responses to   180
  transgenerational   68, 108, 125,
    158, 165, 179, 183
Treaty of Constantinople   163
Treaty of Lausanne   166, 173
Treblinka   41
trials
  of Islamic State (IS) members   172
  of Myall Creek massacre
    perpetrators   155
  of Nazi 'euthanasia' doctors   100
  of Nazi 'euthanasia' nurses   99,
    104, 105

tribal memory 107, 108, 125
Tsangirai, Morgan 20
Tunisian National Dialogue
    Quartet 31
Turkey 29, 166, 175, 191
    see also Armenian genocide
Turkish-Armenian Reconciliation
    Commission 186

U

Union of the Physically Impaired
    Against Segregation
    (UPIAS) 72
United Nations 168
    see also Annan, Kofi; Ban
    Ki-moon
United Nations Human Rights
    Committee 36
United Nations Preventive
    Deployment Force
    (UNPREDEP) 24
United States of America 136, 165,
    170, 184
Universal Declaration of Human
    Rights 35
University of Newcastle,
    Australia 159

V

Veidt, Conrad 66
Vienna, Austria 53, 54, 56–57, 62
violence, slow 131, 134, 137, 140,
    141–142, 145, 148, 152
visual art 131, 140

W

war crimes 157
Weisberg, Marian 179
Wekstein, Louis 120
Wentzler, Ernst 94
West Papua, Indonesia 135
Western Australia 117–118, 126
'wild euthanasia' 103
witness testimony 39, 45, 60, 111,
    161, 173
women
    Armenian genocide 40, 111,
        164, 171
    Cambodian genocide 45
    Myall Creek massacre 157
    suicide during genocide 111
    Yazidi genocide 168–169, 172
World War One 161, 174
    see also Armenian genocide
World War Two 56, 57–58, 179
    see also Holocaust; Nazis

Y

Yazidis 112, 167, 172–175
Yintayintin ('Davy', stationhand at
    Myall Creek) 155–156
Young Turks 38, 162, 174, 187
Yugoslav National Army (JNA) 23
Yugoslavia, former 23, 27, 50, 112

Z

Zambia 11
Zimbabwe 20

www.ingramcontent.com/pod-product-compliance
Lightning Source LLC
Chambersburg PA
CBHW040253170426
43191CB00019B/2393